THE ACCOUNTABLE SCHOOL COUNSELOR

The Accountable School Counselor

SECOND EDITION

Larry C. Loesch
Martin H. Ritchie

CAPS Press
An independent imprint of

An International Publisher
8700 Shoal Creek Boulevard
Austin, Texas 78757-6897
800/897-3202   Fax: 800/397-7633
www.proedinc.com

© 2005, 2009 by PRO-ED, Inc.
8700 Shoal Creek Boulevard
Austin, Texas 78757-6897
800/897-3202   Fax 800/397-7633
www.proedinc.com

All rights reserved. No part of the material protected by this copyright notice may be reproduced or used in any form or by any means, electronic or mechanical, including photocopying, recording, or by any information storage and retrieval system, without prior written permission of the copyright owner.

Cover photo by Garry R. Walz, Ph.D., NCC, CAPS Press, LLC. This photo was selected because we felt that a book on accountable school counseling should itself be accountable by using a photo of a real school setting on its cover.

Library of Congress Cataloging-in-Publication Data

Loesch, Larry C.
  The accountable school counselor / Larry C. Loesch, Martin H. Ritchie.—2nd ed.
       p.   cm.
  Includes bibliographical references and index.
  ISBN 978-1-4164-0380-7
  1. Educational counseling—United States. 2. Educational accountability—United States. I. Ritchie, Martin H.   II. Title.
LB1027.5.L572 2009
371.4—dc22

                                                          2008048841

This book was developed and produced by CAPS Press, formerly associated with ERIC/CASS, and creator of many titles for the counseling, assessment, and educational fields. In 2004, CAPS Press became an independent imprint of PRO-ED, Inc.

Art Director: Vicki DePountis
Designer: Vicki DePountis
This book is designed in Trump Mediaeval and Scala Sans.

Printed in the United States of America

1 2 3 4 5 6 7 8 9 10   17   16   15   14   13   12   11   10   09   08

CONTENTS

List of Figures and Tables   ix

Preface   xi

CHAPTER 1

The Need for School Counselor Accountability   1

Accountability and Program Evaluation Viewpoints   2
    School Counseling Program Evaluation   4
    School Counselor Accountability   6
Our View of Accountability and Program Evaluation   8
The Need to Improve School Counselors' Professional Image   11
Changing Roles: Trying to Evaluate a Moving Target   14
School Counselor Accountability and Educational Reform   21
Accountability in the Context of the ASCA National Model   25
From the Idealistic to the Actual   31
Conclusion   32
For Thought and Deed   33

CHAPTER 2

Accountable for What, to Whom, and How?   35

What and Why *Data?*   37
Accountable for What?   40
Fun With Numbers?   45
Accountable to Whom?   49
    Parents and Families   51
    School Administrators   54
    Teachers   56
    School Boards   57
    Other School Personnel   58
    Students   59
    Members of the Community   60
    The School Counseling Profession   61
    Self   63

vi   Contents

Accountable How?   64
   Written Report   66
   Verbal Presentation   67
   Multimedia Presentation   69
   Journal Articles   70
   Web Page and/or Blog   72
   Television   74
   Videos   74
   Posters   75
   Products Showcase   76
   Office Showcase   76
   Electronic Communications   77
   Newspaper Article   79
   Pictures   80
Conclusion   80
For Thought and Deed   00

CHAPTER 3

Common Accountability Resources for School Counseling Functions   83

Questionnaires and Surveys   86
Rating Scales   91
Checklists   91
Semistructured Interviews   93
Standardized Tests   95
School-Counselor-Made Tests   98
Academic Performance Indicators   103
Distal Academic Performance Indicators   105
Proximal Outcome Indicators   106
School-Counselor-Made Accountability Data Forms   108
Conclusion   116
For Thought and Deed   116

CHAPTER 4

Accountability for School Counseling - Curriculum Functions   119

Classroom Instruction   119
Interdisciplinary Curriculum Development   124
Group Activities   126
Parent Workshops and Instruction   131

Conclusion 134
For Thought and Deed 134

CHAPTER 5

Accountability for School Counseling - Individual Planning Functions 135

Individual and Small-Group Appraisal 136
Individual and Small-Group Advisement 140
Conclusion 143
For Thought and Deed 144

CHAPTER 6

Accountability for School Counseling - Responsive Services 145

Consultation 146
Personal Counseling 153
Crisis Counseling/Response 167
Referrals 169
Peer Mediation and Conflict Resolution 171
Conclusion 176
For Thought and Deed 177

CHAPTER 7

Accountability for School Counseling - System Support Functions 179

Professional Development 179
Partnering and Teaming 184
Program Management 187
  Budget Management 188
  Resource Development 190
In-service Activities 191
Conclusion 193
For Thought and Deed 194

CHAPTER 8

School Counseling Program Evaluation 195

Context Evaluations and Needs Assessments 198
Focus Groups 204
  Nominal Group Technique 207

Input Evaluations   211
Process Evaluation   213
Product Evaluation   216
Conclusion   220
For Thought and Deed   220

CHAPTER 9

Implementing an Accountability Plan   223

About Informed Consent   223
Adopt a Positive Self-Perception About Being Accountable   225
Resist Being Resistant to Being Accountable   231
Embrace Change   231
Develop an Action Plan   232
Focus on a Specific Purpose   235
Determine Needed Resources   237
Determine the Measurements   238
Establish a Time Schedule   239
Monitor Plan Implementation Progress   240
Try Parallelism   241
Reap the Benefits of Being Accountable   242
Go to the Top of the RAMP   244
Conclusion   249
For Thought and Deed   250

References   251

About the Authors   263

FIGURES AND TABLES

LIST OF FIGURES

Figure 1.1. School Mission Statement

Figure 1.2 . School Counselor Work Assignment Self-Evaluation

Figure 1.3. Analysis of a School Counselor's Work Situation

Figure 1.4. A School Counselor Knowledge and Skills Self-Assessment

Figure 2.1. Listing of School Data

Figure 2.2. Parent Informing and Involving Form

Figure 2.3. Listing of People School Counselors Might Try to Influence

Figure 2.4. Resources and Priorities for Presenting Accountability Information

Figure 2.5. Disseminating Accountability Information to Stakeholders

Figure 3.1. Survey Instrument to Assess the Frequency of Bullying in School

Figure 3.2. Checklist of Possible School Counselor Activities for Freshmen Students

Figure 3.3. School-Counselor-Made True–False Test

Figure 3.4. School-Counselor-Made Sentence Completion Test

Figure 3.5. Free-Association Data-Collection Activity

Figure 3.6. Data Form for Attendance Improvement Activities

Figure 3.7. Data Form for College Scholarship Planning and Counseling

Figure 3.8. Data Form Showing How Students Use the Internet for Career Information

Figure 3.9. Form for FAFSA Activity and Time Project

Figure 4.1. A Hypothetical Sociogram

Figure 4.2. Data Form for the Ropes Course Project

Figure 6.1. Data Form for the Student Success Skills Project

Figure 6.2. Counseling Treatment Plan

Figure 6.3. An A-B Single-Subject Design

Figure 6.4. An A-B-A Single-Subject Design

Figure 6.5. An A-B-A-B Single-Subject Design

Figure 7.1. Professional Development Opportunities

Figure 7.2. Rating Partners and Teams

Figure 7.3. School Counseling Program Budget

Figure 7.4. Three Possible In-service Activities

Figure 8.1. Intermediate Elementary Students Counseling Needs Survey (IESCNS)

Figure 8.2. Middle or High School Counseling Needs Assessment

Figure 8.3. Introduction to a Needs Assessment Focus Group

Figure 8.4. Stakeholders, Outputs, and Outcomes

Figure 9.1. Informed Consent Form for an Individual Counseling Research Activity

Figure 9.2. Informed Consent Form for a General Research Activity

Figure 9.3. The New Me?

Figure 9.4. School Counselor Self-Evaluation Form

Figure 9.5. Best-to-Least-Best School Counseling Activities

Figure 9.6. Needed Resources for an Accountability Project

Figure 9.7. A Response for an ANSSCI Specific Component Standard

Figure 9.8. Another Response for an ANSSCI Specific Component Standard

LIST OF TABLES

Table 1.1. School Counselors' Relative Emphases on Programmatic Goals

Table 2.1. Equal Time Allocations

Table 2.2. Different Time Allocations

Table 2.3. Different Time Allocations, Per Student

Table 2.4. Time Estimator Template

Table 3.1. Information About Tests and Testing

PREFACE

One of the really nice things about developing a second edition of a book is the opportunity to benefit from reviews and use of the first edition. We had sought to provide a book that was of *practical* value to school counselors, one they could use easily to initiate and conduct accountability activities in their schools. We were fortunate to have received many compliments about the first edition. The feedback we received suggested that we were, in the main, successful in achieving that goal. However, we also received a considerable number of suggestions for how the book might be improved. It is this that guides our revision. We want to acknowledge and extend appreciation to all of our readers and, in particular, to those who took the time to provide feedback and suggestions to us. We also want to extend our appreciation to the various editors who contributed to the production of this book. Their understanding of the needs and wants of our readership and their expertise in developing resources that are beneficial to the members of the school counseling profession were invaluable to us.

We had five major goals in mind as we developed this second edition. First, we wanted to provide a broader context for school counselor accountability; specifically, how an individual school counselor's accountability efforts are integrated with overall school counseling program evaluation and accountability. Thus, we have enlarged the discussion of program evaluation. Second, we wanted to make it easier to locate specific ideas and elements in the text. To address this issue, we have reorganized the framework, added more subsection identifiers, and enhanced the table of contents. Third, we wanted to increase the number of usable resources. Toward this goal, we have added a CD-ROM that contains diagrams, forms, and other reproducible resources so that the conduct of many of the activities presented are easier. Fourth, we added activities in a "For Thought and Deed" subsection in each chapter to suggest activities that should enhance understanding of the major ideas presented in the respective chapters. Finally, we wanted to increase the number of accountability activities presented so that readers would have even more ideas for their individual accountability efforts and activities. Many of these new activities were suggested by readers of the first edition, others came from new ideas in the school counseling literature, and a few came from our own continued thinking about school counselor accountability.

We present this second edition with essentially the same intention we had for the first edition. We hope that school counselors will take the initiative to demonstrate that they are indeed effective and successful in their professional activities, with the ultimate result being that the majority of children in schools become better learners and experience positive development from the activities of professional school counselors.

Larry C. Loesch, PhD
University of Florida
Gainesville, Florida

Martin H. Ritchie, EdD
University of Toledo
Toledo, Ohio

CHAPTER 1

THE NEED FOR SCHOOL
COUNSELOR ACCOUNTABILITY

If you are a school counselor, or intend to become one, and want to engage in some interesting professional self-abuse, ask a few teachers, school administrators, and parents this question: *Why do we have school guidance counselors in schools?* We don't know exactly the answers you'll receive, but we are confident that you won't find many of them that will reassure you about your chosen career. We also are confident that you'll most frequently receive answers that reflect stereotypical ideas about why there are school counselors in schools, such as "to help kids get into colleges," "to do testing," or "to help kids with problems." It is true that school counselors often do the activities upon which the stereotypes about them and their activities are based, however, it is also true that you as a school counselor do much, much more than such simplistic responses suggest. Current and "wannabe" school counselors still face a big challenge: How do they get people to understand what they do? Unfortunately, the real challenge is even bigger than that: How do you get people to *appreciate* what you do?

We believe that efforts to confront and overcome these challenges (e.g., to promote school counselors and school counseling in significantly positive ways) are interrelated. In general, the myriad and diverse activities that are conducted to *inform* teachers, administrators, parents, students, and others involved with schools about what school counselors do are not successful, or at least not successful to any great extent in improving peoples' attitudes about school counselors and school counseling. Please understand that we are not impugning school counselors' public relations activities. Quite the contrary. We believe that school counselors' PR activities are important and that they serve to enlighten *some* audiences about *some* aspects of school counseling for *some* time. However, we have not seen a great impact from such activities. Somehow, the information presented just doesn't seem to stick with the people who are exposed to it. Could it be that people want more than just information about your school counseling activities and programs? Could it be that people want to know if your activities accomplish something that might be of value to them? We think so. It is our contention that the various groups of people with whom you and other school counselors interact and to whom you have some responsibility want to know how your activities, both individually and collectively, benefit them or the people about whom they care. That is, people who are interested in education want to know if your activities are doing any good, and if so, for whom and to what extent.

The best-educated human being is the one who understands most about the life in which [s]he is placed.

—Helen Keller

ACCOUNTABILITY AND PROGRAM EVALUATION VIEWPOINTS

A mosaic is a visual image (i.e., picture, pattern, or design) that is created from an assembly of tiles (see the illustration). Typically the tiles are quite small (i.e., a half inch or less per side), but may also be larger, such as when the tiles for a mosaic are the bricks on the side of a building. The visual image of a mosaic is created by the careful placement of adjacent tiles with gradations or differences in color.

As is true for any visual image, mosaics appear smaller when viewed from a distance. However, unlike other visual images, the perceptual interpretation of a mosaic changes rather dramatically at some point as the viewing distance increases. If a mosaic is viewed from a relatively close distance, the image appears to include something akin to a grid because the lines between the tiles are evident. The mosaic thus appears to be much more a collection of individual, smaller pieces than of an integrated, composite image. The individual tiles retain a large portion of their uniqueness. However, if the mosaic is viewed from far away, the lines between tiles are not evident (i.e., the grid disappears), and the visual image is viewed and interpreted as a composite image,

The Need for School Counselor Accountability 3

PHOTO 1.1. An ancient mosaic from the Ravenna region of Italy. View this mosaic at different distances, and see how your view of the image changes.

not as a collection of pieces. At such a distant view, the individual tiles lose their uniqueness.

A mosaic is a good analogy for viewing and evaluating the effectiveness of your school counseling activities. The phrase *school counselor accountability* applies to the assessment of the effectiveness of your *individual* professional school counseling activities. Similarly, the phrase *school counseling program evaluation* applies to the assessment of the effectiveness of the *composite* (overall) results of your professional school counseling activities. (The phrase *school counseling program accountability* is used sometimes, but technically it is a misnomer.) The mosaic analogy comes into play when one considers the viewpoint (i.e., distance from the image) of the person or persons interested in the effectiveness of your professional activities. If the viewer's interest is only in accountability for your *individual* activities (i.e., the close-up view), he or she will not necessarily obtain good understanding of the results of your school counseling program (i.e., the distant view). Conversely, if the viewer's interest is only in your school counseling program (composite) results, the person will not necessarily achieve good understanding of your individual activities. Thus, although your individual activities and the composite results of your school counseling program are related (as are the individual tiles and the larger image in a mosaic), the viewpoint of the person interested in and viewing the results determines the level of understanding of the information under consideration.

Don't like the mosaic analogy because you haven't seen a mosaic lately? How about one that's more common? Imagine that you are watching an American football game on television. For most plays in the game, the television camera will view the game from a relatively long distance so that all the players (and most of the field) can be seen. This viewpoint allows you to see the overall result of the play. While viewing the play from afar, you know that all the football players on the field are doing *something*, but your viewpoint makes it impossible to comprehend what each of the players is doing during the particular play. The television networks know this. So what do they do? That's right! They use instant replay to show what a few of the players did specifically during the play. The instant replay viewpoint is much closer because the camera has zoomed in on those few players. But have you ever been away from the television long enough so that when you came back you saw only the replay of what a few players did? Unfortunately, you missed the total play from which the replay was taken, and therefore you do not know the overall result of the play! Again, it's all about the viewpoint taken. School counseling program evaluation is the long view of the overall results of all of the school counselor's professional activities. School counselor accountability is the close-up view of the school counselor's individual professional activities.

SCHOOL COUNSELING PROGRAM EVALUATION

Your collective activities as a school counselor (allowing that there may be other school counselors in your school) constitute the school counseling program because *having school counselors* in schools is synonymous with *having a school counseling program* in the school. That is, school counselors are inextricably linked to the context in which they perform their activities, and that context is understood to be the school counseling program. All school counseling authorities agree that it is desirable for a school counseling program to be a well-conceptualized, well-developed, well-implemented, and well-coordinated set of activities (e.g., Baker & Gerler, 2004; Brown & Trusty, 2005; Gysbers & Henderson, 2006; Myrick, 2002; Sink, 2005). However, even if the activities of school counselors in a school are ill conceived, under developed, poorly implemented, or disorganized, their activities nonetheless constitute the school counseling program. It's really quite simple: What the school counseling program *is*, is what you and/or other school counselors in the school do.

School counseling program evaluation is important because of the often substantial human, monetary, and physical resources invested in and assigned to school counseling activities and programs. In addition, school counseling program evaluation is necessary for the improvement of school counseling programs (and school counselor activities, by association) through knowledge gained of what is and what isn't effective and successful for most students (Cobia & Henderson, 2006; Erford, 2007a; Gysbers, 2004). And finally, school counseling program evaluation, and the activities within it, is important just because it is *part of what good professionals do* (Whiston & Sexton, 1998). Unfortunately, most school counselors have not been trained substantively or effectively to conduct school counseling program evaluation (Astramovich, Coker, & Hoskins, 2005; Lapan, 2005; Trevisan & Hubert, 2001). The overall result is that the majority of school counselors simply have done little or no school counseling program evaluation. However, the good news is that the situation is changing and improving. Gysbers, Lapan, and Stanley (2006) wrote that

> Two major developments over the past few decades have facilitated school counselors' direct involvement in results evaluation. The first development is the comprehensive approach to school counseling. The second development involves technology and the widespread use of personal computers.
>
> With a program approach, results-based evaluation is not an added duty; it is an expected part of all school counselors' work.
>
> All the tools school counselors need to do results-based evaluation are at their desks in their personal computers. (p. 35)

School counseling program evaluation may not be as simple as these brief statements imply; nonetheless, it is time for you and all other school counselors to get on the evaluation bandwagon to be able to be the best school counselors you can be and to do what is professionally appropriate.

SCHOOL COUNSELOR ACCOUNTABILITY

Similar to school counseling program evaluation, *school counselor accountability* is a phrase that strikes terror into the hearts of most school counselors. The most frequently used reason for school counselors to be accountable is so that they will not lose their jobs. Again, a simple logic is applied: If no one knows that what you do in your school is of any good to students and/or others interested in schools, then why continue to employ you, especially when educational funding is so limited, and other priorities are demanding attention? Unfortunately the majority of school counselors have not defended or justified (or, in some cases, have not been able to defend or justify) their activities with accountability data (Baker & Gerler, 2004; Hughes & James, 2001; L. S. Johnson, 2000). School counselors thus have contributed to the misunderstandings of their work and the school counseling profession and in the process have contributed to their own vulnerability. Obviously this situation must change if the school counseling profession is to endure, grow, and improve (Erford, 2007b).

Education professionals in general and school counseling professionals in particular acknowledge the need for school counselor accountability. As Studer, Oberman, and Womack (2006) noted, "School counselors can no longer sit back and hope that others will recognize the good things they are doing" (p. 385). However, the fact that so few school counselors actually demonstrate accountability implies that there are major (real or perceived) impediments to school counselors like you collecting and disseminating evidence to demonstrate your effectiveness (Curcio, Mathai, & Roberts, 2003; Fairchild, 1993; Myrick, 2003). Many reasons have been offered as to why school counselors don't do a better job of collecting accountability data, such as they are too busy working with students, they have heavy workloads, there isn't enough secretarial or administrative support, they are not good at research and statistics, they don't understand good assessment procedures, they have too many nonguidance duties, their role expectations are unclear, and on and on (e.g., Frith & Clark, 1982; Sciarra, 2004; Shaw, 1973; Stone & Dahir, 2006). As daunting as some of these reasons might be, the fact remains that some school counselors are being accountable, so it is by no means impossible for you and other school counselors to be accountable as well. Most importantly, there are compelling reasons why school counselors should be accountable

> Goodtown Elementary School exists to serve the academic, physical, social, and emotional needs of students as they develop through childhood into early adolescence. Our school staff is committed to creating and maintaining an educative, trusting, and caring environment in which teaching, learning, and developing are exciting, and students are assisted to develop responsibly. All of our activities are child centered and designed to accommodate individual learning styles so that all may experience success.

FIGURE 1.1. School mission statement.

now, including saving their jobs and perhaps even saving the school counseling profession (Cobia & Henderson, 2006).

It is worth repeating that while school counseling program evaluation and school counselor accountability are integrally related, technically they are not the same thing: School counseling program evaluation involves examining the total impact and outcomes of the *collective* school counseling activities conducted in the school, while school counselor accountability involves examining the impact and outcomes of each school counselor's *individual* activities. It also is important to emphasize again that achieving one does not mean achieving the other. For example, knowing that underachieving students who participated in your school counseling program activities improved their standardized test scores by an average of three percentile points does not explain (or allow evaluation of) the specific activities in which the students participated, the extent to which various activities (and therefore specific school counselors) were successful, or the contributions of different school counselors to the overall result. Conversely, the collective information from individual school counselor accountability activities may not provide information about the broader impacts of the school counseling program. For example, knowing that you conducted small-group counseling sessions with a focus on study skills to help six underachieving students improve their standardized test scores by an average of three percentile points does not explain the overall effectiveness of your school counseling program. These distinctions allow school counselor accountability and school counseling program evaluation to be discussed separately, with the understanding that each can and should be used in the service of the other.

Our View of Accountability and Program Evaluation

There is one thing about which we are absolutely certain: In order for you to be accountable as a school counselor, you have to have an appropriate perspective on being accountable. Gysbers (2005) laid it out clearly:

> A critical lesson we have learned and continue to learn is the importance of evaluating the work we do so we are accountable. You may have already discovered there is a good deal of work involved in developing and implementing comprehensive school counseling programs. But it is the evaluation phase of the process that often creates work overload and the most activity in the minds of school counselors. Thus, the first task in evaluation is for school counselors to rid their minds of the phobia of evaluation, of the persistent fear of evaluation that often leads to a compelling desire to avoid anything that has to do with evaluation. What is required is a mindset that evaluation is a part of school counselors' work that is done in schools each and every day. (pp. 27–28)

In general terms, being accountable means taking responsibility for one's actions (and conversely, not being accountable necessarily means accepting the consequences of not accepting responsibility). In a professional context, there are three primary elements to being accountable. First, the professional must have a clearly defined set of responsibilities or duties. For you as a school counselor, defined responsibilities may be assigned by your school administrator or self-determined. Obviously, most school counselors would prefer that their professional activities be self-determined, but rarely do they have a choice. Second, the professional's performance of the responsibilities and duties must be assessed and evaluated. For you, the evaluation process may be self-conducted, done by a school administrator or supervisor, or both. Unfortunately, the common default choice of most school counselors is to let others evaluate their performance, which among other things means they have little control over the evaluation criteria applied. Third, the results of

The Need for School Counselor Accountability   9

WORK ASSIGNMENT SELF-EVALUATION

In the first column, list up to eight (8) of your *primary functions* (activities) as a school counselor. That is, list those activities that take up most of your time, such as counseling students, classroom guidance, scheduling, test coordination, consulting with teachers, or whatever else you do. List them in descending order from the one that occupies most of your time at the top of the list to the one that occupies the least of your time at the bottom. In the second column, put a check mark by those functions you consider *appropriate* for school counselors. In the third column, identify *who is responsible* for you having to perform each function (e.g., a school administrator, your guidance coordinator, a school system policy, yourself, someone else who has control over what you do). In the fourth column, identify who evaluates your performance of the function.

Function	Appropriate	Function Designator	Function Evaluator
1. Counsel students individually	✓	Self	Guidance coordinator
2. Conduct classroom guidance	✓	Self	Guidance coordinator
3. Monitor student attendance		Principal	Principal
4. Maintain student records and data		Guidance coordinator	Guidance coordinator
5. Lunchroom duty		Principal	Principal
6. Counsel students in small groups	✓	Self	Guidance coordinator
7. Consult with parents or teachers	✓	Self	Guidance coordinator
8.			

How to you feel about the information you provided? What would you like to change in the listings?

FIGURE 1.2. School counselor work assignment self-evaluation.

professional evaluations must be reported to others (Baker & Gerler, 2004; Cobia & Henderson, 2003; DeVoss & Andrews, 2006). For you and other school counselors, this means that evaluation results most certainly must be reported to your administrators or supervisors. However, there are many other audiences interested in your school counseling activities and the school counseling program.

It is our view that being accountable means that you document the effectiveness of your individual professional activities through the generation and dissemination of data that reflect the actual results and outcomes of your various activities. Similarly, providing program evaluation means that you document the effectiveness of your collective (i.e., programmatic) professional activities through generation and dissemination of data that reflect the composite, broad-scale results and outcomes of your school counseling program. In simple terms, our view is that you must generate *evidence* that what your activities produce are valued by the various constituencies (i.e., stakeholders) you serve.

In general, your accountability and program evaluation processes are both part of the general, larger process of providing school counseling services that include (a) identifying needs, (b) setting goals based on those needs, (c) implementing activities to achieve those goals, (d) assessing the results and outcomes of your activities, (e) using the results to modify and refine your activities, and (f) sharing the results with various audiences (Fairchild & Seeley, 1995; Isaacs, 2003, Myrick, 2003). Because most of your school counseling activities involve work with students, a point emphasized in the *ASCA National Model: A Framework for School Counseling Programs* (American School Counselor Association [ASCA], 2005)[1], school counselor accountability and school counseling program evaluation primarily address the following question: How are *students* different as a result of the school counselor's activities and/or the school counseling program? This focus on students suggests that educators are the people most interested in a school counselor's activities. However, there are others interested in your school counseling work who are deserving of attention and who should receive information. These groups are discussed further in Chapter 2.

---

[1]Because the contents of this resource are referred to frequently throughout this book, we will hereafter refer to it as the *ASCA National Model.*

The Need to Improve School Counselors' Professional Image

Accountability in the context of our focus here is a *professional* responsibility, which of course begs the question, Is school counseling a profession? The American School Counselor Association promotes the use of the term *professional school counselor* (e.g., ASCA, 2005). Does that automatically make you, as a school counselor, a professional? What are the criteria achieved by a *recognized* profession (such as law or medicine), and how does school counseling stack up against those criteria? And will increased school counselor accountability and program evaluation activities enhance the reputation of school counseling as a profession?

To be a true profession and be widely recognized as a profession by the public, the activities performed by members of the alleged profession must meet certain criteria, including having (a) a distinctive body of knowledge underlying the profession and activities, (b) high standards of training for the activities, (c) an identifiable set of skills, (d) broad levels of autonomy over practice, (e) legal recognition as relatively exclusive providers of the services, (f) enforceable ethical (behavioral) standards, and (f) broad-based sanction by members of the community (McCully & Miller, 1969; Ritchie, 1990; Vacc & Loesch, 2000). The knowledge base underlying school counseling is interdisciplinary in nature. It certainly is derived substantially from psychology, particularly including developmental, social, personality, educational, and perceptual psychology. Of course, it also derives in large part from educational research and literature. However, the school counseling knowledge base also derives somewhat from sociology and anthropology, particularly including the multicultural elements of those disciplines. And finally, to far lesser extents, it derives from the other social sciences, and perhaps even a few ideas from the physical sciences. Thus, the knowledge base for school counseling is broad, but it is recognizable, and more importantly, it is growing.

High standards of training (i.e., professional preparation) for school counselors require that they earn at least a master's degree, and there are strong accreditation standards for school counselor preparation programs (e.g., those of the Council for the Accreditation of Counseling and Related Educational Programs [CACREP]). The skills school counselors need have been specified and emanate from a variety of sources; however, the best and clearest expositions about and summaries of needed school counselor skills have come from ASCA. In addition, school counselors have legal recognition in that all states and the District of Columbia require school counselors to hold state certification or licensure in order to provide school counseling services in schools.

School counselors are supposed to, and in the majority of cases do, operate within ASCA's ethical standards as well as those of the American Counseling Association (ACA). The primary purpose of ethical standards is to provide guidelines for professional behavior so that counseling service recipients will be protected from harm. However, ASCA's *Ethical Standards for School Counselors* (ASCA, 2004) also delineate many of your professional responsibilities as a school counselor, including the need to be accountable and to conduct program evaluation in various ways and for various constituencies. For example, in section "A.3 Counseling Plans" (ASCA, 2004), school counselors are charged to develop effective counseling plans and to review them regularly to ensure the continued viability and effectiveness of the plans. Similarly, in section "A.9.g Evaluation, Assessment, and Interpretation," school counselors are specifically admonished to assess the effectiveness of their individual and programmatic activities, particularly as they relate to the enhancement of students' academic, personal/social, and career developments. In section "D.1.g(3) Responsibilities to the School," school counselors are charged to assist in developing "a systematic evaluation process for comprehensive, developmental, standards-based school counseling programs, services, and personnel. The counselor is guided by the findings of the evaluation data in planning programs and services." And finally, in sections "F.1.c Responsibilities to the Profession" and "F.2.b Contribution to the Profession," school counselors are charged to conduct appropriate research and share their findings with professional colleagues.

Thus far, it appears that school counseling meets *most* of the criteria for a profession. For example, Ritchie (1990) assessed the extent to which school counselors met the specific criteria for a profession proposed by McCully and Miller (1969) and found that school counselors met most of the criteria. However, there were noticeable deficits in achievement of at least two of the criteria: broad levels of autonomy over practice and broad-based sanction by members of the community (i.e., the public). Ritchie (1990) suggested that a major obstacle to meeting these criteria was a lack of consensus about the roles of the school counselor, in part based on school counselors' general inability to convey their roles to the community effectively. This problem persists today and, unfortunately, the problem is circular. The variation in what school counselors do is immense and therefore it is more difficult for them to demonstrate accountability and program evaluation to a public that is ignorant of or confused about what it is that school counselors *should* be doing. Further, if school counselors themselves are not sure what it is they should be doing, it is difficult for them to be accountable consistently for their own services and programs or those they have in common with other school counselors, and if school counselors are not consistently accountable for the services and programs they provide, it is impossible for the general public to sanction their activities.

What we must decide is how we are valuable rather than how valuable we are.

—Edgar Friedenberg

Numerous and comprehensive efforts to define school counselors' roles have been only moderately successful. That is, while there appears to be some agreement about some school counselor functions, there remains considerable disparity in opinions about what are appropriate school counselor activities. Given this situation, a school counselor's accountability and program evaluation activities must, at least for now, be taken on as a highly personalized initiative. That is, each school counselor must engender an individual responsibility to be accountable. Without doubt, demonstrating accountability and engaging in program evaluation are requisites to school counseling being recognized as a true profession, and in turn to school counselors being recognized as true professionals.

You and other professional school counselors are obliged to monitor and evaluate your services and to provide evidence to the public that your services are valuable and effective. You as a professional school counselor must gather evidence from which to improve the services you provide, add to the school counseling profession's knowledge base, and enhance the skills available for your use. You also must share your results with other audiences through a variety of dissemination activities and outlets. Effective and accountable school counselors all embrace these responsibilities, evaluate their services, and share their evaluations; and through these activities and processes, improve the services they provide and the profession in which they are members. Therefore, becoming more accountable is tantamount to becoming more professional.

CHANGING ROLES: TRYING TO EVALUATE A MOVING TARGET

Since the inception of school guidance services in the early 1900s, school counselors' roles have evolved to reflect changes in our society's norms and values as well as changes in demands for public and private education (Baker & Gerler, 2004). As school counselors adapted to these changes, differences emerged in what school counselors do from one school to the next, from one school system to the next, and from one region to another.

School counseling evolved in the United States from events and social forces shaping this country in the early 20th century. At the turn of that century, the United States was rapidly changing from a rural and primarily agrarian society to an urban and primarily industrial society. People flocked to cities, especially in the Northeast and Midwest United States, looking for employment or better paying jobs. Out-of-work farmers, minorities, and a large influx of immigrants, mainly from Europe, were among them. Because schooling was compulsory in most of the United States, large numbers of children flooded the school systems. Unfortunately, there arose fear that these children, particularly those of immigrants and poor farmers from the South, being in schools would lead to economic and perhaps even moral crises. Some even feared that these children would not be educable and therefore would be unemployable. Others feared that their strange new customs might challenge the so-called American moral code. Therefore, there was a push to create vocational training and moral guidance. Responding to these challenges were the pioneers in school guidance who would become known as the founders of school counseling, including Jesse B. Davis, in Detroit; Frank Parsons, in Boston; and Eli Weaver, in New York City (Aubrey, 1977).

The first school counselors were teachers or administrators who taught guidance lessons on vocational and moral education. Many of these early school counselors advanced Parson's trait-and-factor model in their vocational guidance activities, a model that primarily consisted of assessing students' traits and aptitudes and then attempting to match them to educational and/or vocational paths presumed to be consistent with those traits and aptitudes. When the Soviet Union's *Sputnik* satellite was launched in 1957, fear of falling behind in the quality of American education arose among many people in the United States. Consequently, the U.S. Congress passed the National Defense Education Act (NDEA) of 1958. This act included funding for rapid training of guidance counselors who could appraise and assess American students and presumably steer those with appropriate intelligence and aptitude into advanced science and mathematics courses. Thus, for approximately the first 50 years of what we now know as school counseling, the school counselor's role was primarily concerned with vocational guidance for students, with heavy emphasis on testing and appraisal of students' characteristics, knowledge, and abilities.

When you aim for perfection, you discover that it is a moving target.

—George Fisher

The NDEA established centers across the United States to train guidance counselors. Many of the first trainers (i.e., counselor educators) of guidance counselors for these institutes were influenced by the work of Carl Rogers, who advocated a nondirective, person-centered approach to counseling and education. Consequently, many school counselors embraced a role that included substantial individual and group counseling, a role akin to a mini-therapy model centered in Rogerian counseling techniques. ASCA, which became a founding division of the American Personnel and Guidance Association (now the ACA) in 1952, recommended uniform training standards for school counselors that included educational and career information, guidance, record keeping, placement, and follow-up and evaluation within a framework that emphasized individual and group counseling. It is also noteworthy that, in the early years of the school counseling profession, school counselors were trained almost exclusively to provide counseling services in secondary schools. However, in 1962, C. Gilbert Wrenn admonished secondary school counselors to give up concentrating their efforts on the remedial needs of relatively few students and challenged school counselors instead to address the developmental needs of all students (Baker & Gerler, 2004).

A school counseling program is comprehensive in scope, preventative in design, and developmental in nature.

—ASCA, 2005, p. 13

The 1964 amendments to the NDEA provided funding for training the first elementary school counselors and thus created opportunity to provide developmental and preventative school counseling services. Soon after, ASCA began to advocate school counselor roles that addressed and enhanced the academic, personal/social, and vocational (career) developments of all children (Baker & Gerler, 2004; Sciarra, 2004). However, shrinking enrollments and economic problems in the 1970s and 1980s resulted in large-scale reductions in school personnel in general and in fewer school counselors in particular. Among those who were retained, many school counselors had caseloads of well over 500 students, even though ASCA recommended a student-to-counselor ratio of 250:1. In view of the high student-to-counselor ratios, it was impossible to provide direct services to all students. Thus, many in the school counseling profession and in school counselor education began to advocate for more indirect services, such as large-group guidance, consultation, and coordination. In addition, to a great extent, the specific roles of school counselors had become dependent on and unique to the work setting (i.e., school counselors' roles and functions were different for those working in elementary, middle/junior high, or secondary/high schools). As a result, what school counselors actually did depended largely on their respective school settings, a situation that remains to the present. Unfortunately, however, even today, many school counselors do not have or operate from within a role statement (i.e., a relatively specific list of duties, responsibilities, and assigned functions). Rather, their duties are often simply defined and assigned by school administrators and just as often include noncounseling activities (see Figure 1.3 for a sample analysis of a school counselor's situation).

The Need for School Counselor Accountability   17

ANALYSIS OF A SCHOOL COUNSELOR'S WORK SITUATION

In the first column, list all the functions (activities) in which you engage as a school counselor. In the second column, put a check mark by those activities that you consider to be your (personal and professional) priorities for your work as a school counselor. In the third column, put a check mark by those activities you believe are *your school principal's priorities*. In the fourth column, put a check mark by those activities you think are *priorities of teachers* in your school. In the fifth column, put a check mark by those activities you think are *priorities of students* in your school.

Function	Priority for			
	Personal	**Principal**	**Teachers**	**Students**
1. Advise students	✓	✓	✓	✓
2. Counsel students in small groups	✓			✓
4. Counsel students individually	✓	✓	✓	✓
5. Work with teachers	✓	✓	✓	
6. Work with parents	✓	✓	✓	
7. Coordinate/implement testing program	✓	✓		
8. Do accountability work	✓	✓		
9. Administrate/develop guidance program	✓	✓		
10. Maintain student records	✓	✓		
11. Coordinate students' peer mediation program	✓			✓
12. Provide classroom guidance	✓		✓	
13. Liaison with community resources	✓	✓		

Look at the pattern of check marks. For which activities is there most priority agreement? For which activities is there least agreement?

FIGURE 1.3. An analysis of a school counselor's work situation.

Burnham and Jackson (2000) found that 40% of the school counselors they surveyed reported spending at least a quarter of their time on nonguidance activities. While such activities may be needed or useful in schools, they do not contribute to a school counselor's effectiveness, and they certainly confuse any attempt at a school counselor's accountability and/or program evaluation. Partin (1993) surveyed school counselors to determine how they spent their time, and what they considered the greatest robbers of time from performing professionally endorsed school counseling and guidance-related activities. A variety of activities that interfered with endorsed school counseling functions were identified, including scheduling, supervising students (e.g., bus, hall, lunch room, or study hall duties), nursing duties, substitute teaching, secretarial duties (e.g., answering the telephone or filing paperwork), and other administrative tasks (e.g., recording grades or administering standardized tests). According to Partin, on average, these nonguidance activities accounted for nearly 20% of the school counselor's time. In a 10-year follow-up, Partin, Huss, and Ritchie (2003) found that relatively little had changed, except that school counselors were spending even more time on noncounseling tasks, notably, administering standardized tests.

The issue of the school counselor's role has received more attention than any other topic in the school counseling literature.

—Brown & Trusty, 2005, p. 152

There certainly is no lack of opinion today about what are the appropriate roles for school counselors. The widespread differences of opinion have led to misunderstandings and doubts by teachers, administrators, parents, the community, and even students as to the appropriate roles of the school counselor (Johnson, 2000). Counselor educators, other school counseling authorities, and school counselors themselves have lamented the lack of consensus of what it is that school counselors are supposed to do (Burnham & Jackson, 2000). Baker and Gerler (2004) wrote that "the enduring nature of this role confusion indicates that school counselors and counselor educators were not very successful in meeting the challenge [to define school counselor roles effectively] during the twentieth century" and that "a profession that agrees on its mission, role, and functions may be more likely to achieve dramatic change collectively rather than individually"(p. 305). In particular, this role confusion has hampered and still does hamper school counselors' efforts to demonstrate accountability and/or to do program evaluation effectively (Johnson, Johnson, & Downs, 2006). Most authorities argue that school counselors must better define their roles as partners in the educational enterprise before they can demonstrate their effectiveness and become fully accountable (ASCA, 2005; Herr, 2003; Johnson, 2000).

Because there is confusion about school counselors' roles and functions, it is no wonder that they are sometimes viewed as nonessential personnel. For example, Hughey, Gysbers, and Starr (1993) assessed the perceptions of students, parents, and teachers of a comprehensive guidance program and found disagreement about appropriate school counselor roles and functions. Hagborg (1992) found that parents showed general satisfaction for their respective school counselors but also found confusion about the school counselor's role. Similarly, in a study of future school administrators' perceptions of the school counselor's roles and functions, respondents identified many administrative, disciplinary, and nonguidance duties as important for school counselors to fulfill (Fitch, Newby, Ballestero, & Marshall, 2001). Ironically, however, when future school principals were presented with vignettes of school counselors performing appropriate and inappropriate school counselor activities relative to recommendations in the ASCA National Standards, they were able to distinguish inappropriate from appropriate performance in accord with ASCA's recommendations (Chata & Loesch, 2007).

True professionals have a clearly delineated scope of practice, based upon their training and experience, and often as defined by law. Currently, most school counselors perform a wide variety of duties, some of which pertain to their training and experience and some of which do not. The role confusion apparently starts early in the life of a school counselor. For example, students in some school counselor preparation programs are sometimes asked to interview and shadow practicing school counselors and then to write a report on what they perceive as the school counselor's duties and responsibilities. Invariably, a hodgepodge of activities is reported, with little consistency from one situation to the next. Many of the duties thus reported do not require master's-level training, and many are outside of any recommended scope of practice. These additional duties not only interfere with the school counselor's ability to provide appropriate school counseling services but also undermine reasonable accountability efforts.

ASCA (2006) has attempted to provide role clarity for school counselors through dissemination of *The Role of the Professional School Counselor*. This document intimates school counselor roles by defining what a school counselor is:

> The professional school counselor is a certified/licensed educator trained in school counseling with unique qualifications and skills to address all students' academic, personal/social and career development needs. Professional school counselors implement a comprehensive school counseling program that promotes and enhances student achievement. Professional school counselors are employed in elementary, middle/junior high and high schools and in district supervisory, counselor education and post-secondary settings. Their work is differentiated by attention to developmental stages of student growth, including the needs, tasks and student interests related to those stages. (p. 1)

The ASCA role statement also advocates that school counselors provide services through delivery of (a) the school guidance curriculum (e.g., large-group guidance activities); (b) individual student planning (e.g., helping students make and achieve goals); (c) responsive services (e.g., individual and small-group counseling); and (d) system support (e.g., management of the school counseling program). This role statement helps to clarify what you as a school counselor should be doing in general, but like other models available in the professional literature, it doesn't really provide much *specific* information about what you should be doing. However, the ASCA role statement is clear about the need for school counselors to be involved in accountability and program evaluation activities:

> To demonstrate the effectiveness of the school counseling program in measurable terms, professional school counselors report on immediate, intermediate and long-range results showing how students are different as a result of the school counseling program. Professional school counselors use data to show the impact of the school counseling program on school improvement and student achievement. Professional school counselors conduct school counseling program audits to guide

future action and improve future results for all students. The performance of the professional school counselor is evaluated on basic standards of practice expected of professional school counselors implementing a school counseling program. (p. 2)

SCHOOL COUNSELOR ACCOUNTABILITY AND EDUCATIONAL REFORM

Most school counselors have quietly gone about providing their services for many years, satisfied that they were helping children and that they were, at least nominally, accepted and valued as part of the educational team. Those few school counselors who did bother to file yearly reports typically compiled process data that documented only the number of student contacts and/or the number of different services they provided. Some even shared their daily calendars to let others know how they spent their time, as a preliminary attempt to be accountable. Administrators, teachers, parents, and other stakeholders seemed to be fairly content with the roles of the school counselor, their services and activities, and their general lack of accountability. However, in the early 1980s, public perception of education began to change. The release of *A Nation at Risk* (US Department of Education National Commission on Excellence in Education, 1983) began an educational reform movement that popularized the notion that American students were not performing at acceptable levels and that schools must be held more accountable for the academic performance of students. This reform movement swept aside decades of public complacency about public education. The hue and cry for better education in America brought with it mandatory proficiency tests, increased standards of preparation for school personnel, evaluations of both school systems and individual schools, and outcome-based assessments. In addition, increased scrutiny was placed on how auxiliary personnel (such as and including school counselors) actually affected students' academic achievement.

At the beginning of this century, U.S. President George W. Bush shepherded through the U.S. Congress revised legislation that has dramatically impacted practices in American schools. Popularly known as No Child Left Behind (NCLB; U.S. Department of Education, 2006), this legislation was the reauthorization of the Elementary and Secondary Education Act of 1965, the long-standing federal government program through which federal funds for education are dispersed to schools for a wide variety of purposes and uses. NCLB has had a profound effect on the American education system. Among other goals and directives, a primary focus of NCLB is that schools receiving *any* federal funds (which of course includes the majority of schools in the United States) shall be accountable for their educational practices through the measurement of student achievement by tests based on state standards. One result of NCLB is that entire school districts, and *all* the school personnel within them, seem to be being held accountable solely on the basis of student achievement as evidenced by standardized test scores (Isaacs, 2003).

The No Child Left Behind Act (NCLB) brought academic achievement to the top of education reform priorities. The new emphasis on achievement for all coincides with a movement among school counselors to move from the periphery to the center of a school's mission.

—American Counseling Association, 2005, p. 2

NCLB justifies latitude in school counselor's activities in that the act emphasizes that students will be educated in learning environments conducive to learning. Just what constitutes a "conducive learning environment" has not been defined to any great extent; yet, it seems obvious that such an environment would be one in which students are comfortable with themselves and others, both inside and outside of the school (i.e., they feel safe); are assisted to set appropriate and meaningful personal, career, and life goals; and, in general, are helped to experience normal development in positive ways. You and other school counselors certainly have responsibility to help students be the best possible learners they can be; however, just as certainly, you have responsibility to help students develop effectively as people. If a rationale is needed for such emphasis within the context of NCLB, clearly it is that good people are good learners. Thus, if you and other school counselors do not seize the opportunity to demonstrate that you are accountable for the effects of your activities on the personal/social, career, and academic developments of students, surely you will suffer the consequences of being held accountable to effects (in particular, test scores) over which you have little direct control.

With the advent of NCLB (2001), school counselors have to work much harder to show that the work they are doing is helping school systems to meet the mandates established by this legislation.

—McGannon, Carey, & Dimmitt, 2005, p. 4

T. Davis (2005) wrote that "we must recognize that as society continues to grow and change, the [school counseling] profession must continue to be responsive to the needs of society" (p. 27). Whether we, as members of the school counseling profession, agree with all the societal and political changes around and upon us is far less important than is our dedication to serving society's needs as best we are able. And lest there be any doubt that the current educational reform movement in the United States is having an impact on school counseling activities, consider Table 1.1 from Parsad, Alexander, Farris, and Hudson (2006) about school counseling emphases in schools in the United States in 2002.

For this national sample of high school counselors in 2002, the most emphasized aspect of school counseling services was helping students with academic achievement (48%), followed by helping students prepare for postsecondary schooling (26%), helping students with personal growth and development (17%), and helping students prepare for their work roles after high school (8%). These data compared to the following percentages for 1984: helping students with academic achievement (35%), followed by helping students prepare for postsecondary schooling (27%), helping students with personal growth and development (27%), and helping students prepare for their work roles after high school (11%). Clearly the shift is toward emphasis on academic performance, primarily at the expense of helping students with personal growth and development. But is academic performance, as measured by test scores and the like, the primary criterion to which school counselors want to be held accountable?

Coupled with the educational reform movement, budget cuts have forced many school boards to trim or eliminate programs and to lay off school personnel. However, even within the educational reform movement and its sometimes negative repercussions, school personnel who can demonstrate that their services impact students positively, particularly in regard to academic achievement, are more secure in their positions than those who cannot or will not be accountable. (It

24   The Accountable School Counselor

TABLE 1.1.

SCHOOL COUNSELORS' RELATIVE EMPHASES ON PROGRAMMATIC GOALS

Goal	Most Emphasis	Second-Most Emphasis	Third-Most Emphasis	Fourth-Most Emphasis
		2002		
Help students plan and prepare for their work roles after high school	8	12	30	51
Help students with personal growth and development	17	21	31	31
Help students plan and prepare for postsecondary schooling	26	39	26	9
Help students with their academic achievement in high school	48	29	14	9
		1984		
Help students plan and prepare for their work roles after high school	11	17	33	39
Help students with personal growth and development	27	28	16	29
Help students plan and prepare for postsecondary schooling	27	32	29	12
Help students with their academic achievement in high school	35	23	22	20

Note. Detail may not sum to totals because of rounding. From "High School Guidance Counseling," by B. Parsad, D. Alexander, E. Farris, & L. Hudson, 2006, *Education Statistics Quarterly,* 5(3).

is ironic that some school personnel who enjoy popular support from the community, such as athletic coaches, are often spared when budget cuts are necessary. Unfortunately, school counselors like you are not usually in those groups.) School boards and school administrators often find it easier and perhaps more popular to lay off or fail to replace educational personnel such as school counselors and other support personnel whose roles in the schools are less well understood or appreciated by the public. Clearly, as a school counselor you can no longer assume that your services are valued and that your position in the schools is safe. You must take responsibility for demonstrating the effectiveness and contributions of your activities and services in schools, and you must share this information effectively with the public.

As a [school counseling] profession, we cannot become disgruntled or jaded by a cursory consideration of this [NCLB] legislation; instead, school counselors must be aware of and compliant with the changing emphases of the educational discourse without losing the benefits that school counselors offer students. The emphases on academics and accountability can be framed in a positive light.

—Dollarhide & Lemberger, 2006, p. 303

ACCOUNTABILITY IN THE CONTEXT OF THE *ASCA NATIONAL MODEL*

Today, school counselors like you feel pressure to present evidence of their effectiveness to be seen as integral players in the reform movement in general, and in their respective schools in particular (Johnson, et al., 2006; Myrick, 2003). Years of neglecting to be accountable have caught up with the school counseling profession, and the topics of accountability and program evaluation appear with increasing frequency at professional conferences and in professional journals. A charge to action was heard, and responses have begun. For example, the DeWitt-Wallace Education Trust launched the Transforming School Counseling project to assist school counselor education programs prepare school counselors to advocate for and foster effective and successful learning for all students (Johnson, 2000). Similarly, ASCA developed the National Standards for School Counseling Programs (Campbell & Dahir, 1997), which encompass program goals, student competencies, and performance indicators across academic, career, and personal/social developmental domains. These standards were designed so the student competencies specified in them could be observed and/or measured by the performance indicators, thus providing a broad-based foundation for school counselor accountability and program evaluation (Dahir, Sheldon, & Valiga, 1998). Building upon and encompassing their National Standards, ASCA subsequently developed the *ASCA National Model* (ASCA, 2005).

Using the [ASCA] national standards as a foundation for program content, the ASCA model offers a standards-based approach to school counseling that is aligned with the mission of schools, proactively responds to school improvement, and is intentional in its support of every student's development.

—Stone & Dahir, 2006, p. 217

The *ASCA National Model* provides a framework for school counseling programs that includes attention to leadership, advocacy, collaboration and teaming, and systemic change. The *ASCA National Model* thus provides information relative to a sound basis for your school counseling program and to its delivery, management, and accountability systems. The *ASCA National Model* has four basic components: (1) Foundation provides the *what* of your school counseling program and covers what students should know and be able to do as a result of your program; (2) Delivery System, covers *how* your school counseling program should be implemented; (3) Management Systems addresses *when*, *why*, and on *what authority* your school counseling program should be implemented; and (4) Accountability covers how you should respond to a question such as "How are students different as a result of the program?" (ACSA, 2005). The four components of the model are encompassed by four themes to guide your functioning as a school counselor: leadership, advocacy, collaboration and teaming, and systemic change (ACSA, 2005). Briefly, these themes suggest that school counselors should be educational leaders in the school, should advocate for students and respond effectively to their needs, work with all of the school's stakeholders, and strive to provide services for all students in the school as their respective individual needs may require. (See Figure 1.4 for an example of a school counelor's knowledge and skills self-assessment.)

KNOWLEDGE AND SKILLS SELF-ASSESSMENT

On the lines following, list up to eight of the knowledge areas (e.g., those in the CACREP Core Curriculum standards) pertinent to your work as a school counselor for which you have the greatest knowledge, starting with the area about which you are most knowledgeable.

1. Helping Relationships (individual counseling) _____

2. Professional Orientation and Ethical Practice _____

3. Group Work _____

4. Social and Cultural Foundations (multicultural counseling) _____

5. Assessment (testing) _____

6. Career Development _____

7. Human Growth and Development _____

8. Research and Program Evaluation _____

On the lines following, list up to eight of your best *skills* (e.g., those presented throughout the *ASCA National Model*) as a school counselor, starting with your best skill.

1. Individual or Small-Group Advisement/Counseling _____

2. Consultation with Teachers and Parents _____

3. Crisis Counseling _____

4. Classroom Guidance _____

5. Guidance Program Management _____

6. _____

7. _____

8. _____

FIGURE 1.4. A school counselor knowledge and skills self-assessment. *Note.* CACREP = Council for Accreditation of Counseling and Related Educational Programs.

Obviously, all the components of the *ASCA National Model* must be addressed effectively to have a fully successful school counseling program. However, our focus here is on the Accountability and

Delivery System components of the model. Most of the remainder of this book addresses specific aspects of your accountability as a school counselor. However, before those topics can be covered, it is appropriate to examine what you should be doing as a school counselor in a broad context, and that is what is presented in the Delivery Systems component of the *ASCA National Model*.

The Delivery System covers four components of school counselor functioning: School Guidance Curriculum, Individual Student Planning, Responsive Services, and System Support. Each component encompasses a variety of specific services that you should be providing, including the following:

School Guidance Curriculum

Classroom Instruction

Interdisciplinary Curriculum Development

Group Activities

Parent Workshops and Instruction

Individual Student Planning

Individual or Small-Group Appraisal

Individual or Small-Group Advisement

Responsive Services

Consultation

Individual and Small-Group Counseling

Crisis Counseling/Response

Referrals

Peer Facilitation

System Support

Professional Development

Consultation, Collaboration and Teaming

Program Management and Operation (ASCA, 2005, p. 39)

These four Delivery System components and the services within them form the framework for discussion of accountability in this book.

These services include most of the activities you do as a school counselor, or at least what you *should* be doing. While the actual amount of time spent on the various components and services varies from one school counselor to another, depending in large part on their respective school settings, the importance of providing these services and evaluating their effects across settings is evident. Specific suggestions for evaluating these services and their component activities are presented in Chapter 3. We provide brief, introductory descriptions of major school counselor services and activities here because we believe that providing them later would detract from coverage of specific accountability and program evaluation activities. The following summaries are derived from information in the *ASCA National Model* (2005).

Classroom Instruction includes a variety of activities designed to deliver the school guidance curriculum, such as classroom guidance and other learning activities, in the classroom or other school facilities (such as the career and/or media center).

Interdisciplinary Curriculum Development occurs when the school counselor teams with teachers to integrate the school guidance curriculum into the school's academic curriculum.

Group Activities refers to group activities conducted by school counselors outside of the classroom that are designed to be responsive to identified student needs or interests. Small-group *counseling* is not included in this context.

Parent Workshops and Instruction are conducted to address identified needs and to support the school guidance curriculum.

Individual or Small-Group Appraisal involves measuring and evaluating students' abilities, interests, skills, and achievement through standardized and other testing and/or consideration of grades and other student data. Typically, in this context, the school counselor meets with students to design and revise academic plans.

Individual or Small-Group Advisement helps students set realistic educational, vocational, and/or personal goals based on a variety of data. Some specific examples include helping students with their annual course selection, helping students choose postsecondary options, assisting students in locating financial aid, or teaching and/or facilitating students' test preparation and/or taking skills.

Consultation is an indirect service in which school counselors consult with parents, teachers, and other community members to help students and their families.

Individual and Small-Group Counseling involves short-term counseling for students experiencing personal/social concerns or difficulties with normal developmental tasks.

Crisis Counseling supports students and families in emergency situations, is short-term, and is often accompanied by referral.

Referrals are made to a variety of professionals and agencies in the local community that offer services that the school counselor cannot provide and also support the school counselor's services.

Peer Facilitation involves training students to be peer mediators, conflict managers, tutors, or mentors.

Professional Development occurs regularly and involves the school counselor updating her or his skills through in-service training, other professional development activities (e.g., attending professional conferences), or postgraduate education.

Consultation, Collaboration, and Teaming encompass myriad activities that school counselors perform to inform school personnel and the community about the school counseling program and to enlist their cooperation and support. Some specific examples include working with advisory boards, parent–teacher organizations, and community organizations.

Program Management and Operations includes planning and management activities necessary to conduct the school counseling program effectively, analyzing data, establishing policies and procedures, and managing budget and facilities.

These services and their associated activities can be used to meet all of the program goals and student competencies listed in the ASCA National Standards. Ideally, as a school counselor you would develop a comprehensive school counseling program that incorporates the ASCA National Standards and delivers your school counseling program using the services suggested in the *ASCA National Model*, and then evaluate the effectiveness of those services. If the latter idea seems daunting, not to worry; it is not as difficult as you might think.

FROM THE IDEALISTIC TO THE ACTUAL

So how do you become accountable? First, you must decide that you *want* to be accountable. The importance and necessity of having an appropriate perspective on being accountable is covered further in Chapter 9. You also must have a well-conceived school counseling program to evaluate, a program in this context meaning an organized, planned, and systematically implemented set of school counseling activities. If you do not already have one in place, the *ASCA National Model* is a good starting place to develop a program. And even if you have a program in operation, it should be compared to and eventually aligned with the *ASCA National Model*.

The work will teach you how to do it.

—Estonian Proverb

You should also implement a professional role statement. If you do not have one, the ASCA Role Statement (ASCA, 2006) is a good one to follow. Further elaboration of specific roles for elementary, middle/junior high, secondary, and postsecondary school counselors, respectively, can be found at the ASCA Web site (www.schoolcounselor.org). You also will need a framework for evaluating your school counseling program, and again, the *ASCA National Model* is a good one to follow. More specific plans for program evaluation and accountability activities are presented in the following chapters, which you can use to develop an effective work plan. Also, those chapters contain specific suggestions for how to implement the various aspects of a plan and the activities within it.

After collecting program evaluation and accountability data, you must be able to disseminate them effectively; suggestions for effective dissemination are presented prior to planning and specific program evaluation and accountability activities because often the activities selected and/or how they are conducted are shaped by the audience for which the results are intended.

You should not feel alone in what might be perceived as a program evaluation and accountability quagmire. Other school counselors across the country are also starting their accountability activities. Is it easy and effortless? No. But most things important and worth doing require effort.

CONCLUSION

As a school counselor you must be prepared to (a) define your roles, (b) delineate your program, and (c) defend both by collecting and disseminating data which demonstrate that they have a measurable impact on the lives of students, both academically and personally. As an accountable school counselor, you must provide evidence that your school counseling program affects students in positive ways and helps students become more effective learners. As an accountable school counselor, you are also responsible for your actions and must provide evidence that your activities are beneficial to students as well as others interested in or associated with the educational mission of the school. In sum, as an accountable school counselor, you must demonstrate that you make a positive difference. Accountability is accomplished through commitment. From commitment comes the motivation, ideas, resources, and strength to be a truly accountable school counselor, and therefore to be a truly professional school counselor.

The Top 10 Reasons to Become an Accountable School Counselor

(with apologies to David Letterman)

1. You will discover that you are better than you thought you were.

2. Others will learn what you do, and that you do a darn good job.
3. You will earn the respect of your colleagues.
4. You can share your accountability data with other professionals.
5. You will increase the security of your job as a school counselor.
6. Students will know how they benefited from your work.
7. Teachers will know how you helped students.
8. Parents will know how you helped their children.
9. You will feel better for doing what is best for you and your students.
10. You will be a better, professional school counselor!

FOR THOUGHT AND DEED

1. Look over the information you were asked to provide, including your school's mission statement, your primary functions and who determines and evaluates them, the various perspectives on priorities for your school counseling activities, and your knowledge and skills. What is your sense of how it all fits together? Does the information you provided seem to be an integrated whole? If not, what are the aspects that don't seem to fit together?

2. Create three different forms of a letter of request for written comments about the work of school counselors. For the first form, start with the salutation "Dear Teacher" and follow it with the question, "How do school counselors help children?" as the text of the letter. For the second and third forms, use the salutations "Dear Parent" and "Dear Student," respectively, followed by the same question. Make five copies of each letter, and give one copy and an envelope to each of five parents, five teachers, and five students associated with the same school. Instruct each recipient not to put her or his name or other identifying information on the response and return the letter to you in a sealed envelope. After the responses have been returned, read each response. Are there commonalities, or themes, in the responses? How extensive are the responses? Do parents, teachers, and students value school counselors in the same ways or for the same things?

3. Read the mission statement for your school. Inquire at your school about the process used to develop the mission statement. When was it writ-

ten? Who was involved in writing it? Specifically, was a school counselor involved in the process? Certainly, the mission statement addresses students' academic development; does it address other aspects of students' development? How often is it reviewed and/or changed? What is the process for changing it? Write a revised mission statement that you believe incorporates the emphases of school counselors.

4. Find the ethical (or professional) standards for teachers in your state, and compare them to ASCA's (2004) *Ethical Standards for School Counselors*. What are the major similarities and differences in the respective ethical standards? Are there any points of conflict in the respective ethical standards? Investigate the processes for handling cases of alleged ethical misconduct by teachers and by school counselors. What are the similarities and differences in the processes? Visit a school and see if the ethical standards for teachers and/or school counselors are on public display.

CHAPTER 2

ACCOUNTABLE FOR WHAT, TO WHOM, AND HOW?

It is unlikely that any document resulting from the collaborative efforts of school counseling professionals has had (or is likely to have in the foreseeable future) as much and as significant an impact as the *ASCA National Model*. Even at this relatively recent date from its initial and revised versions (released in 2003 and 2005, respectively), this document has spawned widespread, renewed interest in the school counseling profession; generated substantial and substantive professional literature and research; elevated school counseling closer to a level of credibility similar to that of other education professions; and above all, provided direction for the evolution of the school counseling profession. Recognizing that its National Model would be best understood and used if school counseling professionals were cognizant of how it was developed, ASCA included an appendix in the document to present and explain the theory behind it. Briefly, the underlying theory of the *ASCA National Model* is that it was developed as a way to be responsive to seven fundamental questions that must be addressed by the school counseling profession:

1. What do students need that the school counseling profession, based on its special body of knowledge, can address?
2. Which students benefit from activities designed to address these needs?
3. What are school counselors best qualified to do to help them?
4. How do guidance and counseling relate to the overall educational program?
5. How can guidance and counseling be provided most effectively and efficiently?
6. How is a good school counseling program developed by a school?
7. How are the results of school counselors' work measured? (ASCA, 2005, p. 83)

Clearly, these are important questions for you as a school counselor to address, and the *ASCA National Model* provides an effective theoretical basis of response to them. In regard to actual responses to these questions, it is also obvious and emphasized in the National Model that effective responses to these questions must be data-based, that is, responses must include evidence from which arguments for individual school counselor and program effectiveness are derived. Thus, the major focus in the *ASCA National Model* is on generating evidence (i.e., data in various forms) of the results of school counselors' work. That much is abundantly clear, and certainly appropriate. However, merely generating evidence of the results of your school counseling activities and programs will not in and of itself achieve the desired goals. Therefore, we believe that another question should be in the list: How is evidence best used to enhance school counseling practice and programs and the school counseling profession? The point of this question has been noted by other professionals. For example, Baker and Gerler (2004, p. 328) wrote that "collecting evaluative information, though important, is not an end in itself; the information is inert data unless understood by those who have collected it and *presented to others in an informative fashion*" [emphasis added]. Simply put, even good evidence will go to waste if you do not use it properly after it is generated.

If you don't know where you are going, you'll probably wind up someplace else.

—Laurance J. Peter

We find it interesting and perhaps ironic that, in general, the professional literature and research emanating from and including the *ASCA National Model* fail to address with any degree of specificity how the results of measurements of school counselors' work activities should be used. While it would be nice to believe that the data speak for themselves, our experience is that the data rarely do, and even when they do, they are frequently misinterpreted! Therefore, it is important to focus on how generated evidence will be used. In fact, we believe that the important first step in any evidence-generation process is the careful consideration of how evidence of school counselors' work will be used. Therefore, we address how the results of your accountability and program evaluation activities might be used before we discuss how to generate evidence.

What and Why *Data?*

Lapan (2001) wrote that "school counselors are continually immersed in the search for more effective ways to bring about results that are valued by students, parents, school personnel, and the local community" (p. 293), a statement that both speaks to a noble goal and alludes to the idea that information about activity results must be used effectively. The majority of school counselors strive to provide student service activities and programs to the best of their abilities, but how would anyone know that? Inherent in Lapan's statement is the assumption that school counselors can show how, when, where, or in what regard their activities resulted in helping students effectively. Unfortunately, this assumption remains questionable in the eyes of various stakeholders because the majority of school counselors don't demonstrate their effectiveness in delivery of the various services they provide. Even more unfortunately, historic methods of attempting to demonstrate school counselor accountability have been largely unsuccessful.

I always find that statistics are hard to follow and impossible to digest. The only one I can ever remember is that if all the people who go to sleep in church were laid end to end, they would be a lot more comfortable.

—Mrs. Robert A. Taft

School counselors' services would be valued if people knew that the services were being delivered effectively, especially if it were required that the evidence of effectiveness were available for public scrutiny. However, making evidence available to a variety of audiences likely is not enough; it must be the right kind of evidence. Therefore, given that school counselors need to be and can be accountable, a logical question arises: What is the best basis of (or evidence for) school counselor accountability? Clearly the answer is *data*. This emphasis pervades current expectations for education in the broadest contexts. For example, Lewis (2003) wrote that

> in the *No Child Left Behind Act*, Congress refers to evidence-based or research-based education at least 130 times. Every program and initiative wears this requirement, presumably as an antidote to 30 years of considerable federal government invest-

ment in improving education that critics contend has yielded a succession of fads rather than proven success. (p. 339)

The word *data* usually connotes "numbers." However, technically, data are defined simply as "factual information," which allows data to be information in many different forms. Further, data can be generated in different ways (i.e., through different types of processes), so relatively simultaneous consideration must be given both to what and how data are generated. The *ASCA National Model* includes clarification that is specifically relevant for school counselor accountability and program evaluation activities:

> School counseling programs are data-driven. Data create a picture of student needs and provide an accountable way to align the school counseling program with the school's academic mission. Although it is certainly important to know what services are provided for students (process data), this doesn't provide the complete picture. Collecting process data, which is evidence that an event or activity occurred, without a clear understanding of the activity's impact (perception and results data) is less meaningful because it does not provide enough information. Results data answer the question, "So what?" Results data show proof that a student competency is not just mastered but has affected course-taking patterns, graduation rates, knowledge attainment, attendance, behavior or academic achievement. (ASCA, 2005, p. 16)

Stone and Dahir (2007) provided a good, clarifying example of the distinction between process and results data as presented in the *ASCA National Model*:

> Just totaling the number of student contacts made, group sessions held, and classroom guidance lessons delivered is "so what" data in the eyes of legislators, school board members, and other critical stakeholders. In other words, what do these totals really mean if students are being left out of the academic success picture and their future opportunities are adversely stratified? Counting what we do will not demonstrate to our colleagues and community stakeholders that we are powerful contributors in our schools. (pp. 1–2)

Thus, the evidence (data) of the results of school counselors' activities should be any type of information that serves to communicate the outcomes and/or effectiveness of an activity, including numeric information, visual information (e.g., charts, graphs, pictures, diagrams, PowerPoint presentations, objects, or videotapes), or even auditory information (e.g., verbal presentations or audio tapes). Data are clearly the basis for being accountable, but your collection of accountability data need not be impeded by narrow interpretation of what constitutes data. (See Figure 2.1 for an example of school data.)

SCHOOL DATA

Think about the different types of data that your school regularly collects (e.g., standardized test scores, attendance records, graduation rates, referral records, students' grades) and consider how these data can be used for school counseling accountability purposes. In the left column, list the different types of data your school collects. In the second and third columns, list one or two school counseling activities that are related to each of those types of data.

Type of Data	School Counseling Activity	School Counseling Activity
Attendance records	Individual/small-group counseling	Parent consultation
Referral (discipline) records	Individual counseling	Parent consultation
Student grade data	Small-group counseling	Classroom guidance
Standardized test data	Classroom guidance	Teacher consultation
Student retention (in grade) records	Parent consultation	Individual counseling
Parent contacts/inquiries	Parent consultation	Teacher consultation
IEP meeting records	Teacher consultation	Consultation with other school personnel

FIGURE 2.1. Listing of school data.

ACCOUNTABLE FOR WHAT?

A reasonable and logical first question that you as a school counselor should consider is, For what should I be accountable? The easy answer is that you should be accountable for all the activities you perform in your job as a school counselor. However, there is a trap in relying on this easy answer. If this perspective is adopted, then you and other school counselors will find yourselves trying to be accountable for activities that have not been endorsed by the school counseling profession as appropriate for and to school counselor functioning. It is well-known and well-documented (e.g., Burnham & Jackson, 2000) that school counselors perform many functions that fall outside of recommended and professionally endorsed school counselor functions and activities. For example, school counselors who have bus duty or lunch-room duty can generate accountability data for their effectiveness in such functions. But is generating performance data for those activities really desirable? To generate and disseminate such information would in fact be a disservice to the school counseling profession, serving only to promulgate the impression that many nonprofessional activities are appropriate for school counselors. Therefore, you, other school counselors, and the school counseling profession, are better served by generation and dissemination of accountability data for appropriate professional activities. But that begs the question, What are a school counselor's "appropriate" activities?

Determine the thing that can and shall be done, and then we shall find a way.

—Abraham Lincoln

A wide variety of school counselor functions and activities have been identified and recommended in the professional literature, including several comprehensive overviews of potentially appropriate school counselor functions as well as their integration into an effective school counseling program (e.g., Baker & Gerler, 2004; Cobia & Henderson, 2003, 2006; Erford, 2007b; Gysbers & Henderson, 2006; Paisley &

Hubbard, 1994; Myrick, 2002; Schmidt, 2002). Further, ASCA (2006) provided a role statement that delineates much of what is deemed important for school counselors. However, perhaps the strongest endorsement for various, presumably most appropriate and important, school counselor functions is inclusion in the *ASCA National Model*. Even prior to its initial official release, Hatch and Bowers (2002) wrote that

> the [ASCA] National Model for School Counseling Programs is written to reflect a comprehensive approach to program foundation, delivery, management and accountability. It provides a framework for the program components, the school counselor's role in implementation and the underlying philosophies of leadership, advocacy and systemic change. (p. 15)

Thus, the four Delivery System components in the *ASCA National Model* (i.e., School Guidance Curriculum, Individual Student Planning, Responsive Services, and Systems Support) encompass the major school counselor functions and activities widely endorsed in the school counseling profession. But again, although valuable and helpful, these resources don't denote the actual activities to be performed by individual school counselors.

One method to determine which activities (i.e., manifestations of roles and functions) would be appropriate for your use as a school counselor would be to scour the professional literature and then select those activities you believe are most relevant to your situation. This tactic would have the advantage of identifying professionally endorsed activities. However, this approach also has some major limitations. For one, the activities thus identified may not be viewed as appropriate by others who have interest in and perhaps control over the activities in which a school counselor engages. For another, the activities thus identified may not include all the activities you deem appropriate (and important) in your situation. And finally, and most importantly, success in implementing the results of this approach is yet again contingent upon your ability to argue for whatever it is that you should be doing, a tactic that historically has not been productive for most school counselors.

An alternative and relatively widely endorsed (e.g., Hadley & Mitchell, 1995; Houser, 1998) approach is to consider your appropriate activities within the broad context of program evaluation. The essence of program evaluation is to use data to make decisions. For example,

Royse, Thyer, Padgett, and Logan (2006) wrote that "program evaluation is applied research used as a part of managerial process. Evaluations are conducted to aid those who must make administrative decisions about human service programs" (p. 11). Similarly, Hadley and Mitchell (1995) noted that "program evaluation involves collecting, analyzing, and interpreting data to make or support decisions about a service program" (p. 61). Certainly, deciding in which activities to engage is an important decision you and every other school counselor (and/or others who determine the activities) must make.

Within the professional program evaluation literature, determining in which activities a service provider (here, a school counselor) should engage falls under the general rubric of program planning. In turn, good program planning starts with needs assessment. Some authors present needs assessment as an integral part of any program evaluation process (e.g., Hadley & Mitchell, 1995) while others suggest that needs assessment is in and of itself a specific program evaluation process (e.g., Unrau, Gabor, & Grinnell, 2001). Regardless, the basic idea is that before you can decide what to do, you must decide what needs to be done. Unrau et al. (2001) wrote that "the evaluation of need, more commonly called 'needs assessment,' is a type of evaluation that aims to establish the degree to which a social need...actually exists..., as well as corresponding solutions" (p. 60). The term *social need* in this context encompasses any of a wide variety of needs that students may have, specifically including those related to their academic, personal, and career developments. The importance of effective needs assessment was emphasized by Royse, Thyer, Padgett, and Logan (2006) who wrote that "needs assessments should be conducted to ensure that scarce resources are being utilized in the best ways, as well as to determine further programming issues. Needs assessment is also the measure against which program implementation and outcome will be compared" (p. 54). Popham (1993) noted that "the most popular needs-assessment models emphasize the accumulation of a considerable amount of *preference* data, typically from a variety of *different* educational clienteles, such as pupils, teachers, and parents" (p. 67). Therefore, wants often are an integral part of any needs assessment process, allowing that some peoples' "wants" are other peoples' needs. For example, parents want their children to be well-prepared to move through the world of work, which translates to students having a need for effective career development services.

One would not want to develop a program, even a great program, if the need was not there.

Houser (1998)

The activities in which school counselors routinely engage are supposed to be professional, behavioral responses to students' (and perhaps others') needs as determined through systematic investigation of what their most important needs are. We will revisit program evaluation procedures, including needs assessments, in Chapter 3. Our more immediate point here is that the definition of appropriate activities for you or any individual school counselor are those that are responsive to (locally) identified student needs. Of course, the delicacy in this position is that besides students, others associated with schools also have needs. For example, parents, school and district-level administrators, members of the community, and teachers, among others, all have needs to which they want you as a school counselor to attend. The needs of people other than students associated with schools are of course important, warrant attention, and are supposed to be attended to as reflected in professional school counseling recommendations (e.g., as in the ASCA National Standards). Nonetheless, we believe that activities specifically intended to be responsive to students' needs are the most appropriate activities in which you should engage as a school counselor and therefore should be given your highest priority.

Unfortunately, even assuming that the professional school counseling activities in which you engage have been determined from an effective needs assessment, it remains likely that there are many more activities that are deemed important than you can actually engage in. In other words, you have to establish behavioral (i.e., professional activity) priorities, even in the best of circumstances.

School counselors sometimes are viewed as ineffective because they are perceived as spending too much time with too few students. It is easy to see why school counselors fall into this trap. After all, school counselors are trained as helpers, and the students with the most severe problems typically are perceived as the ones most in need of help. However, is providing one-on-one counseling and other direct interventions with a small number of the most troubled students really the best use of your time as a school counselor?

The *ASCA National Model* indicates that school counselors should provide counseling services to *all* students in their respective schools. However, if a school counselor is responsible for 500 or more students and tries to give equal attention to all of them, it is unlikely she or he will have much effect on any of them. Imagine a philanthropist who has $500,000 to donate to alleviate poverty in a community of 100,000 people. The philanthropist could give each person $5, but that would probably have little impact on each person's situation. Alternatively, the philanthropist could identify the 100 neediest people and give them each $5,000, but a lot of people would not be helped at all.

Even donating money can involve difficult choices. A school counselor with an overload of students is faced with a similar situation. To maximize effectiveness, you must prioritize the school counseling services (i.e., activities) you provide for students, and in so doing must allocate your time among activities in a way that is most likely to maximize the benefits of your efforts. Making such decisions isn't easy and isn't fun, but it must be done.

As popularized in the television show *M*A*S*H*, the medical profession developed triage procedures as a way of coping with large-scale medical emergencies. In triage, a medical staff very quickly makes decisions about initial treatment priority, usually in three categories of attention, including those with (a) minor injuries who can wait for treatment; (b) serious injuries who cannot wait and need immediate attention; and (c) injuries so severe that they likely will not survive, even if all available resources are devoted to them. Again, tough decisions to make! Nonetheless, triage was and is essential to ensure that limited medical personnel and supplies can be used to maximize the effects of the services that can be provided.

School counselors facing unreasonable student-to-counselor ratios (i.e., well above the ASCA recommended ratio of 250:1) knowingly or not engage in school counseling triage. Consider a junior high school counselor responsible for 500 students. Suppose there are 25 students (about 5%) who present the biggest problems in the school (e.g., numerous behavioral infractions, suspensions, low academic achievement, excessive absences, low parental involvement). These students likely have presented these problems consistently through elementary school. Teachers and administrators certainly want the school counselor to straighten out those kids. How much time and effort should the school counselor spend on these 25 students? Finally, imagine that the school district is on Academic Emergency status because it meets 7 or fewer of the state's 27 academic performance indicators. Quite a quandary for the school counselor, isn't it?

FUN WITH NUMBERS?

Just to illustrate a point, assume you are a school counselor with a student load of 500 students. Also assume that you have 40 work hours per week to devote to your students and that there are 36 weeks in the academic school year. And finally, assume that administrative, clerical, indirect service, and other miscellaneous tasks take away 15 of those work-week hours, leaving you 25 hours per week to allocate to appropriate school counseling services such as individual and small-group counseling, classroom guidance, and parent and teacher consultation. Under those conditions, you would have a total of 1,500 minutes per week or 54,000 minutes per year [(25 hours/week) × (60 minutes/hour) × (36 weeks/year)] for appropriate school counseling activities. That means that you would have 108 minutes for each student for the year, or, alternatively, 3 minutes per student per week. Somehow, the 108 minutes per student per year doesn't seem too bad, but the 3 minutes per week seems pretty awful!

If only we'd stop trying to be happy, we could have a pretty good time.

—Williard R. Espey

Now assume that among the 500 students for whom you are responsible over the 36 weeks, 450 are typical, average students and that the others are mildly, moderately, and severely at-risk for behavior and/or academic problems. Assuming you spend an equal amount of time with each student each week, Table 2.1 shows how your time allocations would change for various combinations of numbers of students in the various categories. The data in Table 2.1 are essentially self-evident; they simply show a shift in your time allocations as a function of type of student under the assumption of spending an equal amount of time (i.e., 3 minutes per week) with each student. Unfortunately, this table is of little value (other than as a visual stimulus) because the under-

46 The Accountable School Counselor

TABLE 2.1.
EQUAL TIME ALLOCATIONS

Average Students		Mildly At-Risk Students		Moderately At-Risk Students		Severely At-Risk Students		Total Minutes Available
Number	Minutes Per Week	Number	Minutes Per Week	Number	Minutes Per Week	Number	Minutes Per Week	
450	1,350	20	60	20	60	10	30	1,500
430	1,290	40	120	20	60	10	30	1,500
410	1,230	40	120	40	120	10	30	1,500
400	1,200	40	120	40	120	20	60	1,500
380	1,140	60	180	40	120	20	60	1,500
370	1,110	60	180	40	120	30	90	1,500

Note. School counselors' minutes-per-week allocations for various types of students, assuming equal time allocation for each type of student.

lying assumption is faulty. That is, neither you nor any other school counselor functions so as to spend an equal amount of time with each student each year. Clearly students who are at-risk require more of your time and attention than do average students. So, let's change the assumption and reconstruct the table.

We do not know of a fully valid way to determine the differential time allocations in the various categories presented because we do not know how to provide operational (behavioral) definitions of the students in the respective categories. Who knows how much more time must be spent with, for example, a severely at-risk student as compared to an average student? However, for illustrative purposes, assume that a mildly at-risk student requires twice as much time as an average student, a moderately at-risk student requires three times as much time as an average student, and a severely at-risk student requires four times as much time as an average student. Table 2.2 shows the impact of this assumption on a hypothetical school counselor's time for the same distributions of students as are in Table 2.1.

As before, the time available for the average student decreases as the time devoted to at-risk students increases, but the effect for average students is much more dramatic. Now consider the same data, but on a weekly time-per-student basis, as shown in Table 2.3. Notice in particular that as the number of at-risk students increases from 50 to 130, the time available for each average student decreases approxi-

TABLE 2.2.
DIFFERENT TIME ALLOCATIONS

Average Students		Mildly At-Risk Students		Moderately At-Risk Students		Severely At-Risk Students		Total Minutes Available
Number	Minutes Per Week	Number	Minutes Per Week	Number	Minutes Per Week	Number	Minutes Per Week	
450	1,080	20	120	20	180	10	120	1,500
430	960	40	240	20	180	10	120	1,500
410	780	40	240	40	360	10	120	1,500
400	660	40	240	40	360	20	240	1,500
380	540	60	360	40	360	20	240	1,500
370	510	60	360	40	360	30	270	1,500

Note. School counselors' minutes-per-week allocations for various types of students, assuming different time allocation as a function of type of student.

TABLE 2.3.
DIFFERENT TIME ALLOCATIONS, PER STUDENT

Average Students		Mildly At-Risk Students		Moderately At-Risk Students		Severely At-Risk Students	
Number	Minutes Per Week	Number	Minutes Per Week	Number	Minutes Per Week	Number	Minutes Per Week
450	2.40	20	6.00	20	9.00	10	12.00
430	2.24	40	6.00	20	9.00	10	12.00
410	1.91	40	6.00	40	9.00	10	12.00
400	1.65	40	6.00	40	9.00	20	12.00
380	1.43	60	6.00	40	9.00	20	12.00
370	1.38	60	6.00	40	9.00	30	9.00

Note. School counselors' minutes-per-student-per-week allocations for various types of students, assuming different time allocation as a function of type of student.

mately 42% per student per week! Remember that this example started with data for an entire academic school year. Given the unpredictable variations in students' behavior throughout the school year, is it any wonder that school counselors have a difficult time figuring out how to spend their time?

We presented this example for two reasons. First and foremost, it illustrates in general the difficulty a school counselor faces in trying to prioritize activities, and in particular how even a relatively small shift in time allocated to a relatively few students substantially affects the time available for the majority of students. Second, it illustrates the use of data (in this case numbers) to make a point, which we have been emphasizing. This is, in a sense, a frustrating example in that it presents a scenario that guarantees that you as a school counselor cannot provide direct interventions effectively to all students who need them. Of course, in reality, you could provide some indirect services (e.g., consultation and referral) to try to reach more of the students or to try to increase the 25 hours of direct intervention time by reducing the 15 hours per week devoted to other activities. Otherwise, you could try to convince the administration to hire another school counselor. In any case, many school counselors find themselves in this exemplified situation. And again, prioritizing and targeting effort is necessary to maximizing functional effectiveness *and* efficiency and also to be accountable.

Let's personalize this example for you. First, determine the number of students for whom you are responsible in your school (i.e., your student load), and identify that number as SL. Next, estimate as realistically as possible the number of hours per week (on average) that you can devote to direct student service, and designate that number as HPW. Multiply HPW times 60 to give your weekly total minutes available (TMA). Next, divide your TMA by your SL, which can be identified as your time-per-student-per-week (TPS). In other words, calculate [(hours/week $\times$ 60 minutes/hour) / (number of students)] = TPS.

Now, estimate as accurately as possible the numbers of average (NAS), mildly (MAS), moderately (MDAS), and severely (SAS) at-risk students, respectively, among your students, using your own definitions of those categories. Next, complete the first row below the column headings in Table 2.4, which will give you an estimate of how you spend your time for various types of students. Finally, see what would happen if the numbers of students in the MAS, MDAS, and SAS categories, respectively, increased by 50% (i.e., complete the bottom row of the table). To do this, first calculate the new estimated numbers of students in the EMAS, EMDAS, and ESAS categories, respectively, by multiplying each of the original numbers by 1.5 and rounding to the nearest whole number. You can best complete the second row of the table by working from right to left. That is, first determine ESAS and

TABLE 2.4.
TIME ESTIMATOR TEMPLATE

Average Students		Mildly At-Risk Students		Moderately At-Risk Students		Severely At-Risk Students		Total Minutes Available
Number (NAS)	Minutes (NAS × TPS)	Number (MAS)	Minutes (MAS × TPS)	Number (MDAS)	Minutes (MDAS × TPS)	Number (SAS)	Minutes (SAS × TPS)	TMA
Number (ENAS)	Minutes (ENAS × TPS)	Number (EMAS)	Minutes (EMAS × TPS)	Number (EMDAS)	Minutes (EMDAS × TPS)	Number (ESAS)	Minutes (ESAS × TPS)	TMA

Note. Minutes-per-student-per-week time estimator template for your work as a school counselor. NAS = number average students, TPS = time-per-student-per-week, MAS = mildly at-risk students, MDAS = moderately at-risk students, SAS = severely at-risk students, TMA = total minutes available, ENAS = estimated number average students, EMAS = estimated number mildly at-risk students, EMDAS = estimated number moderately at-risk students, ESAS = estimated number severely at-risk students.

then calculate ESAS × TPS. Follow the same procedure to calculate (EMDAS × TPS) and (EMAS × TPS). Finally, determine the number of minutes available for average students by finding the sum of [(ENAS × TPS) + (EMAS × TPS) + (ESAS × TPS)] and then subtracting that sum from TMA. We know it's a bit confusing, but play with the numbers for a while, and the right numbers will fall out.

Look at the numbers of minutes in the (NAS × TPS) and (ENAS × TPS) cells in Table 2.4. How dramatic is the change in the time available for average students if the numbers of at-risk students changes even 50%? Remember that the calculations used to fill this last row of the table are based on the assumption that an equal amount of time is spent with each type of student (i.e., TPS is constant across categories), and that assumption is certainly never valid in real school counseling situations.

ACCOUNTABLE TO WHOM?

A next logical question is, To whom should school counselors be accountable? The general answer is to the stakeholders of the school counseling program. Stakeholders are the people who have a vested interest in the effectiveness of a school counseling program. The term *vested interest* means that stakeholders care about the effectiveness of the school counseling program because they stand to achieve personal gain if, and only if, the school counseling program is effective. The personal gain may be direct and observable (e.g., for teachers when students' test scores improve substantially) or indirect and subtle (e.g., when real estate agents are able to brag about how good the local schools are). However, more often, the personal gain is psychological and emotional; it is a feeling of satisfaction that good things are happening as a result of the school counseling program. Stakeholders achieve a feeling of satisfaction about the school counseling program when they are presented with evidence of its effectiveness. Therefore, in a sense, you as a school counselor must be accountable to make the stakeholders feel good about what is happening in your school counseling program.

Unfortunately (or fortunately, depending on your personal viewpoint), school counselors do not get to choose the stakeholders for their school counseling programs. Rather, a wide variety of stakeholders (or stakeholder groups) always exists for school counseling programs. Baker and Gerler (2004) wrote that "theoretically, the consumers of school counseling are the children and adolescents served by the school district. Realistically, parents, guardians, school board members, and all the citizenry have expectations of the school counselor, too" [sic] (p. 327). What differentiates various stakeholders is the relative directness of their demands for school counselor accountability. Some, such as school administrators, are forthcoming and explicit in their expectations of school counselor accountability. Others, such as community members, typically are far more passive in expressing their accountability expectations. Unfortunately, school counselors often make the mistake of assuming that more obvious stakeholders are somehow more important, and therefore restrict the focus of their accountability activities to those perceived as more important. Such a perspective and the behaviors associated with it are regretable for two major reasons. First, directing accountability activities only at those perceived as more important often leads to alienation of other stakeholders, who in fact may be far more important than is realized. For example, performing clerical and administrative duties specifically to satisfy a principal detracts from a school counselor's ability to demonstrate effectiveness with the teachers and parents. Second, restricting accountability activities leads to the restriction of program services based on what is perceived to be valued by the important stakeholders. As a truly accountable school counselor, you should not assume that some stakeholders are more important than others, but rather strive to be accountable to all stakeholders. Following is a discussion of some of the stakeholder groups to whom school counselors should be accountable. They are not presented in any particular order of importance.

PARENTS AND FAMILIES

Popularizing the old African proverb, Senator and former First Lady Hillary Clinton achieved a degree of notoriety by proclaiming that "it takes a whole village to raise a child." The obvious implication is that many, many people must be involved in positive and significant ways for a child to develop into a well-adjusted adult. Clearly, parents and other family members are at the center of a student's village, and therefore have ultimate responsibility for the student's effective development. However, a school counselor also is an important member of a student's village. And it is precisely because a school counselor has the privilege of being a part of a student's village that the school counselor must be accountable to the parents and family for their part in the student's development.

In general, parents and family members want a student to develop into a good person, get a good education, and get a good job. Most parents and family members recognize that they have primary responsibility for helping their child to become a good person. However, they rightfully expect help from the schools with the process. Most parents and family members also rightfully expect the schools to have the primary responsibility for their child's education and subsequent attainment of a good job or postsecondary placement. However, most also expect to have to assist with these processes. Clearly, the roles of parents and families and the schools in helping each student develop into an effective, educated, and productive member of society are interrelated. They are also presumably mutually supportive. Therefore, as a school counselor you must be accountable to parents and families for their contributions to each student's development. In fact, parents who understand and support the activities of school counselors may be the most influential group in preserving and/or expanding school counseling services. (See Figure 2.2 for an example of a parent informing and involving form.)

52   The Accountable School Counselor

The most basic element of promoting the school counseling program to parents is educating them about the role of school counselors in the school program.

T. Davis, 2005, p. 197

PARENT INFORMING AND INVOLVING

Being accountable to parents and guardians is essential to gaining their support for your school counseling activities and services. The column on the left lists the school counseling services delineated in the *ASCA National Model*. In the second column, list ways that you can inform parents of the service and how it may benefit their children. In the last column, list how you might involve parents in delivering the services or evaluating them.

Service Offered	How to *Inform* Parents	How to *Involve* Parents
Classroom Instruction	School newsletter PTA newsletter Guidance department Web site School Web site Announcement sent home with students	Serve as role models and/or presenters for large-group guidance activities
Interdisciplinary Curriculum Development	Announcement sent home with students	Serve on guidance department advisory committee Provide suggestions for school counseling program involvements
Group Activities	Announcement sent home with students	Serve on guidance department advisory committee
Parent Workshops and Instruction	School newsletter PTA newsletter Guidance department Web site School Web site Announcement sent home with students	Lead subgroups for the activities Make presentations on selected topics

FIGURE 2.2. Parent informing and involving form.

Accountable for What, to Whom, and How?   53

Service Offered	How to *Inform* Parents	How to *Involve* Parents
Individual or Small-Group Appraisal	Announcement sent home with students	Serve on guidance department advisory committee
Individual or Small-Group Advisement	School newsletter PTA newsletter Guidance department Web site School Web site Announcement sent home with students	Assist with dissemination for advisement information
Consultation	School newsletter PTA newsletter Guidance department Web site School Web site	Serve on guidance department advisory committee Liaison with other parents to promote parent contact with school counselors
Individual and Small-Group Counseling	School newsletter PTA newsletter Guidance department Web site School Web site Announcement sent home with students	Provide opinions on preferred activities
Crisis Counseling/ Response	School newsletter PTA newsletter Guidance department Web site School Web site Announcement sent home with students	Help to identify community resources
Referrals	School newsletter PTA newsletter Guidance department Web site School Web site	Help to identify community resources

continues

FIGURE 2.2. (*continued*)

Service Offered	How to *Inform* Parents	How to *Involve* Parents
Peer Facilitation	School newsletter PTA newsletter Guidance department Web site School Web site Announcement sent home with students	Provide opinions on preferred activities Serve on guidance department advisory committee
Professional Development	School newsletter PTA newsletter Guidance department Web site School Web site	Help to identify needed school counseling program improvements that could be facilitated by professional development/ continuing education
Consultation, Collaboration, and Teaming	School newsletter PTA newsletter Guidance department Web site School Web site	Serve on guidance department advisory committee Identify needed school counseling program improvements
Program Management and Operation	School newsletter PTA newsletter Guidance department Web site School Web site	Serve on guidance department advisory committee

FIGURE 2.2. (*continued*)

SCHOOL ADMINISTRATORS

Melton (2003) wrote that "because the principal defines the school's educational mission, school counselors should view principals as one of their most important stakeholders" (p. 4). Note that in concert with the previous recommendation, principals are one of the most important stakeholder groups but are not the only stakeholders who are important. Regardless of the level of importance attributed to principals, however, the importance is often not reciprocal. Indeed, it is ironic that while the school principal is usually the school counselor's boss and therefore has responsibility (e.g., to the school board) for what the school counselor actually does, most school principals have little knowledge of currently recommended school counseling practices. Johnson (2000) put it succinctly:

> If truth be known, most educational administrators...have little understanding of what counselor education is all about and what school counselors are qualified to provide in terms of developmental, responsive, and consultative services as a result of their graduate training. (p. 32)

Knowledgeable or not, a principal directs the school. Baker and Gerler (2004) noted that

> principals clearly influence the environment in their schools. What they value most will influence their own behavior and what they reinforce positively or negatively in the values and behaviors of their subordinates, in their school rules, and in the assignment of responsibilities within their purview. (p. 353)

Obviously this situation does not bode well for school counselors who are not aware of and responsive to their school administrators' importance. It also implies that school counselors must strive to educate their school principals about what constitutes an effective and comprehensive school counseling program and their specific roles and functions within such a program. This is not a new implication and, in fact, there is much discussion in the professional school counseling literature about how you as a school counselor can best educate your school principal. What is perhaps new is the generation and presentation of accountability evidence as a means to educate school principals. Advocacy for a comprehensive school counseling program is certainly important. However, when advocacy is supported by evidence of the effectiveness of activities endorsed by the school counseling profession, the impact of the advocacy is improved significantly. It is one thing for you to simply recommend certain school counseling functions to your school administrator, but it is quite another to show that implementation of those functions has had positive and desirable outcomes for your school administrator.

A great teacher never strives to explain his vision – he simply invites you to stand beside him and see for yourself.

—Rev. R. Inman

TEACHERS

The primary purpose of schools is to educate students. This statement is at once both profound and overly simplistic. It is profound in its implications for the tremendous responsibility given to schools in our society. It is overly simplistic in that it implies that teachers are the only people who educate students. However, school counselors can and should contribute to the educational mission of the schools, a perspective clearly reflected in the school counseling profession:

> The ACSA National Model supports the school's academic mission by promoting and enhancing the learning process for all students through an integration of academic, career and personal/social development. (ASCA, 2005, p. 15)

School counseling services are designed to promote and enhance students' learning processes in many ways. Perhaps the most obvious one is when school counselors work directly with teachers for a variety of purposes, such as facilitating classroom management, improving students' in-class behaviors, facilitating teacher–parent interactions, enhancing teacher–student interactions, or assisting teacher performance of noninstructional activities. School counselors spend a significant amount of their time in these activities, which vary from brief comments while passing in hallways to formal and structured interactions such as collaborative consultation (Kampwirth, 2006).

Typically, school counselors' interactions with teachers are brief because both have tremendous demands on their time. Unfortunately, as a result of their brevity, teachers often don't think very much about these activities and the impact of these activities commonly goes unnoticed for the same reason. School counselors should therefore be especially diligent in the generation of accountability data for their work with teachers because it goes directly to the educational mission of the schools. Teachers should and *deserve* to know that school counselors' activities facilitate and enhance student learning. When the teachers in your school come to understand how you serve the educational mission of the school, they view you as part of the educational team, support your school counselor work and activities, and endorse your school counseling program and the school counseling profession.

SCHOOL BOARDS

The members of school boards are directly responsible and accountable to the people of the community. Unfortunately, people in the communities to which school boards are accountable typically hold them responsible only for more obvious criteria, such as changes in standardized test scores, numbers of student graduating from high schools, or numbers of students attending college after graduation. It is even more unfortunate that school boards often only provide community members types of data with which to be accountable. School counselors can and should provide information that is distinct from these more common indicators of a school system's success (Gysbers, Lapan, & Jones, 2000).

Power undirected by high purpose spells calamity; and high purpose by itself is utterly useless if the power to put it into effect is lacking.

—Theodore Roosevelt

Typically, the school counseling accountability information of most interest to school boards is program evaluation results. School boards are charged to oversee the entire school system operation and therefore must embrace a macro (i.e., large-scale, broad overview) perspective to fulfill their responsibilities. In that context, school board members are likely to be most concerned about a school's entire school counseling program rather than its specific activities. (While presenting the effectiveness of specific activities to school boards is not inappropriate, it should be restricted to activities that are especially noteworthy.) If you present substantive information about the effectiveness of your school counseling program to your school board (either of the entire program or of a specific activity), you stand to benefit not only yourself but also your school board, who can then use the information for their own accountability purposes. It is a unique win-win situation for all.

OTHER SCHOOL PERSONNEL

Obviously, there are many people who work in or with schools who are far less recognized than teachers or school administrators. Media and curriculum specialists, secretarial and clerical assistants, maintenance personnel, school resource officers, school bus drivers, school nurses, school psychologists, speech and hearing therapists, occupational therapists, school social workers, and many others all contribute significantly to the educational mission of the schools. School counselors have much in common with these other school personnel. For example, Simcox, Nuijens, and Lee (2006) delineated some the commonalities between school counselors and school psychologists:

Both school counselors and school psychologists are being called upon to assume an advocacy role in their work with students and their families....

Both school counselors and school psychologists are viewed as systemic change agents....

School counselors and school psychologists are being challenged to assume a greater leadership role in both the school and the community....

Both professionals are being called upon to increase their involvement in crucial educational decision-making processes and initiate evidence-based programs for enhancing student achievement....

School counselors and school psychologists must establish and assess measurable goals for student outcomes....

> School counselors and school psychologists are increasingly acting as collaborators with other educational stakeholders. (p. 273)

Similarly, Barnes, Friehe, and Radd (2003) described the advantages of school counselors and speech–language pathologists working together effectively. And finally, Moore (2005) highlighted the advantages of effective collaboration between school counselors and counseling psychologists who work with students. Thus, school counselors interact with other school personnel in many different ways because of their shared mission and therefore have an obligation to be accountable to them. Unfortunately, these other school personnel rarely know how the work of school counselors interacts with their work or what they can and should expect from school counselors. However, this circumstance does not absolve you as a school counselor from the obligation to be accountable to them. In fact, it heightens that obligation. Here, too being accountable to other school personnel has significant educational value to help them more fully and appropriately understand what you do and how your effective services help everyone in the schools.

STUDENTS

It would be easy to suggest that because students receive the direct benefits from school counselors' services, there is no need to be accountable to them. However, it is precisely because students know school counselor's roles that they should be informed of school counselor's effectiveness. Students rarely have comprehensive knowledge of all the services school counselors can provide. Even students who have had occasion to interact with a school counselor are likely to have uniquely personal perspectives on the school counselor's effectiveness. Conversely, students who have not interacted with a school counselor have no direct way of knowing how a school counselor might be helpful to them. In either case, student perspectives on what school counselors do is likely to be restricted, which means that students generally are unaware of the many ways that school counselors can be helpful. We have discovered a crude but simple way to get a sense of a school counselor's effectiveness. When we visit a school, we ask a few students who their school counselor is and what he or she does. There's an obvious message if most of the students answer, "I don't know." What would your students tell us if we visited your school?

Every adult needs a child to teach; it's the way adults learn.

Frank A. Clark

Students obviously change as they proceed through school, as a function of normal human growth and development. A unique way to view school counseling is to suggest that it is intended to optimize each student's normal development. That is, by intervening in students' lives, school counselors seek to direct them toward fully positive educational and personal development and to help them avoid the pitfalls of what is otherwise relatively random development. For example, a school counselor who assists a student effectively with a problem situation has helped the student to alter what would otherwise have been a negative or inhibiting situation in the student's normal development. Similarly, developmental guidance and other activities having similar purposes are intended to help children choose more effective behaviors than they might choose if simply left to their normal development. Because school counselors, at least potentially, can have a highly significant impact on students' development, they must be accountable for their activities. In particular, they must be directly accountable to the students whose lives they affect.

MEMBERS OF THE COMMUNITY

It takes tremendous resources to operate a school, and someone has to pay for those resources. Community members (i.e., the citizenry of the local community) pay for schools either indirectly (such as through payment of various taxes) or directly (such as through payment of tuition). It is because they pay for schools that community members have a right to know if their payments are being used effectively. Therefore, school counselors have an obligation to be accountable to the members of their schools' communities.

Unfortunately, school counselors often assume that accountability activities directed toward more obvious stakeholders, such as school administrators or school boards, will somehow filter out into the community at large. Perusal of the editorial page of most newspapers is but one way to verify that this assumption typically is invalid. In fact, most people in most communities actually know very little about what is going on in their local schools in general and in their school counseling programs in particular—a situation acknowledged by many school counseling authorities. For example, Baker and Gerler (2004) wrote that "the roles and functions of school counselors...have not been fully understood by a large part of the public" (p. 329). Fortunately, there is a great opportunity in this rather unfortunate situation. Specifically, because so little is known about what goes on in schools, dissemination of information about effective school activities is always well received. Therefore, by being accountable to members of the community, you not only fulfill an accountability obligation but also stand to improve attitudes and perceptions substantially about what you and other school counselors actually do. Further, the mere act of attending to the school-related concerns of a community would be a welcome change in most communities. Providing actual evidence of effectiveness likely would result in very positive responses from community members and therefore greatly enhance support for your school counseling services from a highly significant stakeholder group. (See Figure 2.3 for an example of a list of people school counselors might try to influence.)

THE SCHOOL COUNSELING PROFESSION

Being a member of the school counseling profession is a privilege, but not one without concomitant obligation. For example, you as a school counselor are obligated to have successfully completed appropriate preparation to be a school counselor (as well as to continue to improve your skills), adhere to the behavioral guidelines (such as ethical standards and legal requirements), and use your skills as best as you are able. Far less recognized, however, is your obligation as a school counselor to give something back to the school counseling profession. In particular, you carry the obligation to contribute to the knowledge base of the profession. Sharing evidence of effectiveness of your school counseling activities with other school counselors is a primary way to fulfill this obligation. True professionals are people who care not only about what they do, but also about what other members of their respective professions do; they seek to improve not only what they do, but also

62   The Accountable School Counselor

PEOPLE SCHOOL COUNSELORS MIGHT TRY TO INFLUENCE

It's easy enough to think about and identify *categories* of stakeholders to whom a school counselor should be accountable, especially since we listed most of them for you. However, that doesn't do much to personalize the accountability process, and school counselors like to have personal involvements with people. So, to personalize the idea of your stakeholders, think of people who are representative or typical of the various stakeholder groups to whom you should be accountable. Then, write the names of four representative people in each stakeholder category to whom you would like, or feel it necessary, to be accountable.

Parents	(PTA president) LaKesha Adkinson	(Fellow school counselor) Ed Turnerman
	(Class guest) Thurmond Jenkins	(Teacher) Adriana Barmeister
Administrators	(Principal) Monte Deshead	(Superintendent) Lamond Kefauver
	(Assistant principal) Harriet Shevelman	(Curriculum coordinator) Jake Haskins
Teachers	(Math) Linette Monro	(Social studies) Annette DiMarco
	(Spanish) Juanita Vicenzo	(Language arts) Manfred Wilson
School Board Members	(Board president) J. Miller Higgins	(Member) Frieda Mecurrie
	(Member) Tommy Thompson	(Member) Othello Jones
Other School Personnel	(Nurse) Talia Hickerstam	(Occupational therapist) Ted Gingerman
	(Custodian) Jake Westerman	(School psychologist) Xaiodi Nuygen
Students	(Senior class president) Mary Anne McPhee	(Junior class president) Ed Munsterman
	(School council president) Amanda Blakely	(Head football manager) LaBrian Agee
Community Members	(Judge) Derrick Thompson	(Public defender) Mastriano Barnes
	(Parole officer) Harry Mansenio	(Newspaper editor) Joel Cunningham
Members of the Profession	(State ASCA president) Marti Benshoff	(State ASCA president-elect) Ty Addlemeier
	(State ASCA newsletter editor) Ben Dickman	(ACA regional representative) Marie Olaf

FIGURE 2.3. LISTING OF PEOPLE SCHOOL COUNSELORS MIGHT TRY TO INFLUENCE.

what every other member of the profession does. What better way to enhance and improve the school counseling profession than for you to share what is effective, or even what isn't effective, with other school counselors?

SELF

Being a school counselor is not an easy job. The needs of the service recipients are enormous and complex, the resources are limited, and the pay isn't commensurate with the demands of the job. Dollarhide (2003b) noted that

> There are many sources of stress for a school counselor...from the working with others who don't understand the work that counselors do, from struggles of students, and from budgets that do not keep up with needs. Other stressors include a lack of privacy and anonymity due to heightened visibility as a mental health professional and feelings of isolation. (p. 326)

Is it any wonder that burnout is a significant problem in the school counseling profession? If school counselors are to continue to perform at an effective level, they must do things that are meaningful in deeply personal ways. In particular, they must maintain a sense that what they do is good and noble, and worth doing. They must overcome the temptation to question whether anything they do actually makes a difference in people's lives. It is easy to get discouraged as a school counselor and it takes concerted effort to avoid feelings of discouragement. One of the ways school counselors can avoid feelings of professional and personal discouragement it to be accountable to self; that is, as a school counselor, you should act purposefully to generate information that will allow you to feel good about yourself and what you do. It is good news that the generation of accountability data for any stakeholder group necessarily results in data that serve this purpose. Indeed, the primary benefit of generating evidence of effectiveness for others is that it provides evidence of effectiveness for you, the school counselor. The way to feel good about being a school counselor (and more importantly, to maintain that feeling), is to be able to generate and point to evidence of your personal effectiveness.

Accountable How?

A final question in this logic sequence is, *How* should school counselors be accountable? "How" in this context reflects the means by which school counselors disseminate the results of their accountability activities, not how the activities should be conducted. The general answer is, "broadly, purposefully, and tailored to the respective audiences." More specifically, school counselors should (a) disseminate the results of their accountability activities to as many stakeholder groups as possible; (b) follow an organized, systematic plan for dissemination of information; and (c) strive to provide information in a form specifically suitable to each stakeholder group. The importance of distributing your accountability activity results effectively should not be minimized because, as Fitzpatrick, Sanders, and Worthen (2004) wrote, "communicating with... stakeholders is as critical as the data collection itself, for without involvement, participation, and effective two-way communication, the most valid data in the world will not have the intended effect" (p. 413).

Dissemination of the results of your school counseling accountability activities is an element of the marketing of school counseling. Carlson and Yohon (2004) wrote that

> professional school counselors need to perform three types of marketing activities to reach three different audiences: internal marketing (marketing between school counselors and [school] faculty, administrators, and staff), external marketing (marketing between the counseling program and the community), and client marketing (marketing between the counseling program and students).
>
> A professional school counseling program's marketing plan focuses on the program's audiences and what messages these audiences need to hear. (p. 81)

In sum, you, as a school counselor, should disseminate the results of your accountability activities to as many stakeholders as possible, but not in an indiscriminate manner. Rather, your presentation of accountability activity results should be well-planned and organized and tailored specifically to each stakeholder group (for an example of how

RESOURCES AND PRIORITIES FOR PRESENTING ACCOUNTABILITY INFORMATION

The following are 12 ways that school counselors can present evidence for accountability purposes, but not everyone will prefer each of the 12 ways equally. Therefore,there is need to prioritize. However, presenting accountability information need not be a singular activity. School counselors know people who can help with the presentation process, and it is important to identify who those people are, because their help might change the priorities.

In the left column are the 12 ways of presenting accountability information. In the second and third columns, write the names of two people who could help with the presentation of accountability information in each row. Finally, in the right column, prioritize the activities by assigning 1 to your most preferred method of presenting information, 2 to your next most preferred method, and so on through 12, your least preferred method.

	Resource Person 1	Resource Person 2	Priority
Written Report	Language arts teacher	Professional colleague	2
Verbal Presentation	Speech teacher	School principal	1
Multimedia Presentation	AV support person	Tech-savvy student	9
Journal Articles	Professional colleague	Former professor	12
Web Page and/ or Blog	Tech-support person	Tech-savvy student	10
Television	Local TV personality	Local entertainer	11
Videos	AV-support person	Talented parent	8
Posters	Art teacher	Talented parent	7
Products Display	Local business person	Talented parent	5
Office Display	Art teacher	Talented student	6
Electronic Communication	Tech-support person	Tech-savvy student	4
Newspaper Article	Journalism teacher	School newspaper editor	5
Pictures	Journalism teacher	Talented parent	3

FIGURE 2.4. Resources and priorities for presenting accountability information.

66 The Accountable School Counselor

to propritize accountability resources, see Figure 2.4). If a stakeholder group receives results in a form that is either unacceptable to them or incongruent with their level of understanding, your entire accountability effort may be defeated or damaged. It is therefore important for you to consider carefully the form and/or method of dissemination of your results. Fortunately, there are a variety of ways and means that you can use to distribute the results of your accountability efforts effectively.

WRITTEN REPORT

Probably the most common way that school counselors distribute accountability information is through a written report. The major advantages of a written report include that it (a) can be easily given or sent to various stakeholders, (b) is a relatively permanent record of the activity, and (c) can be developed relatively efficiently. In addition, development of a written report allows creativity in what is presented in regard to both format and content. For example, through the use of word processing and/or graphics programs, a school counselor can develop a substantive document relatively quickly while also creating one that has strong visual appeal. Graphics, page format variations, borders and/or trim elements, pictures, and other visual enhancements can be used easily to improve the document's appeal and acceptance. At a minimum, the content should include what was done, who participated and in what ways, and what were the primary results. However, your presentation also can be enhanced significantly through inclusion of quotes or narratives or other indicators of personal reactions (assuming that the necessary and appropriate permissions have been obtained; see Chapter 9).

Although it is a common means of results presentation, a written report is not without its limitations. For example, it requires effective document development, content organization, and written communication skills. The latter is particularly important because the language used to express the content must be adapted to the nature of the audience that will receive the report. For example, the words and grammatical structures for a report that is to be distributed to students should be different compared to one that is to be distributed to members of a school board. The costs of duplicating the written report also may be an important consideration, because the cost could be substantial if the report is large and/or the stakeholder group to which it is to be distributed is very large. And finally, careful attention must be given to the amount of content included in the report; too much detail will bore some audiences and too little will disappoint others.

No one can write decently who is distrustful of the reader's intelligence, or whose attitude is patronizing.

—E. B. White

We must add a caution about using good and appropriate writing skills, particularly in regard to using of good grammar. School counselors mostly talk in their work, and while it is true that school counselors do a fair amount of writing, it is mostly informal writing, which requires little attention to the fine points of good writing. The typical outcome of this commonality among school counselors is that their writing skills decline over time, and although informal written communications are sufficient for most of what school counselors do, it is not appropriate for written accountability reports. In fact, a poorly written accountability report not only will not achieve its intended purposes, it may be a source of embarrassment. Therefore, you should make every effort to ensure that any written accountability report you distribute is well written, includes good organization, proper grammar, spelling accuracy, and careful editing. Get help with your writing if you need it, and do everything you can to avoid distributing a poorly constructed report.

VERBAL PRESENTATION

Regardless of their highly developed skills for and the significant emphasis given to listening in their work, most school counselors like to talk, and usually do so, given an opportunity! Therefore, oral presentation of accountability information often is the delivery mode of choice for school counselors. It is an especially appropriate delivery mode for large audiences such as school assemblies, school staff in-service meetings, PTA meetings, or school board meetings. Verbal presentation is an efficient means of communication, and most people have better verbal skills than written communication comprehension skills. Clearly it is a more efficient use of a school counselor's time to make a verbal presentation than it is to write the same information. It also is clear that the same idea applies to the recipients of the information; they hear faster (and usually with better comprehension) than they read. However, there also are several disadvantages. One is that the amount of information people can remember from a verbal presentation is relatively limited; therefore, it is essential that a few, and only a few, carefully selected points be emphasized in an oral presentation. Another is that people generally have selective memory in regard to what they have heard; they remember that which is important to them. In that regard, it also is important to be cognizant that people remember best that which they heard most recently, so the most important points should be presented near the end of a verbal presentation. A third is that it is easy to slip into a presentation mode that is over or under the appropriate mode for a particular audience, thus causing them to become either bored or overwhelmed. A fourth is that many people are hesitant to make speeches and become anxious about actually doing so. A fifth and final limitation of an oral presentation is that there is no lasting record of it, save those few parts people remember.

Presentation at a professional conference or convention is a unique opportunity for school counselors to give something back to the school counseling profession through sharing their activities with their peers and/or other professionals who have interest in their work. Although time and cost considerations must be overcome, presentation at a professional meeting is a meaningful contribution to the school counseling profession and also is likely to be a great source of personal pride in accomplishment. The significant advantage of making a presentation at a professional meeting is that there is usually opportunity during the presentation for dialogue between the presenter(s) and those attending. Like most other professionals, school counselors seem to learn best from their peers and most effectively through meaningful communications with them.

Look out how you use proud words. When you let proud words go, it is not easy to call them back.

—Carl Sandburg

Written and verbal presentations are often used in conjunction as results-delivery modes, particularly if a school counselor wants the results to be both distributed quickly (through verbal presentation) and available for later access (through written presentation). Well-prepared and coordinated written and verbal presentations of accountability information have the advantage of maximizing the advantages of each mode while minimizing their disadvantages. It is a good tactic to use, as long as the verbal presentation is not simply an oral reading of the written presentation. Reading a document to a group of people is usually lethal behavior in regard to dissemination effectiveness. Conversely, a well-prepared speech used in conjunction with a well-developed written report is an excellent way to disseminate accountability information.

MULTIMEDIA PRESENTATION

A multimedia presentation, such as PowerPoint, made from a computer-based projection system can be a particularly effective way to present the results of accountability activities. PowerPoint slide shows are particularly interesting because of their visual appeal, and they are an efficient way to communicate the most important information. When used in conjunction with a verbal presentation, a PowerPoint slide show helps to ensure that all the major points to be covered are in fact addressed, and addressed in the desired order. They are, in effect, visual notes for the presenter as well as for the audience.

One limitation of the use of a PowerPoint presentation is the need for computer and projection equipment to develop and present the slide show effectively. (Fortunately, such resources increasingly are available to school counselors.) Another limitation is that effective use of a PowerPoint slide show necessitates that the lighting in the room be lowered. The reduced lighting causes the audience to focus on the slides and away from the presenter, thus possibly detracting from what is being said. In addition, lowered lighting inhibits audience members from taking notes on what is being presented. However, this latter problem can be minimized by printing the slides as handouts (from the PowerPoint print menu) and distributing them to audience members.

The major limitation of a PowerPoint presentation is that it can be incredibly boring if it merely lists words or phrases at which the audience stares while someone off in the dark lectures. To make a PowerPoint presentation interesting, include audio highlights (both sounds and voice clips), clipart and/or photos (assuming appropriate permissions have been obtained), and varied animation (i.e., slide element entry and removal) sequences. It should be emphasized, however, that if an enhanced PowerPoint slide show is used in conjunction with a verbal presentation, the total presentation should be practiced carefully before it is presented to an audience.

Home computers are being called upon to perform many new functions, including the consumption of homework formerly eaten by the dog.

—Doug Larson

A unique PowerPoint option is the continuous play mode. A slide show can be set to play itself repeatedly, with each of the slides being shown at a predetermined interval (e.g., every 5 seconds). Therefore, the slide show can be set up and shown without the need of someone to run it. Placement of a stand-alone showing of the slides in a school cafeteria, display case, hallway, or office allows persons to view it at their convenience. Of course, this presentation mode requires that the PowerPoint slide show be carefully and fully developed, but it does have the distinct advantage of being convenient for various stakeholder groups.

JOURNAL ARTICLES

Unfortunately, professional publication by practicing school counselors is relatively rare. This situation is unfortunate indeed because the school counseling profession is in great need of information from school counseling practitioners about what does and does not work. "The profession is in short supply of good empirical studies (either quantitative or qualitative) that take the time to systematically observe what counselors do and how students benefit from these efforts" (Lapan, 2006, p. iii). As is true for a presentation at a professional conference, writing for publication is a significant way for school counselors to contribute to the knowledge base of the profession and can be a source personal pride. And with the exception of best-selling books, journal articles typically reach larger school counselor audiences than other print media (Ritchie, 1997). For example, the ASCA journal *Professional School Counseling* has over 18,000 subscribers, and many more nonsubscribers who access its content in libraries and/or computer databases. Although many school counselors engage in activities that are worthy of publication in a professional journal, it is unfortunate that most do not even attempt to publish their activities, even the highly successful ones.

Writing for publication in a professional journal is not all difficult, but it does involve skills other than those typically used in school counseling practice. In particular, it involves communicating information in writing in a formal style, one both structurally correct and specific to the journal's readership. Good professional writing takes time and practice, and the ability to receive feedback without becoming emotionally injured. However, most importantly, it is a skill that can be learned by anyone, not an innate ability enjoyed by only a chosen few. It takes practice, practice, and more practice to be successful in writing for publication, but the resultant self-satisfaction is well worth the effort.

In a very general sense, the publication requirements for local or state school counseling newsletters are less rigorous than those for state school counseling journals, which in turn are less rigorous than those for national school counseling journals. Therefore, it makes sense for you to learn to write for publication by submitting manuscripts about your accountability activities and results to local or state school counseling newsletters first, and then to progress to publication outlets with more stringent publication requirements. A crucial step in this learning process is proactive solicitation of professional feedback about the manuscript. This is the part in which avoiding emotional injury comes into play; feedback should always be considered as potentially helpful, not as an affront to one's personality. Writing with a coauthor (particularly one who is an experienced, published coauthor) also may be helpful in the learning process. Again, collaborative and/or peer learning is often the best and most effective learning strategy for beginning authors.

School counselors learning to write for publication also are well advised to submit manuscripts to publications whose primary readership consists of professionals other than school counselors. For example, publications intended primarily for school administrators, curriculum specialists, or other educational personnel may be more receptive to a manuscript that is outside of their respective professional fields.

In other words, many journals for, say, school administrators like to publish articles from professionals other than school administrators, such as articles from school counselors. There are literally hundreds of professional publications to which manuscripts may be submitted. Accountable school counselors should disseminate their activities and results to many different audiences.

Writing articles for state and national journals in which you present a report of your research is an important contribution to the field [of school counseling].

Bauman, 2006, p. 363

WEB PAGE AND/OR BLOG

Increasingly, the Internet and World Wide Web are becoming primary sources of information for all members of society, particularly for young people. Therefore, it also is becoming a primary means of disseminating information. Want to get information out quickly to a lot of young people? Put it on the Web! Creating a Web page is not particularly difficult, but it involves skills that many school counselors do not have. Fortunately, there are many good resources available, including human resources at your school or school district level, books, and computer software. A variation on this theme would be to have the students who participated in your activities create Web pages that describe the respective activities. This approach can be used with all children, even elementary school–age children (e.g., see Havens, 2003). For examples of how school counselors' activities can be disseminated via the World Wide Web, visit the Saint Paul Public Schools Educational Technology Web site (http://mis.spps.org/counselors/articlesHome.html). And, of course, a school counselor can always ask a teenager for help with development of a Web page!

Dr. Russ Sabella, former ASCA president, provided an excellent set of content elements that can or should be addressed in a local school counseling Web site in the August 15, 2006, *eNewsletter* (# 66) distributed from www.SchoolCounselor.com. He also identified common target audiences for such a Web site, all of which are stakeholder groups for a school counseling program. We would add to his suggestions that accountability information should be presented on a local school counseling program's Web site because it is a highly effective way to disseminate such information.

The advantages of using a Web page to distribute accountability information include (a) a Web page can be developed relatively easily and relatively quickly, (b) there is widespread access to Web sites, and (c) the costs associated with dissemination are usually minimal. Perhaps most importantly, information on the Web is often shared quickly through electronic communications that refer to the Web site. But if putting up a Web page still is too slow or too complex for you, consider blogging. In so-called geek speak, a *blog* is an abbreviation for "Web log." In essence, a blog is a personal journal that is put out on the Web. As such, it is a quick and easy way to communicate current information. A typical blog has a main page and no others. Sequential entries to a blog are put at the top of the page such that previous entries are pushed down, thus maintaining the entries in reverse chronological order. A blog may just contain a blogger's thoughts and comments about anything or informational content such as links to Web sites. A significant advantage to blogging is that readers subscribe to a blog and therefore are notified automatically when new entries are posted. For more information about blogging and what's involved in it, visit www.blogger.com, or use a search engine with the key word *blog*.

We certainly do not recommend that you develop a blog just to spout off about whatever is on your mind each day. However, we do recommend that you develop a blog as a means of professional communication, especially to students and parents. Students in particular are into blogging because the communications posted usually are informal and informative. You can use a blog to inform recipients of your current and/or forthcoming school counseling activities, important information, or communicate whatever you want to share. In particular, you can blog about the results of your school counseling activities, thus, a blog is yet another contemporary and popular way to inform your stakeholders about what you are doing and what is happening as a result.

The limitation of putting information on the Web or in a blog is that the information is public, anyone with a connection to the Internet can read it. Therefore, it is extremely important that the information you put on a Web page be accurate, legally defensible (e.g., not subject to allegations of libel or copyright infringement), and presented in an appropriate professional manner. Be careful about what you post!

TELEVISION

Many local public or cable television channels air broadcasts focused on local school events. A well-developed school counselor accountability activity should be a welcomed topic for such broadcasts. A significant advantage of using television to disseminate school counseling activities and results is that both school counselors and the participants can be featured. In addition, it brings positive publicity to the schools in which the events occurred. Importantly, the television personnel do most, if not all, of the work necessary to prepare the broadcast; you would need only to present the content of the programming.

Although representatives of these television outlets are always seeking topics of local interest, it is likely that school counselors who want to use television as a means of disseminating results will have to initiate contact with a television station. After all, a tenet of this book is that the results of school counselors' activities are not well known. Therefore, you and other school counselors must be proactive in using television for your purposes.

I find television very educating. Every time someone turns on the set I go into the other room and read a book.

—Groucho Marx

VIDEOS

A video presentation (e.g., videotape, CD, DVD) of an actual school counseling activity, particularly a videotape that demonstrates clearly the effectiveness of the activity, can be a powerful communication of a school counselor's effectiveness. People who view the video should come away from it with a good understanding of what a school counselor did and how it impacted the participants. In addition, people in our society are quite used to learning by viewing, and use of a video is an accepted way of disseminating results. Similar to PowerPoint continuous-play presentations, videos can be set up on a CD or DVD for repeated (i.e., stand alone) showings which allow people to watch them at their convenience (e.g., as an adjunct to other activities at a PTA meeting).

Development of videos that show your school counseling activities can also be a powerful way to involve students in your school counseling program, because students can assist with the development of the videos. For some activities (such as students role-playing as part of a large-group guidance activity or students demonstrating how to use selected school counseling resources), students at any school level can develop or help to develop the script for whatever is shown and/or said during the activity being videotaped. At middle or high school levels, students might do the taping of the activity or direct whatever is taped. The result of student involvements such as these would be a student-produced video of your school counseling activity. If the student-produced videos are of relatively short duration (e.g., 5 minutes or less), you could even put them on your school counseling program Web site (see www.SchoolCounselor.com, *eNewsletter* #68, September 4, 2006, for examples and guidance about how to incorporate videos into your Web site). A student-produced video not only would serve as evidence of accountability but also might serve as an incentive for other students to get more involved in your school counseling program activities.

There are, however, limitations to the use of videos as a means of accountability information dissemination. One is that parental permission (vis-à-vis informed consent; see Chapter 9) is needed for the participants, and some parents may be unwilling to provide their permission. Another is that technical assistance may be needed to develop the master video into one suited for public showing (although there is usually some one in a school system who can provide such assistance). The most important limitation is that the activities shown should be limited to those that are not deeply personal in nature (e.g., most career development or classroom guidance activities are better for this purpose than are individual or small-group crisis counseling activities). Videos can be powerful, but their use should be considered carefully and with due consideration of all involved.

POSTERS

Schools are full of posters. Why shouldn't there be some for school counseling activities? In general, they are inexpensive to create, don't require great artistic skills, are easily distributed, and are viewed by many people. The limitation is that relatively little information can be communicated on them.

A simple and effective use of posters would be to have student participants of a school counseling activity present statements, drawings, or other graphical information about what they got from and/or learned from a school counseling activity. Posters can be an effective way to share accountability information with members of a school community if they are developed carefully and creatively (e.g., school counselors should supervise and/or retain approval rights for students' posters) and if they are appropriately placed in schools.

PRODUCTS SHOWCASE

School counselors frequently develop personal resource materials as they perform their day-to-day activities. Such resources may take the form of crib sheets for advising students about class schedules, notes and reminders about forthcoming school events and activities, lesson plans and/or materials for classroom group guidance activities, forms and charts used to help students, lists of professional resources, and other things school counselors use to fulfill their responsibilities. Unfortunately, these materials often get set aside, to be used only when needed and with little thought given to their potential as accountability indicators. However, they are not without value in regard to accountability (vis-à-vis the marketing ideas covered previously), and you should share with some stakeholders. For example, these products in a school help other school personnel have a better understanding of what school counselors do *and* how they do it. Basically, you develop a lot of stuff as you go about your daily activities, and that stuff is evidence of your activities.

OFFICE SHOWCASE

Walk into most professionals' offices, and one of the first things you notice is their diplomas and other professional credentials. Similarly, walk into just about any classroom in any school and you pretty quickly get a sense of what is taught in that classroom. Pictures, posters, displays, student work samples and the like adorn the walls, and it is easy to figure out what goes on in that room. Walk into the typical school counselor's office and you immediately get the sense that you're in a(n)...? Where are the school counselor's diplomas; professional credential certificates; registration badges, programs, or posters from professional conferences attended; professional resources such as books, tests, group work kits, drawing media, audiotapes, or videotapes; pictures of the school counselor with students; or other indicators that the office occupant is a professional school counselor? While some may disdain displaying such materials as braggadocio, the reality is that such showcasing is an excellent way to communicate what a you are and what you do.

ELECTRONIC COMMUNICATIONS

Most adults have a love–hate relationship with e-mail. They love it as a way to send communications quickly and efficiently. They hate it because so much of it is essentially useless information and/or is highly impersonal communication. Therefore, a blanket mailing of the results of a school counseling activity to people in the school's community, no matter how effective the activity, is simply a bad idea. A better tactic is to select the recipients carefully and then to provide the information in a manner that makes it a *personal* communication. For example, sending the same e-mail to each recipient individually is much preferred over sending it to many recipients simultaneously. Who feels special when their e-mail address is one among a huge list of other recipients? In addition, if the communication is substantive and extensive (such as sending a written report and/or pictures), it is better to send the main information as an attached document rather than in the main text of the e-mail (because variations in e-mail programs may make what is received difficult to read). The main text should contain only a brief overview of and comment about what is in the attachment. Finally, consideration should be given to the nature of the software program needed to open an attached file. In particular, sending graphics, spreadsheets, or photos to recipients in a file format that they cannot view defeats the purpose of the communication.

E-mail has tremendous potential as a means of effective communication between school counselors and their various stakeholder groups. We emphasize groups because distributing information to all members of a group simultaneously is a good way to get the message out far and wide. Sending individual e-mail correspondence is powerful because of its personalization, but it's also a very inefficient way to inform members of even relatively large stakeholder groups. Most e-mail programs allow set up of distribution lists, in which each name and e-mail address is entered once, a name for the entire distribution list is entered, and subsequently, an e-mail sent to the list name goes to all members of the distribution list. For example, school counselors often are members of a group that meets to develop interventions for particular students, the groups typically being known as student intervention teams or student assistance teams. You can communicate the results of interventions to the entire group by sending one e-mail message to the distribution list. Similarly, distribution lists can be created to allow you to share information about your school counseling program and significant activities to any and all of your important stakeholder groups.

Listservs can serve a similar function, but the workings of a Listserv are slightly different. Listservs have subscribers; that is, people who voluntarily agree (through subscribing, which is usually free) to receive via e-mail anything that is posted (sent) to the Listserv by anyone. Subscribing to Listservs is an increasingly popular way for people with common interests to share ideas, questions, and/or information. For example, as a professional school counselor, you certainly should join the Listserv for the Center for School Counseling Outcome Research (http://www.umass.edu/schoolcounseling). Similarly, many professional organizations or associations have Listservs for their members, and some may be of direct or tangential interest to you. For example, CESNET-L is a Listserv (http://www.lsoft.com/scripts/wl.exe?SL1=CESNET-L&H-LISTSERV.KENT.edu) intended primarily for counselor educators and supervisors, but it often has information useful to school counseling professionals. A good list of electronic discussion groups (a special type of Listserv) can be found at http://wwwcsun.edu/edpsy/links-discussion.htm. The discussion groups listed reflect focused, specific professional topics, some of which may be of interest to you. Finally, school counselors in a school district or state could set up a Listserv to share their ideas and plans for being accountable as well as for other topics of common interest.

Message boards and their subdivisions, known as forums, are popular among students of all ages. Message boards are similar to Listservs in that members must subscribe in order to be able to post messages for other members to read. However, they are more sophisticated than Listservs because messages are posted to specific forums (i.e., to specific topic areas.) A member of a Listserv receives an e-mail whenever someone sends a message to the Listserv. A subscriber to a forum or message board does not receive e-mails. Instead, a subscriber logs on to the message board, peruses the topics or forums that are active (i.e., in which members are posting messages), and opens only the messages in the forums that are of interest. A subscriber can respond to a message and the response is posted on the particular forum for others to read. School counseling message boards are beginning to appear on the Internet. (One example can be found at http://www.wa-schoolcounselor.org). Wouldn't it be great if each school system had a message board, and one of the forums was for school counseling? Thus, message boards are another way that you as a school counselor can disseminate information about your services and activities, promote your accomplishments, and participate in discussions with stakeholders.

NEWSPAPER ARTICLE

Like television stations, newspapers are always looking for local news stories about what goes on in area schools. Here, too, school counselors should be proactive in seeking coverage of what they do and of the positive results the activities have had for children. The primary advantage of a newspaper article is the same as that of a television broadcast: wide distribution. However, there is the significant limitation that only a small amount of information can be included in a newspaper article. Journalists want the story to be interesting, which means that they want to determine what is presented. This may result in conflict if what they want to present is not in line with what school counselors want to present. In some cases, you may request and receive editorial control over what is to be printed; however, such control is not commonly given, and, more likely, you will have to rely on the journalist's judgment about what is important to present. Therefore, although newspapers are a good means to distribute activity and accountability information, care should be used in choosing this approach.

It is well to remember that freedom through the press is the thing that comes first. Most of us probably feel we couldn't be free without newspapers, and that is the real reason we want the newspapers to be free.

—Edward R. Murrow

PICTURES

People enjoy looking at pictures, and while we are not exactly sure how many words a picture is actually worth, we do know that they communicate a lot of information very quickly. Therefore, pictures are a very effective way to communicate information about your school counseling activities. The most informative pictures for accountability purposes are those that show you actually working with students, teachers, parents, or others. For example, you could display pictures of you conducting a large-group guidance activity, doing small-group counseling, helping students use the Internet for career education or development, consulting with a teacher or parent, or even organizing materials for the school's testing program. In general, displaying pictures that show you doing something in your role as a school counselor informs others of the nature of your activities. Pictures are not data (in the traditional sense of the term) that demonstrate the effectiveness of your activities, but they are evidence of the things you do.

Of course, if you are going to display pictures, you need someone to take the pictures. One possibility is to have a parent volunteer come into your school and take pictures of you in action. Another possibility is to have one or more students take pictures of you while you do your various activities. A third is to have a colleague take the pictures. The pictures do not have to be of professional quality; they will be informative to the extent that they show you actually doing our job as a school counselor. There are lots of places in schools where pictures are or could be displayed. It would be helpful to your professional functioning if the pictures displayed were of you being a school counselor. (For an example of pairing accountability distribution methods to various stakeholders, see Figure 2.5.)

CONCLUSION

The questions to whom should school counselors be accountable, for what, and how are not answered easily. The school counseling profession and the services you, like other school counselors, provide are multifaceted, and so effective responses to these questions necessarily involve multiple parts. However, the complexity of the responses should not impede your efforts to be accountable. Rather, the numbers stakeholder groups, responsibilities, and ways of being accountable should be

Disseminating Accountability Information to Stakeholders

Combining the many stakeholders to which school counselors should be accountable and the many ways of disseminating accountability information results in many audience–method combinations. Unfortunately, there are no firm guidelines about which dissemination methods should be used with which stakeholder groups. However, recommendations can be made for general guidance. The following are *suggested* combinations that have good potential for successful distribution. These suggestions were derived from experience, the school counseling professional literature, and other indicators that the combinations have good potential for success. However, the choice of which means of dissemination of accountability results is paired with which stakeholder group is ultimately left to you in your particular situation. No combination is inherently better than another. It all depends on *what* you want to communicate, *to whom* you want to communicate, and *how* you want to communicate.

	Written Report	Verbal Presentation	Multimedia Presentation	Journal Article	Web Page	Television	Video	Posters	Products Display	Office Display	Ee-mail	Newspaper Article	Pictures
Parents & Families	✲	✲	✲			✲	✲	✲	✲	✲	✲	✲	✲
School Administrator	✲	✲						✲	✲	✲			✲
Teachers	✲	✲	✲					✲	✲	✲	✲		✲
School Board Members	✲	✲	✲									✲	
Other School Personnel								✲	✲	✲	✲	✲	
Students						✲	✲	✲	✲	✲		✲	✲
Community Members						✲						✲	✲
School Counselor Professionals		✲		✲									
Self	✲	✲	✲	✲	✲	✲	✲	✲	✲	✲	✲	✲	

FIGURE 2.5. Suggestions for disseminating accountability information to stakeholders.

viewed opportunities to try different things, starting with those within your comfort level and moving to more complex and involved accountability activities. Over time, you can indeed be accountable to all the stakeholder groups, for all the important things that you do, in a variety of ways. The important thing is to start!

For Thought and Deed

1. Design what you would consider to be the ideal school counseling suite of offices and resource space in a school. In other words, design your ideal school counseling physical facilities. Next, describe in as much detail as possible how you would decorate the school counseling area in the school.

2. Imagine that you have been invited to make a 15-minute presentation at a PTA meeting for your school to explain your school counseling program. Develop an outline of what you would present, and explain how you would make the presentation.

3. Attend (or watch on local-access television) several meetings of your local school board. While you watch the proceedings, identify three or four of the primary topics discussed at the meetings. Next, consider how your activities as a school counselor relate to those primary topics. Finally, imagine that you were asked to present to the school board how your school counseling activities relate to those topic areas. What would you present, and how would you present it?

4. Identify three activities that you do as a school counselor that are particularly helpful to students in your school. Then, describe three ways you could inform students that you can be particularly helpful to them in regard to those activities.

5. Demonstrating cultural sensitivity is certainly an important emphasis in the school counseling profession. Describe two ways that you could inform parents that you are a culturally sensitive school counselor.

6. Who are the members of your local school board? List who they are, their occupations, and other information about them that would better help you understand them. Make an appointment with one or more of them to explain your role and services as a school counselor, and ask them what they think of school counseling services.

7. Write a letter to your local newspaper that includes brief description of your school counseling roles and services, points out recent accomplishments, and requests that a reporter do a community interest story on your activities.

CHAPTER 3

Common Accountability Resources for School Counseling Functions

The general framework for the next five chapters is based on the Delivery System subsection of the *ASCA National Model*, because that subsection provides a comprehensive overview of important school counseling, and by direct implication, school counselor functions. The four major elements of this framework are (a) the school guidance curriculum, (b) individual student planning, (c) responsive services, and (d) system support. Presumably, each and all of your activities as a school counselor can be assigned to one of these four categories. However, program evaluation activities encompass the composite results of all, or at least a major portion of, your professional school counseling activities. Therefore, because of its central importance to your accountability activities, program evaluation is covered separately in Chapter 8.

There are two perspectives presented in the *ASCA National Model* that should be kept in mind when considering, planning, and/or conducting accountability and program evaluation activities. The first is that the *ASCA National Model* was not intended to be prescriptive or restrictive; it is a conceptual framework, not a mandate for a school counselor's activities. "Although the ASCA National Model serves as a framework for the development of a school counseling program, it is not meant to be replicated exactly as written" (ASCA, 2005, p. 10). This means that you should be involved only in accountability activities specifically related to the activities you are performing in your school counseling program and recognize that those activities are not necessarily specific to the functions and activities delineated in the *ASCA*

83

National Model. Basically, the activities you perform should be the focus for your accountability methods and activities.

A second important perspective acknowledged in the *ASCA National Model* is that various school counselor activities have varying time frames in which results may be achieved. Thus, ASCA (2005) recommended that

> data are collected at three time intervals. Short-term data provide immediate evaluation of the activity process on student behavior or student learning. Intermediate data collection occurs over a longer period of time as a benchmark or indication of progress toward the goal. Long-term data collection occurs over an extended period of time and measures the activity's overall results for students. (p. 60)

Most school counselors want to conduct accountability activities immediately upon completion of an activity, in part because it is often the most expeditious time to collect data and in part because they simply want to be done with the activity and move on to another. Collecting data at the completion of an activity certainly is not a bad idea (e.g., obtaining immediate impact data). However, the ASCA data collection schema addresses the importance of follow-up data collection in recognition that the results of school counselors' activities are not always immediately evident.

The time is always right to do what is right.

—Rev. Martin Luther King, Jr.

You can be fully accountable as a school counselor only to the extent that you can generate substantive evidence that your activities have changed students in positive and desirable ways. The resultant changes need not be monumental; in fact, the changes resulting from school counseling interventions often are small or subtle. However, they must be documented through an accountability activity and then made evident to appropriate stakeholders. To fit well within the school counselor's many responsibilities, any accountability method used must be as efficient as possible for each activity that is evaluated. Yet, while efficiency is highly desirable, efficiency should not be achieved at the sacrifice of quality. Analogous to the old computer maxim "garbage in, garbage out" (G-I-G-O), the results of an accountability activity are only as good as the quality of the method used to generate them. Therefore, your accountability strategies must be both effective and efficient; neither alone is a sufficient criterion for successful achievement of accountability.

A few comments about data management are warranted before discussing specific accountability methods. Being accountable is about gathering data and the data, may be either numbers or words. For many of a school counselor's accountability activities, the data may be voluminous; for example, the more students involved, the greater the data that can be collected. Therefore, there is need for an effective and efficient data-management system. The best way for you to engage in good data management is to use a computer-based spreadsheet software program. Current versions of popular spreadsheet programs such as Excel (contained in the Word Office Suite) or QuattroPro (contained in the WordPerfect Office Suite) have an amazing array of options for data management and for generating reports of the data entered. They can also perform the majority of statistical data analyses you or other school counselors will ever need to use. You can be accountable without using a spreadsheet, but it is impossible for you to generate as much data (because there will be less time for data generation), manage it as effectively, and be as efficient in being accountable as a school counselor who uses a spreadsheet. It's simply the best way of doing things. Excellent examples (including pictures of actual spreadsheet pages) of how school counselors can use spreadsheets effectively are provided by Ware and Galassi (2006).

The first rule of any technology used in a business is that automation applied to an efficient operation will magnify the efficiency. The second is that automation applied to an inefficient operation will magnify the inefficiency.

—Bill Gates

Some accountability activities (i.e., evidence gathering methods) can be applied to a variety of school counseling activities and some are restricted to use with specific activities. The extent to which a particular method can be used in various contexts is not in and of itself an indication of its worth; both generalized and specific activities have their advantages and limitations. However, for the sake of organizational convenience, some accountability resources and methods commonly used in different contexts are discussed in this chapter, and resources and methods specific to various school counselor functions are presented in the chapters following.

QUESTIONNAIRES AND SURVEYS

Paper-and-pencil, and increasingly online electronic, measurement instruments are popular methods for gathering data because of their efficiency; large amounts of data can be gathered in a relatively short time period. Questionnaires and surveys are measurement techniques that have particular favor in this regard. A questionnaire is used to gather *factual* (e.g., demographic) information, whereas a survey is used to gather *attitudinal* or *opinion* data. However, the word *survey* is commonly used to cover both techniques because most surveys include a questionnaire subsection to collect demographic information. They are distinguished here merely for discussion convenience.

The two fundamental ideas in the development of a questionnaire are to (a) make it as clear as possible for the respondent to understand what information is being requested and (b) make responding as easy as possible. The items of a questionnaire should be singular in the sense that each item should request one very specific type of information. For example, obviously it is inappropriate to assume that all students in a particular grade level are the same age. Therefore, if both age and grade-level information is desired, two separate items should be used.

In regard to the ease of providing information, a decision must be made about what type of response choices should be offered. For example, it is easier for students to write in the number of courses they have completed than it is for them to choose from a long list of numbers. Further, it is easier for a student to check off, bubble in, or circle a response choice (e.g., to indicate the student's gender) than it is for the student to write or type in the information. However, items that provide response choices are particularly appropriate for respondents who might be confused about how to interpret the item. For example, some students may have difficulty understanding an item that asks for race or ethnicity information. In such cases, providing response choices, such as the options used for the U.S. census, makes the item easier to understand. The general guideline is to provide possible responses when there are a very limited number of response choices and to use open-ended (sometimes called free-response) items when there are many possible response choices.

Survey items also should be as clear as possible and singular in nature. One guiding principle is that items on a survey should not contain a conjunction. For example, an item such as, "The job shadowing activity was fun and interesting" is not a good (survey) item because the respondent might have the opinion that the activity was fun but not interesting or vice versa. A variety of response scales may be used appropriately for responding to survey items, but the original Likert scale (*Strongly Agree, Agree, Undecided, Disagree, Strongly Disagree*) is used most often. Variations of it (so-called Likert-type scales) also are used frequently. Common variations for Likert-type scales include not having a middle choice (e.g., *Strongly Agree, Agree, Disagree, Strongly Disagree*), which theoretically forces the respondent to express an opinion, or expanding the number of choices (e.g., *Strongly Agree, Agree, Somewhat Agree, Undecided, Somewhat Disagree, Disagree, Strongly Disagree*), which theoretically allows for greater differentiation among responses across respondents.

The greatest discovery of my generation is that a human being can alter his [her] life by altering his [her] attitude.

—William James

Survey item responses usually are weighted (i.e., a different number is assigned to each response choice) to allow composite scoring (i.e., finding the sum of the response weights for the various items) of the survey or various parts of it. For example, a common weighting system is *Strongly Agree* = 5, *Agree* = 4, *Undecided* = 3, *Disagree* = 2, and *Strongly Disagree* = 1. In general, higher scores on an attitude scale should indicate a more favorable perspective on whatever general concept (e.g., attitude toward a particular counseling activity) is being investigated.

It is desirable to have both positively and negatively stated items on a survey so that respondents attend carefully to each of the items (i.e., do not just respond in a pattern such as choosing *Strongly Agree* for every item). An example of a positively stated item is, "I was able to express my true feelings to my counselor." An example of a negatively stated item is, "I was uncomfortable sharing my true feelings with my counselor." If negatively stated items are included, the response weights for those items *only* should be reversed (e.g., *Strongly Agree* = 1, *Agree* = 2, *Undecided* = 3, *Disagree* = 4, and *Strongly Disagree* = 5) so that again a higher total score will reflect a more favorable attitude toward the concept being investigated.

Increasingly the development and/or dissemination of a survey is facilitated through use of one of the available online Internet-based survey tools, such as Zoomerang (www.zoomerang.com), SurveyMonkey (www.surveymonkey.com), or counselingsurveys (www.counselingsurveys.org). Each of these sites provides for development of an online survey to suit each user's needs. However, each of these services has advantages and disadvantages. For example, there is a charge for using some of the more sophisticated surveying options available in Zoomerang, but some of those options can make the surveying and results reporting processes much easier. SurveyMonkey allows for a wide variety of choices of item, item–response, and results formats, but it has some limitations related to how the resultant data can be downloaded to a spreadsheet or other data analysis program. CounselingSurveys has the advantage of including a general informed consent form (to be discussed further in Chapter 9), but it offers fewer item, item–response, and results report format options. One of the significant advantages of available online survey instruments is that they all include mutually exclusive response options; that is, a respondent cannot choose two or more response choices for a particular survey item. This provision greatly helps to reduce response errors.

Access to current and new technologies will only increase over time. Professional school counselors need to harness the power of the Internet in performing their job functions.

—Wall, 2004, p. 480

We strongly recommend that if you use one of these tools, first develop the survey in a paper format by using a word-processor program such as Word or WordPerfect. The effective development of a survey requires careful, thoughtful, and repeated consideration; therefore, it is much easier to develop the survey into a desired format using a word-processing program that allows easy alteration of the survey as opposed to trying to develop the survey online from scratch.

It is always a good idea to pilot-test questionnaires and surveys before they are administered. In a pilot study, the first version of the survey or questionnaire is given to a small (3–10) sample of the people (e.g., students, teachers, or parents) from among those who will eventually receive the instrument. They are asked to complete the questionnaire or survey and, more importantly, to provide written or oral feedback on how easy it was to understand and how long it took to complete. We believe that no matter how clearly a school counselor thinks the items or questions are worded, they can and will be misinterpreted. Thus, a pilot test of a questionnaire or survey provides valuable information for how to improve the survey or questionnaire such that most respondents will interpret the items or questions as intended.

It also is important to explain and define terms that are used in the instrument, which is easily accomplished by providing written explanations if the instrument is mailed or appears on the Web. If the instrument is to be given in a classroom, a school counselor or teacher also can verbally define or clarify important terms and respond to any questions about the instrument. For example, if you wanted to use a survey instrument to gather data on the frequency of bullying behaviors in your school, you would want to define bullying very carefully because students differ in what they consider to be bullying. You also can provide specific examples of what is and what is not bullying, within the context of the definition of *bullying* being used in the survey or questionnaire. An example of a survey to assess the frequency of bullying in a middle school is provided in Figure 3.1.

There are a few disadvantages to web-based surveys, including that anyone with access to the survey can complete it. Therefore, there is no assurance that the actual respondents are restricted to those for whom the survey was intended. Similarly, it is sometimes possible for anyone with access to the survey to respond multiple times, thereby biasing the data. Security measures such as passwords or identification codes can be used to control for these problems, but their use makes the

The Accountable School Counselor

Assessing School Bullying

In which grade are you? ☐ 6th ☐ 7th ☐ 8th

What is your gender? ☐ Boy ☐ Girl

Have you ever been bullied by another student? ☐ Yes ☐ No

On average, how many times *per week* are you bullied? _____

How many different students bully you? _____

Have you ever bullied another student? ☐ Yes ☐ No

If you were bullied, who would you tell?
(Check all that apply) ☐ Friends ☐ Parent(s) ☐ Teacher(s)
                        ☐ Counselor ☐ No one

For the following items, please circle your answer using this response scale:

SA = if you *strongly agree* with the statement

A = if you generally *agree* with the statement

U = if you are *undecided* about the statement

D = if you generally *disagree* with the statement

SD = if you *strongly disagree* with the statement

I feel safe while I'm in school	SA	A	U	D	SD
I am afraid that I will be bullied	SA	A	U	D	SD
Bullying is okay in school	SA	A	U	D	SD
No one cares if students get bullied	SA	A	U	D	SD
It is good to tell a teacher if I got bullied	SA	A	U	D	SD
I dread coming to school because of being bullied	SA	A	U	D	SD
Bullying is worse for girls than for boys	SA	A	U	D	SD

If you want to tell us else about bullying in the school, you can write about it on the back of this sheet.

Figure 3.1. Survey instrument to assess the frequency of bullying in school.

data-gathering process much more complex. On the other hand, Web-based surveys have several decided advantages. First, they are generally less expensive to implement. Second, they require less activity (such as taking the time and effort to mail or deliver them back) from the respondent. Third, they are easier to distribute and can be distributed to a wider audience (e.g., school graduates who may be far away). And finally, the data are received and compiled easier and faster because they are in electronic form and do not need to be transferred from the response sheet to another format. Web-based surveys are appropriate for use with any stakeholder group.

Helpful guidelines for development of assessment instruments particularly suitable for use by school counselors can be found in Studer et al. (2006), Erford (2007a), and Whiston (2005), or in comprehensive assessment texts.

RATING SCALES

A rating scale is used to assess the relative frequency of events or actions, or the relative intensity of an opinion or feeling about an object. For example, the Likert response scale, commonly used on surveys, actually is a specific type of rating scale. However, the term *rating scale* is more commonly applied to measures of behavior frequency or degree of preference. The items in a rating scale are usually in the form of a question followed by an appropriate response scale. The nature of the information desired must be made perfectly clear in the item stem. For example, suppose it was desirable to get information about an aspect of a person's personal hygiene. The opened-ended question, "How much time to do you spend in the shower each week?" might seem to request the desired information; however, the item "How frequently do you bathe?" with response choices such as Hourly, Daily, Weekly, Monthly, or Yearly gives much more specific, behavioral information. Similarly, a question such as, "How much do you like each of the following foods?" followed by a list of foods and instructions to use a scale of 1 = *not very much* to 10 = *very much* for rating the answer. As with surveys and questionnaires, careful statement of the question and selection of the rating scale is essential to obtaining good information.

CHECKLISTS

Checklists are literally what the name implies. They are lists of words or phrases presented to a respondent, and the respondent is asked sim-

92   The Accountable School Counselor

ply to check or otherwise identify those items on the list that meet a criterion. For example, checklists are frequently used to determine how many tasks a student has completed in a sequence of tasks (e.g., to indicate how may steps in a graduation activity sequence have been completed). Commonly, each respondent's checklist is reviewed separately, and then the school counselor takes whatever subsequent action is appropriate for the student respondent. However, checklists also are a good way to obtain frequency data from a large group of students. For example, if you present a checklist of possible school counseling activities to all the freshmen students in a high school, you can simply compute the various checked frequencies for each of the activities on the list, and then perhaps prioritize activities based on those results. An example of such a checklist is provided in Figure 3.2.

SCHOOL COUNSELOR ACTIVITIES FOR FRESHMEN

Listed are service activities your school counselors can provide to you. Please put a check in the box beside any activities in which you would like to participate.

Large-group guidance lessons covering:

❑ Graduation and school curriculum requirements

❑ College and postsecondary options and opportunities

❑ Time management and study skills

❑ Preparation for state and national tests

Small-group planning and advisement covering:

❑ Career exploration

❑ Goal setting and decision making

❑ Communication and relationship skills

Individual Counseling for:

❑ Academic issues and problems

❑ Career choice and direction issues

❑ Personal/Social Issues

FIGURE 3.2. Checklist of possible school counselor activities for freshmen students.

Checklists have the significant advantage of being an efficient way of collecting data. In addition, checklists are usually nonthreatening in the sense that student respondents don't have to disclose much about themselves in checking any particular item. However, the major disadvantage of using checklists is that they do not allow indication of the intensity of a response. For example, if you give students a list of possible topics that the students would like to discuss with you as a school counselor, different students checking the same item may have widely varying degrees of need intensity or immediacy in their respective desires to talk with you.

SEMISTRUCTURED INTERVIEWS

In a fully structured interview, the questioner asks a specific set of predetermined questions, and the respondents are able to respond only in the context of previously explained response boundaries. For example, a school counselor might ask a student, "Among the individual, small-group, and large-group counseling activities in which you participated this school year, which was the most helpful to you?" A semistructured interview is similar in that the questions asked are determined before the interview is conducted. However, the natures of both the questioner–responder interaction and the allowable responses are different. Although certainly purposeful, a semistructured interview is intended to be a relatively casual interaction between the questioner and responder; the responder should feel free to respond however she or he chooses to respond, including to not respond to a question. For example, you might ask a student, "Which school counseling activity did you like best this year?" Typically, a semistructured interview should be an hour or less in duration.

It was impossible to get a conversation going, everybody was talking too much.

—Yogi Berra

In the context of using semistructured interviews to generate accountability data, school counselors must develop the questions carefully. They should be open-ended, relatively narrow in scope, and presented in the simplest possible language. For example, questions such as "How has your behavior changed as a result of participating in the small-group counseling activity?" "In what ways have the series of career exploration activities we conducted this past semester helped your child make postgraduation plans?" and "What parts of our school counseling program were helpful to you as a teacher?" are focused enough to yield relatively specific responses. A broad question such as "What do you think of the school counseling program?" likely would yield diverse (and interesting!) responses, but the responses would be so disparate and unfocused that they would be of little use. In developing the questions for a semistructured interview, it is helpful to share the questions with a colleague to obtain feedback on the clarity and appropriateness of the proposed questions.

Most professionals think that the data-gathering process for a semistructured interview simply amounts to recording the responses given so that they can be transcribed and intuitively interpreted later. However, data gathering for a semistructured interview is supposed to be a codifying and counting activity. That is, once the questions have been developed, categories of possible response elements for each question should be identified. For example, suppose teachers are asked the question, "How has my consultation activities with you helped you function better in your classroom?" Possible response element categories might be (a) better classroom management, (b) improved communications with students, (c) better student academic performance, (d) better peer relationships among students, or (e) other. When the interview is conducted, each of the respondent's comments in response to the question are coded into, or checked as belonging to, a predetermined response element category. In cases of lengthy and/or complex responses, various elements of the response may be assigned to different categories, which may result in the sum of the counts in the response categories being greater than the number of questions asked. Notes of the respective comments are helpful for subsequent clarification of various responses, but the primary data from a semistructured interview are the category counts. This is how a semistructured interview yields quantitative data.

The purpose of all higher education is to make [wo]men aware of what was and what is; to incite them to probe into what may be. It seeks to teach them to understand, to evaluate, to communicate.

—Otto Kleppner

Semistructured interviews as an accountability method can be used with members of any stakeholder group. However, in general, they are best used with adults, such as parents, teachers, or school administrators. Students may feel that they are being interrogated and/or pressured to respond in what they perceive to be desired ways (e.g., not making negative comments). If the interview interaction is indeed as comfortable as it should be, respondents should be able to make open and honest responses, which is, of course, the best type of information that can be gained. Also, adults are more likely to be willing to invest the time it takes for a semistructured interview and to maintain appropriate focus throughout.

STANDARDIZED TESTS

Most school counselors (as well as most other educators) are of the opinion that there is entirely too much standardized testing going on in schools today. That perspective is easy enough to understand, given the apparently everexpanding use of standardized tests in schools, particularly in the last decade. However, it can be argued that there is not enough standardized testing going on in the schools, or at least that there is not enough of the right kind of standardized testing. The problem appears to be that there is too much standardized testing intended to measure students' academic performance. The deficiency is that there is not enough standardized measurement of students' other characteristics.

In regard to school counselors' use of assessments, Guindon (2003) succinctly captured the role of assessment in the work of school counselors:

> Of the many professional school counselor activities, appraisal is a primary and necessary skill.
>
> Appraisal provides a method by which students and their concerns may be understood, and encompasses a broad range of activities useful to professional school counselors. Appraisal is defined . . . as any function that measures, assesses, tests or sets a value on one or more attributes of individuals. (p. 331)

Nugent, Sieppert, and Hudson (2001) wrote that "measurement helps us [i.e., professional counselors] to tap into the subtle and varied dimensions of client problems. Good measures, particularly standardized measures, help us to more thoroughly and accurately describe client problems" (p. 219). Erford (2007a) noted that there are four primary purposes for assessment in the work of professional counselors: (a) screening, (b) diagnosis, (c) treatment planning and goal identification, and (d) progress evaluation. We would add that, increasingly, outcome assessment is a fifth primary purpose.

Ekstrom, Elmore, Schafer, Trotter, and Webster (2004) surveyed members of ASCA and found that the majority of school counselors are indeed heavily involved with various aspects of testing in their schools, including the use of standardized tests. They noted that school counselors' involvement with testing is a desirable and positive situation in schools, in part because effective use of assessments is in concert with commonly advocated professional roles and functions for school counselors, and in part because school counselors frequently are the most knowledgeable about assessment among professionals in schools. For example, Popham (2001) wrote that "as a rule, school counselors are more conversant with educational measurement concepts than are classroom teachers" (p. 277).

The... evaluation of [school] counseling programs requires that professional school counselors use data from standardized testing... to improve student outcomes.

—Elmore & Ekstrom, 2004, p. 400

School counselors work primarily in the realms of students' affect and behavior. There are hundreds of good measures of affective characteristics and behaviors available. As a school counselor, you should know how to use such measures and should use them frequently, because standardized measures are well suited for use in a wide variety of school counselor accountability activities.

A large part of your work with students lies in the attempt to change and improve their affective characteristics, based on the assumption that improvement of the students' affective characteristics will lead to improvement of the students' academic and other behaviors. Gredler (1996) wrote that

> affective characteristics are nonobservable internal character-
> istics of persons that arise from or include an emotional com-
> ponent. Affective characteristics consist of appreciations, at-
> titudes, adjustments, interests, and values, as well as feelings
> about oneself, such as self-concept, self-esteem, and self-ef-
> ficacy. Affective characteristics are constructs that are indi-
> rectly related to behavior. (p. 167)

In 1918, noted psychologist E. L. Thorndike commented, "Whatever exists at all exists in some amount" (cited in McCall, 1922, p.16)." Psychologist R. B. McCall (1922) added that "anything that exists in amount can be measured." Today, these seemingly obvious but actually profound insights are combined into the commonly espoused dictum that if a thing exists, it exists in some amount, and if it exists in some amount, it can be measured. Similarly, if in fact a school counselor's intervention is successful in changing a student's affective characteristics, then that change must be measurable (Nugent et al., 2001). One of the best ways to measure such change is to administer a standardized (i.e., commercially available, normative, and validated) measure of the student's affective characteristics, preferably before and after the intervention. The change data that result are among the strongest types of evidence that you can generate for accountability purposes, because test-based evidence of change is usually perceived as having much more credibility than subjective reports of change.

Tests or measurements for a variety of student affective characteristics are available. Some of them are diagnostic (used here in a broadest sense of the term) in nature, such as measurements of students' levels of depression, anxiety, suicidal ideology, substance abuse/addiction, attention deficit disorder, or eating disorder. Others are not intended to be diagnostic but instead are designed to provide normative information on levels of student attributes, such as self- concept, self-esteem, self-efficacy, general emotional well-being, or general personality characteristics. A third type is intended to allow students to communicate their concerns nonverbally. For example, there are several different types of problem checklists that can be used to determine relatively specific life-functioning problem areas of either individual students or groups of students. Any of these types of assessments can be used to indicate change if applied before and after intervention. The selection of an appropriate measure is dependent upon a school counselor's purposes, needs, and/or assessment capabilities (e.g., most school counselors are not qualified to use so-called clinical tests, such as diagnostic personality inventories).

When used properly, tests—or more precisely, test results—may enhance the counseling process and facilitate client change.

—Hanson & Claiborn, 2006, p. 349

There also are a number of measurements of students' behaviors. Most often, these measures are in the form of checklists to be completed by a student or the student's parents or teachers. Typically, ratings are made of the relative frequency with which a student engages in each of the behaviors listed. Use of behavior checklists may provide particularly strong accountability data because change in behavior, including its relative frequency of occurrence, is the most commonly desired result of a school counselor intervention.

Please remember that if you use a standardized test, you should read and study the test manual carefully. The manual will explain what the test is designed to measure (and, perhaps, what it is not designed to measure) and how the test is to be administered. (Obviously, if a standardized test is not used for an appropriate purpose or administered properly, the results of its use cannot be valid.)

Information about the many standardized tests suitable for use by school counselors is readily available (see, for example, Table 3.1). All the major test publishing companies now have Web sites, most of which can be found either by doing an Internet search using the phrase "test publishers" or by linking from the ATP Web site. In addition, it is always a good idea for you to get on the postal or electronic mailing lists of the major testing companies to receive catalogs and current information about previously published and new tests.

School-Counselor-Made Tests

Many school counseling authorities, as well as ASCA, advocate that school counselors should fulfill an educational role in the schools. In

Common Accountability Resources for School Counseling Functions   99

TABLE 3.1.
INFORMATION ABOUT TESTS AND TESTING

American Educational Research Association (AERA)
www.aera.net

American Psychological Association–Science Directorate (APA)
www.apa.org/science

Association for Assessment in Counseling and Education (AACE)
http://aac.ncat.edu

Association of Test Publishers (ATP)
www.testpublishers.org

Buros Institute of Mental Measurements
www.unl.edu/buros

Fair Access Coalition on Testing (FACT)
www.fairaccess.org

Joint Committee on Testing Practices (JCTP)
www.apa.org/science/jctpweb.html

National Association of School Psychologists (NASP)
www.nasponline.org

National Association of Test Directors (NATD)
www.natd.org

National Council on Measurement in Education (NCME)
www.ncme.org

---

this view, school counselors may be considered a nontraditional type of educator/teacher in the schools. School counselors are essentially teachers when they engage in large-group guidance activities. In addition, school counselors frequently teach during other interactions with students, such as in individual or small-group counseling. Thus, the teaching function is quite naturally an integral part of a your functioning as a school counselor.

Unfortunately, there is scant evidence that school counselors are effective in their large-group guidance activities. For one thing, there are few studies of the effectiveness of large-group guidance activities in the professional school counseling literature, and those that are presented show mixed results (Whiston, 2003). For another, it may be that the nature of the effectiveness evidence that was sought was inappropriate for the nature of the large-group guidance. For example, most of the studies available for review have investigated whether large-group guidance activities changed global student characteristics, such as their self-concepts or attitudes toward school. Statistically significant differences (e.g., changes over time) have not often been found. But is it any surprise that a large-group guidance activity of only several hours doesn't change the average self-concept of students in the class? While a few students might change their self-concepts substantially as a result of a specific large-group guidance activity, it would indeed be a major accomplishment and surprise if the class average improved significantly. The most unfortunate result of this lack of demonstrated effectiveness of large-group guidance activities is that there are not good models of how to evaluate them.

Again, the usual long-term goal of school counselors' teaching functions is to change students' affective characteristics and/or behaviors. However, if school counselors are in effect teachers, the more immediate result should be that students either learn new material, develop new skills, or both. Of course learning or skill development are the traditionally expected results of classroom teaching activities. It follows that the use of measures modeled after traditional classroom tests is the most appropriate way to evaluate the effectiveness of school counselors' teaching activities, at least in the short-term. Linn and Miller (2005) effectively summarized the role of testing in instructional contexts:

> The main purpose of classroom instruction is to help students achieve a set of intended learning goals. These goals should typically include desired changes in the intellectual, emotional, and physical spheres. When classroom instruction is viewed in this light, assessment becomes an integral part of the teaching learning process. The intended learning outcomes are established by the instructional goals, the desired changes in students are brought about by the planned learning activities, and the students' learning progress is periodically assessed by tests and other assessment devices. (pp. 29–30)

Any of the usual variety of classroom-type tests may be suitable for evaluating a school counselor's teaching activities, including true–false, completion, matching, multiple choice, essay, and simulation tests. Two examples school-counselor-made tests are provided in Figures 3.3 and 3.4 to exemplify how a localized and personalized test might look. Unfortunately, complete discussion of the principles for the development of such tests is beyond the scope of this discussion. However, reading and a little study of any good book on classroom testing (e.g., Linn & Miller, 2005) will provide you with the necessary foundations and test development skills. In addition, you have excellent resources for the development of classroom-type tests: the teachers in your school. Collaboration with teachers on the development of a test suitable for use for a school counselor's purposes not only results in a better test but also fosters better teacher understandings of the work of the school counselor. As Dollarhide (2003a) wrote, "Many teachers will benefit from a better understanding of the role of the school counselor in a comprehensive school counseling program" (p. 252). It follows that school counselors will have better relationships with teachers if the teachers are aware of the commonalities of their respective efforts in the schools, and testing is one of those commonalties.

We emphasize that we believe in change because we were born of it, we have lived by it, we prospered and grew great by it. So the status quo has never been our god, and we ask no one else to bow down before it.

—Carl T. Rowan

Tests are sometimes administered in a pre–post pattern, to assess change or gain from the activity. It is unrealistic to expect a class average on a test to improve significantly, in a statistical sense. It is reasonable, however, to expect some students, particularly those with the lowest scores, to improve. For example, if a physical education teacher trains students to run faster for 100 meters, the fittest and fastest students might not improve their times significantly, but the slowest students will likely run significantly faster. Similarly, if you premeasure individuals before large-group guidance activities, focus on students most in need of improvement rather than looking at the class average, and see if they demonstrate significant improvement via a posttest.

School counselors often find essay tests desirable for evaluating their large-group guidance activities because they think (a) students have a free-response format for communicating the impact of the activities, (b) they are easy ways to assess student outcomes, and/or (c) the

TRUE–FALSE

Think about our classroom lesson on how to prepare for the state examinations. This quiz is to help you and me see how much you learned from it. *Your score on this quiz will not affect your grade in the class.* Please circle a T for True or an F for False for each statement.

T F I should mark the date of the state test on my school calendar.

T F If I get nervous about the test, I should tell only my close friends.

T F I should get as much sleep as possible the night before the test.

T F Eating breakfast the day of will upset my stomach during the test.

T F I should answer each question in order, even if I am unsure about my answer.

T F After the test begins, I will not be allowed to leave the room.

T F I should answer the questions I know first and then go back to more difficult questions.

T F If I don't know the answer to a test question, I should guess at it.

T F I should try to be the first person to finish the test.

T F If I have a question, I should raise my hand and wait for the teacher to come to me.

FIGURE 3.3. School-counselor-made true–false test.

results of essay tests are easy to evaluate or score. However, an essay test is essentially a semistructured interview conducted in writing. It is true that essay tests are a comfortable type of assessment in that student respondents don't feel pressure to find one right answer; the comfort comes from the student's feeling of being able to respond as she or he thinks is appropriate. Therefore, essay tests are a more comfortable interaction with the question asker (in this case, the school counselor) than are most types of tests. However, just as in a semistructured interview, evaluation of responses to essay questions is a codifying and counting task. Here too, categories of response elements (usually including an *other* or *unclassifiable* category) should be developed for each essay question before it is administered. Review and evaluation

> ### Sentence Completion Test
>
> Suppose that you have just presented a large-group guidance unit on the *M.U.R.D.E.R.* (Mood-Understand-Recall-Digest-Expand-Review) approach to studying (e.g., see www.studygs.net/murder.htm). Following are some completion items that might be used to determine what the students learned from the activity.
>
> 1. You will retain information better if you _review_ , which includes thinking about both what you learned and how you learned it.
>
> 2. It is a good idea to separate what you know from what you don't know about a topic and then to concentrate your activities on what you don't know. In other words, you should mark what you don't _understand_ .
>
> 3. Sometimes it is appropriate to ask someone else and/or to use another resource to help you figure out what the information means, or to help you to _digest_ it.
>
> 4. You should select an appropriate time and place for and attitude about studying. In other words, you should set a positive _mood_ for yourself.
>
> 5. In order to _expand_ your knowledge of the topic, you can think about questions that you might ask the source of the information, how it might apply to your life, and how would you explain it to other students.
>
> 6. One good way to _recall_ what you have learned is to put what you know into your own words.

Figure 3.4. School-counselor-made sentence completion test.

of the responses should then include assignment of response elements to predetermined response categories. Again, this is how responses to essay questions become quantitative data.

Academic Performance Indicators

Cobia and Henderson (2003, p. 19) wrote that "the purposes of education relate to intellectual, economic, political, and social purposes. *Schooling is ultimately designed to help students increase their cognitive knowledge and skills, an intellectual goal*" [emphasis added]. Various educational professionals' ideological and philosophical statements aside, the majority of Americans believe that the purpose of schools in America is to "learn 'em somethin'." That is what they believe they are paying for, and that is what they expect for their money. School counselors need to be fully cognizant of this expectation. Most people don't expect school counselors to help their children become better people, better citizens, or even better children. People expect school counselors, under the general rubric of educators to help their children learn as much as possible in school; therefore, it is crucial that school counselors develop accountability evidence to show that they have helped students perform better academically in school.

The ultimate indicator of students doing better in school is of course improvement in their grade point average. The good news is that such data are readily obtained; you don't have to measure anything directly to get the data. The bad news is that you will rarely be able to show that you are the primary or direct cause of improvement in a student's grade point average. There are simply too many factors that influence a student's grade point average to demonstrate that it was specifically whatever you did that caused the improvement. Further, claiming that you were the only cause of improvement in a student's academic performance will not likely be popular among your teacher colleagues. Thus, although you should not shy away from showing that you helped to bring about improvements in students' grades, you should be cautious in making claims about the success of your efforts. Taking credit for improvement in a student's grades when someone or something else was a contributing factor would be a significant, and likely embarrassing, professional and personal blunder.

The education explosion is producing a vast number of people who want to lead significant, important lives but lack the ability to satisfy this craving for importance by individual achievement.

—Eric Hoffer

But if not grades, then what? The best response likely lies in adopting a different perspective on the situation. Grades and test scores can be viewed as *distal* outcomes (Brown & Trusty, 2005); distal in the sense that they usually are not attributable to any one source of influence, including your efforts as a school counselor. However, if you provide an intervention activity designed to improve students' study skills, then study skills are *proximal* outcomes. "Proximal outcomes are those that are targeted directly by the strategic intervention" (Brown & Trusty, 2005, p. 5). So, your best bet to show that your efforts resulted in better student academic performance is to demonstrate that you changed attitudes *or* behaviors generally understood to be associated with better academic performance. For example, improvements in a student's self-concept, attitude toward school, relationship with his or her teacher, perceived self-efficacy, clarity of academic plans and the like all would be positively associated with improved general academic performance. Similarly, improvements in a student's behavior, such as increased school attendance (less absenteeism), decreased tardiness, increased positive classroom behaviors (e.g., volunteering), increased frequency of homework submission, better study habits, decreased discipline referrals and the like would be positively associated with improved general academic performance. These are student attitudes and behaviors to which you can appropriately attend and for which you can legitimately take credit for improvements. Other examples of distal and proximal academic performance indicators are provided as follows:

Distal Academic Performance Indicators

State report card or proficiency rating

State comprehensive examinations results

Standardized achievement test results

College entry examination results

Composite class-level grade point averages

Graduation rates

Number of honor roll students

Number of students in advanced placement

Number of students in international baccalaureate courses

Number of students enrolled in college courses

Number of students in gifted/talented classes

Pass rates by course or grade

Attendance rates

Retention rates

Promotion rates

Dropout rates

Suspension rates

Disciplinary referrals

Proximal Outcome Indicators

Homework completion rates

Classroom participation rates

Membership in extracurricular activities

Motivation self-reports

Self-concept

Confidence in abilities

Attitudes toward school

Number of friendships

Communication skills

Problem-solving skills

Goal-setting skills

Planning and decision-making skills

Study skills

Time management skills

Persistence on-task

Self-knowledge of learning style

Responsibility

Self-directedness

Ability to work in groups

Conflict management skills

Initiative

Ability to identify support system

Organization skills

Ability to avoid peer pressure

Articulation of postsecondary plans

Ability to balance school, leisure, and family

Respect for diversity

Dependability

Punctuality

Identification of personal skills and interests

Career-planning skills

Financial management skills

Employability

Understanding of the importance of work

Cooperation with others

Identification of values, attitudes, and beliefs

Distinguishing between appropriate and inappropriate behaviors

Recognizing personal boundaries and other's boundaries

Accept individual differences

Understanding consequences of decisions and actions

Knowing how to seek assistance

Learning how to manage stress

Learning coping skill

Note that even if you can provide evidence of effectiveness causing improvements in specific student attitudes and behaviors, you will likely have to explain the association between the activity and the resultant improved student general academic performance in any accountability report of the activity. It need not be lengthy, but it should emphasize that most of your successful activities lead to improved academic performance, and stakeholders who receive the information need to be reminded of that.

Demonstrating that you had positive influence on proximal indicators of students' academic performance is relatively easy through the use of many of the accountability activities and resources that have been or will be presented in this book. However, we believe there is need to interject a note of caution at this point. There is an old adage among financial experts that, as an investor, you should take your gains where you can get them. Basically, this means that you should invest most of your money in investment opportunities and/or strategies most likely to provide a sufficient and satisfactory return on your investments. It is okay to invest some money in highly speculative (i.e., high risk–high reward) investments and some money in conservative (i.e., low risk–low reward) investments, but most of your money should go into relatively sound (i.e., moderate risk–moderate reward) investments. An analogous situation exists for your school counseling activities intended to improve students' academic performance (vis-à-vis improvement in proximal indicators). For example, although it is likely that you can help some significantly underperforming students with their academic work (i.e., improve some of their proximal indicators of good academic behavior), it will be difficult, and likely take a long time, to show improvement of their distal indicators of good academic performance (i.e., highly improved grades). Conversely, it is likely that you can help some very well-performing students improve their proximal indicators, and subsequently their distal indicators, of good academic performance. However, because they are already performing well, the amount of change will be small and therefore will not have much impact as accountability information. Most of the students with whom you should work in this regard fall between these extremes. Your best chances for success, both in helping students perform better academically through improvement of their proximal indicators of academic performance and in demonstrating accountability for your activities in this regard, lie in working with students who fall in the *just below average* to *just above average* range of academic performance. Take your gains where you can get them.

School-Counselor-Made Accountability Data Forms

For many, perhaps most, of your accountability activities, it will be necessary to create forms that convey the nature of the activity and the type of data collected. Fortunately, creating such forms is not difficult through the use of a word-processing or spreadsheet software program. The use of personally developed data forms allows you to be both creative and informative. For example, suppose you plan to conduct a large-group guidance activity intended to increase multicultural sensitivity and awareness among elementary school children. One of your goals would likely be to change students' attitudes about other students whose cultural backgrounds are different from their own (i.e., to help children become more accepting of students representing cultures different from their own). If you want to demonstrate change in the students' attitudes, you will need to know attitudes before and after your large-group guidance activity. The words students use to describe people are a behavioral indictor of students' attitudes. One way to assess students' attitudes would be to use a free-association technique before and after your activity. Basically, before your large-group guidance activity, you would ask students to indicate any words that come to mind immediately when they think of a person from a particular cultural background. You would then ask the students again after you have completed the large-group guidance activity. (It would be even better to wait a week or two after the activity to determine if the effects of the activity last.) A form that could be used to collect data for such an activity is shown in Figure 3.5.

FREE-ASSOCIATION DATA COLLECTION

Think about a person who is of [*insert appropriate cultural identifier term*] background. Write down some words that come into your mind when you think about a person who is [*insert appropriate cultural identifier*].

_____

_____

_____

_____

_____

_____

_____

_____

_____

Use multiple copies of this form for several different cultural backgrounds to be addressed.

FIGURE 3.5. Free-association data-collection activity.

The resultant data of a free association data-collection technique are words. Interpreting words as data is, of course, intuitive and subjective; however, if the words change and become more positive and accepting, the data from a free association data collection technique often are obvious and can be very powerful. For another example of using the free-association technique as a data-collection method, see Smith (2004).

Students cannot do well in school if they do not attend school, so, helping students have better attendance is something that most school counselors try to achieve. Myriad school counseling activities have been tried or are used to help students have a better attendance record. However, for the sake of example, suppose you plan to use one or more of five general categories of school counseling activities to help selected students attend school more regularly: (a) individual counseling, (b) small-group counseling, (c) teacher consultation, (d) parent consultation, and (e) other resources (e.g., finding more reliable transportation for a student, improving a student's medical care, changing a student's class schedule). Also assume that each student's attendance will be monitored for a 2-week period, before and after their respective interventions. Figure 3.6 could be used to record activities used and their results for specific students. To gather the data, simply put a check mark in the appropriate cell whenever that type of intervention activity is used with each of the respective students. Note that multiple interventions will be necessary for some students. The totals for all of the relevant activities and the averages for attendance are readily computed and can be shown at the bottom of the form.

Now suppose that you are engaging in a career education or development activity intended to help students use the Internet as a resource for finding career or job information, based on the assumption that if students can identify career goals, they will be more motivated to do better in school. The intent of this activity is to have the students use the Internet more often. To determine if students increase their use of the Internet, you must know how frequently they use the Internet for career-related activities. A simple way to get that information is to ask each student to respond to the question, "How many times during the last 2 weeks have you used the Internet to find information about jobs or careers that you might like?" Their self-reported responses, and possibly changes in them, can easily be shown on the sample data form (see Figure 3.7). It would be best, and less susceptible to social desirability responding, if the students provided their responses anonymously.

Common Accountability Resources for School Counseling Functions   111

Attendance Improvement Activities

	Absences Two Weeks Before	Individual Counseling	Small-Group Counseling	Teacher Consultation	Parent Consultation	Other Resource(s)	Absences Two Weeks After
Student 1	6	✓			✓	✓	4
Student 2	3		✓	✓			2
Student 3	2			✓			0
Student 4	5	✓			✓		7
Student 5	4		✓	✓			1
Student 6	1			✓			1
Student 7	5		✓	✓	✓		2
Student 8	6	✓			✓	✓	1
Student 9	7				✓	✓	5
Student 10	4		✓	✓			1
Student 11	2			✓			0
Student 12	2			✓			0
Student 13	7					✓	9
Student 14	9	✓			✓	✓	4
Student 15	3		✓	✓			1
Student 16	3		✓	✓			1
Student 17	2			✓			0
Totals	71	4	6	11	6	5	39
Averages	4.18	- - - -	- - - -	- - - -	- - - -	- - - -	2.30
s.d.	2.24	- - - -	- - - -	- - - -	- - - -	- - - -	2.64

FIGURE 3.6. Data form for attendance improvement activities.

COLLEGE SCHOLARSHIP PLANNING AND COUNSELING

		Initial Number	Advisement	Counseling	Referral	Number After
Plan A	Low GPA	29	24	0	2	3
Plan A	Low score	42	38	4	1	1
Plan A	Both	21	12	2	3	4
Plan B	Low GPA	15	11	2	0	2
Plan B	Low score	30	19	5	1	5
Plan B	Both	7	2	1	4	4

FIGURE 3.7. Data form for college scholarship planning and counseling.

Therefore, each student could be asked to use the same individual code (e.g., last four digits of home telephone number) on both assessment occasions so that each student's before and after responses could be paired.

An increasing number of states are providing tuition and other scholarships to postsecondary educational institutions for students who have completed a stipulated high school curriculum with a minimum grade point average and have surpassed a minimum criterion score on a standardized test, often administered by the state, in a timely manner. In some of these states, the level of scholarship awarded varies, depending on a student's various academic and/or test-score accomplishments. Therefore, there may be different scholarship eligibility criteria for different students, depending on the level of scholarship sought. Unfortunately, students don't always do what we would like them to do, when we want them to do it. Thus, some students who would like to take advantage of these scholarship opportunities either need to know the requirements or need help to fulfill the various requirements successfully and on time. Now, suppose that in your state there is a minimum GPA and an associated minimum test score for a partial scholarship (Plan A) and another minimum GPA and associated test score for a full scholarship (Plan B). Some students who have not yet fulfilled the eligibility criteria will have a low GPA, some will have a low test score, and some will have both a low GPA and a low test score. Now, suppose you plan to use three types of school counseling activities to help these students: (a) Advisement, which in this case means informing the students of what they need to do and when they need to do it; (b) Counseling, which in this case means working with the student more extensively to overcome obstacles to eligibility; and (c) Referral, which in this case means having the student use an outside resource (such as a tutor). The data form for this activity might look like Figure 3.8.

STUDENTS' USE OF THE INTERNET FOR CAREER INFORMATION

Internet Use 2 Weeks Before		Internet Use 2 Weeks After
1	Student 1	6
2	Student 2	6
0	Student 3	0
0	Student 4	5
2	Student 5	5
0	Student 6	8
1	Student 7	4
1	Student 8	2
0	Student 9	6
3	Student 10	9
0	Student 11	5
0	Student 12	2
1	Student 13	2
5	Student 14	9
0	Student 15	2
0	Student 16	4
1	Student 17	1
2	Student 18	4
4	Student 19	5
3	Student 20	8
2	Student 21	2
0	Student 22	3
0	Student 23	4
1	Student 24	5
1	Student 25	0
30	Total	107
1.20	Average	4.28
1.39	SD	2.57

FIGURE 3.8. Data form showing how students use the Internet for career information.

To complete the form, you would determine how many students are in each plan category initially; provide a school counseling service as appropriate for each student, noting the type of activity provided by putting a check mark in the appropriate categories; and then determine the number of students in each plan category once you have completed your activities.

Keeping with the theme of helping high school students to get to postsecondary education, consider that a rapidly increasing number of students are applying for federal student aid. A student must complete the U.S. Department of Education's "Free Application for Federal Student Aid" (FAFSA) form to obtain financial aid from this source. The form is readily available on the Internet (http://www.fafsa.ed.gov/), but it is not easy to complete fully, accurately, and successfully. Therefore, many students need various types of assistance to complete the form and file it correctly and on time. Suppose that you decide to help students with the FAFSA form by using the same three general activities as in Figure 3.9: (a) Advisement, i.e., informing the students of what they need to do and when they need to do it; (b) Counseling, working with students more extensively to overcome obstacles (e.g., familial problems); and (c) Referral, having students use an outside resource (such as a family's financial consultant). This is an important but time-consuming part of your school counseling activities, so you decide to indicate not only what you did but also how much time it took to do it.

To record the types of assistance provided to each student, put a check mark in the appropriate cell in the row for that student. Sum the check marks in each of the columns to show the total number of each type of assistance that was provided. To keep track of the time you spent in each activity, enter the number of quarter hours you spent with each student for each of the activities provided for the respective students. Subsequently, you could readily convert the total numbers of quarter hours to hours for ease of interpretation.

Forms such as those shown in the preceding examples are easy to create, use, and understand. Recording data for your accountability activities does not have to be, and should not be, an overly complex process. As indicated in the first chapter, engaging in accountability activities should not be at the expense of providing good school counseling services. Using simple forms such as the ones shown in these examples will allow you to maintain priority on providing quality services while also allowing you to generate accountability data for your professional school counseling activities.

FAFSA Activity and Time Project

	Number for Advisement	Quarter Hours for Advisement	Number for Counseling	Quarter Hours for Counseling	Number for Referral	Quarter Hours For Referrals	Application Complete Y/N
Student 1	✓	1	✓	4		0	N
Student 2	✓✓✓	4		0	✓	2	N
Student 3		0	✓	3			Y
Student 4	✓	1		0			Y
Student 5	✓✓	3		0			Y
Student 6	✓	1		0	✓	2	N
Student 7		0	✓✓	4			Y
Student 8		0		0	✓✓	4	Y
Student 9	✓✓✓	3		0			Y
Student 10		0	✓	2			Y
Student 11	✓	1		0			N
Student 12	✓	1		0			Y
Student 13	✓✓	3		0			Y
Student 14		0	✓✓✓	6	✓	3	Y
Student 15		0	✓	5			Y
Student 16	✓	1		0			N
Student 17		0	✓	2	✓		Y
Student 18	✓✓✓	3		0			Y
Student 19	✓	2		0			Y
Student 20	✓✓	2		0			N
Student 21	✓	1		0			Y
Student 22		0	✓	2			Y
Student 23	✓✓✓	4		0			Y
Student 24		0	✓	3			Y
Student 25	✓	1		0			N
Student 26		0	✓✓	6	✓✓		Y
Student 27	✓✓	2		0			N
Student 28	✓✓✓	2		0			Y
Student 29		0	✓✓	2			Y
Student 30	✓	2		0	✓		Y
Numbers Total	33	38	16	39	9	11	Y = 22 N = 8
Hours Total		9.50		9.75		2.75	

Figure 3.9. Form for FAFSA activity and time project.

CONCLUSION

The resources described here can be used in a wide variety of school counselor accountability activities. However, what is needed is creativity and thoughtfulness in their use. Creativity is needed in that most of these resources are best when developed by school counselors specifically for local use. Thoughtfulness is needed in that most of these resources can be used repeatedly over time if they are carefully and sufficiently developed. Obtaining or developing accountability resources is a primary responsibility for you as a school counselor. Effective and successful fulfillment of that responsibility requires that you consider carefully each and every one of your accountability activities and intentions. Therefore, in Chapter 4 we turn attention to more specific accountability activities (i.e., activities presented within the delivery system components of the *ASCA National Model*).

FOR THOUGHT AND DEED

1. Ask a group of school counselors who all work at the same school level (e.g., elementary, middle, or secondary) to (a) list the five most common problems for which students in their respective schools seek their help and (b) prioritize their respective lists from 1 (*most common*) to 5 (*least common*) of the five listed. Compile and edit the items (i.e., problems) provided into a checklist format. Give the checklist to a group of students at the appropriate school level, and ask them to check the problems for which they are most likely to seek their school counselor's help. Tally the results and compare them to the school counselors' prioritizations.

2. Using the items (i.e., problems) previously identified, create a rating scale that would allow students to indicate the frequency of occurrence of various problems among their peers. That is, list each problem and create a rating scale that would allow students to indicate how frequently (on some relative basis, such as from *very frequently* to *very infrequently*) their peers experience the respective problems. Administer the survey to a group of students at the appropriate school level, and summarize the results.

3. Develop a set of five questions that could be used in semistructured interviews with students to gather information about their reactions to a large-group guidance activity that focuses on helping students develop better time-management skills.

4. Examples of distal and proximal indicators of academic performance were provided in the chapter. Create a matrix that shows what you believe about how various distal indicators are associated with various proximal indicators. List the distal indicators across the top and the proximal indicators down the left side, and then put an "x" in the grid cells to indicate which indicators are most closely associated with one another. Note that you may have one or more of the proximal indicators associated with one or more of the distal indicators.

CHAPTER 4

ACCOUNTABILITY FOR SCHOOL COUNSELING CURRICULUM FUNCTIONS

In general, a guidance curriculum is a program that systematically delivers age-appropriate guidance content considered to be important and essential to all (or at least to a large majority) of the students in a school (ASCA, 2005; Cobia & Henderson, 2006; Gysbers & Henderson, 2006; Wittmer, Thompson, & Loesch, 1997). It is also presumed to be developmental and sequential in nature, "with the concepts at one level building on those learned at the previous level" (Cobia & Henderson, 2003, p. 90). Historically, the guidance curriculum has been almost synonymous with classroom (large-group) guidance activities. Sears (2005) wrote that "large-group guidance is defined as an intervention to deliver a curriculum or series of planned activities to help students anticipate problems before they occur or to help them cope effectively with problems after they occur" (p. 190). Because this definition reflects the essence of a *developmental* school counseling program, much of the professional literature on the guidance curriculum is focused on large-group guidance; however, there are other important guidance curriculum activities warrant attention.

CLASSROOM INSTRUCTION

School counselors working in the classroom essentially perform teaching functions, even though the subject matter is different from what is usually taught in the academic disciplines. That is, classroom instruction by school counselors is intended to help students obtain information and to develop skills that will enable them to function more ef-

119

fectively in their lives, both in and out of school. However, even though the subject matter is unique, the techniques of instruction are not very different from those that are, or could be, used in any classroom.

A school counselor may fill one of three roles in the delivery of a classroom (i.e., large-group) guidance unit; that is, a school counselor can (a) conduct the activity entirely by him- or herself, (b) conduct the activity in conjunction with a classroom teacher, or (c) serve as a consultant to a teacher who then conducts the activity by her- or himself (Baker & Gerler, 2004; Goodenough, Pérusse, & Erford, 2003). The first two modes are used frequently. The third mode is less common and probably is better considered as a form of consultation. However, no matter which tactic is used, it is crucial that there be clarity of purpose so that any accountability method applied has a likelihood for success. For example, sometimes the purpose of the large-group guidance instruction is simply to convey information; at other times, it is simply to teach skills. A key point is that *assessment of knowledge learned is different from assessment of skills gained*. It follows that attempting to measure the skills students have developed when only content has been presented, or vice versa, is doomed to failure, both as a large-group guidance activity evaluation and as an accountability activity. The data-gathering methods must fit the instructional goals and activities underlying the classroom activity.

Common developmental curriculum delivery methods include presenting information, discussions, debates, quiet reflection and writing, artwork, journaling, role playing, demonstrations, experiments, and field trips. But don't let this list confine you—be creative!

—Dollarhide & Saginak, 2003, p. 167

Methods that measure the effects of regular classroom instruction in regard to knowledge learned have been developed, and most of them could be used in the evaluation of the large-group guidance activities. Cobia and Henderson (2003) identified quite a few of them in just a few sentences:

> Ways of checking cognitive learning may involve oral questions, classroom interviews, journals, logs, and participation

> in activities and projects as well as tests.... Students could also create, either verbally or orally [sic] a before and after summary of their understanding of the topic.... Measuring attitudes, feelings, and beliefs—the substance of the affective domain—requires different strategies. Using pre- and post-unit questionnaires and checklists; making observations; tape recording class discussions; and monitoring the frequency of using materials such as occupational information are different ways to assess attitudes and beliefs. (p. 102)

In general, any assessment technique that measures the amount of student learning can be used as accountability activity. However, the use of school-counselor-made tests is highly recommended. Not only does using such tests lead to quantitative accountability data, it also exemplifies a parallel between what school counselors do and what teachers do. Again, teachers are often distanced from school counselors because they do not fully understand what school counselors do. Giving a knowledge test before or after a large-group guidance activity is one way to demonstrate to teachers that what school counselors do is less distant from what teachers do than the teachers may have thought.

The assessment of skills learned is somewhat more complex, but, again, many of the traditional methods are applicable. For example, having students role-play using the skills and tape recording the role-play sessions for analysis later is an effective way to determine if the students learned to use the skills properly. Another good technique is to use written simulations of future situations in which the skills might be applied. A simulation is simply a brief description (i.e., a scenario or vignette) of a situation in which the student might find her- or himself, followed by a general question of what the student would do in response to the situation. For example, if the students have been taught some effective interpersonal relationship skills, they might be given simulations of interpersonal encounters, in which use of the skills would be appropriate to assess whether the students apply the skills correctly. Written simulations can be structured in two ways. In one, the student simply identifies the most appropriate out of several provided responses. This approach makes it easy for students to respond and for the resultant data to be compiled. However, it also allows for guessing and therefore lessens the credibility of the assessment, particularly if only a small number of simulations is presented. A better alternative is to present the simulation and have the students write their responses. This is a truer assessment of skills development but requires more effort in the classification and interpretation of the responses given. As for semistructured interviews and essay questions, the possible response categories should be developed when the simulation is created. The general advantage of the written simulation approach is that it is relatively easy to analyze the written responses to determine if the skills have been developed and applied correctly.

If the shared presentation format (i.e., a school counselor and a teacher presenting a large-group guidance unit together) is used, and particularly if the school counselor has used this approach with several teachers in the school, then using semistructured interviews with the collaborating teachers is an excellent way to generate accountability data. The collaborating teachers can be interviewed for their perceptions of the effectiveness of the large-group guidance activity, the impact it had on students in the class, how it fit in with whatever else was being taught in the class, or for whatever other impact it may have had. Again, the mere act of conducting the follow-up interviews is likely to improve teacher–school counselor relationships. Further, the resultant data can be used to establish credibility with other teachers. Similarly, the students can be interviewed post-classroom-guidance activity to determine what impact, if any, the unit had on them. If this tactic is used, it is a good idea to have the cooperating teacher conduct at least some of the interviews. Involving the teacher allows that teacher to get a sense of what the school counselor is trying to do and accomplish, how students react to the large-group guidance activity, and perhaps even to suggest to the school counselor how the activity could be improved.

For every one of us that succeeds, it's because there's somebody there to show you the way out. The light doesn't always necessarily have to be in your family; for me it was teachers and school.

—Oprah Winfrey

One common goal for school counselors' classroom instruction activities is to change and/or improve relationships among students, particularly among students in the same classroom. Development of a *sociogram* is a unique way to assess whether such activities have been effective. A sociogram is a diagram of the relational preferences among people in a defined group. Development of a sociogram begins with asking a simple question, such as, "With which three students in this group (class) would you most like to spend your out-of-class (or recess or lunch or free) time?" The instructions are for the students to list up to three preferences, without regard to order of preference. A hypothetical sociogram that might result from this activity is shown in Figure 4.1.

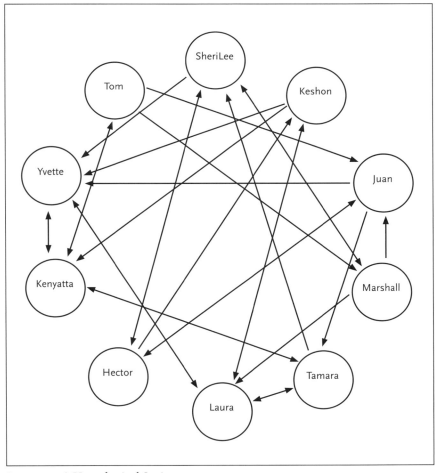

FIGURE 4.1. A Hypothetical Sociogram.

The sociogram is constructed by drawing a line from each student's name circle to the students' name circles representing his or her choices. An arrow pointing from one student to another (e.g., Keshon to Yvette or Keshon to Kenyatta) indicates that the first student (e.g., Keshon) has indicated the second student (e.g., Yvette) as one of his or her preferences. A line with an arrowhead at each end indicates a mutual selection (e.g., Keshon and Laura or Hector and SheriLee). (Some students may not identify three choices, which may be something worthy of a school counselor's attention.)

Sociograms are used most commonly to identify isolates and stars. An *isolate* in this context is a group member who was not indicated as a preference by any of the other group members. In a larger group (such as a class of 20 or more students), the isolate criterion might be raised somewhat to having been selected by very few other people in the group. In Figure 4.1, Tom is the group isolate. Tom indicated choices, but no one listed Tom as being among their top three preferences. Yvette is the star in the example, which means that she was the student listed most frequently as a preference.

In addition to identifying students who may benefit from counseling (i.e., isolates), a sociogram can be used as a pre- and postmeasure of the interpersonal relationships in the group. For example, if a large-group guidance activity results in change in the relational preferences among the group members (and particularly if a former isolate is selected more frequently afterward), presentation of the before and after sociograms is vivid evidence of the effectiveness of the activity.

INTERDISCIPLINARY CURRICULUM DEVELOPMENT

The *ASCA National Model* (ASCA, 2005) stipulates that

> school counselors participate on interdisciplinary teams to develop and refine curriculum in content areas. These teams develop school guidance curriculum that integrates with the subject matter. The scope and sequence of the school guidance curriculum may include units delivered through other classroom disciplines. (p. 41)

Basically, this means that school counselors should work with teachers to integrate some of the topical material (e.g., interpersonal relationship skill development, career development enhancement, intrafamily relationship facilitation) with which school counselors are frequently involved into teachers' regular classroom instruction. The extent to which school counselors do this is unknown; however, school counselors are admonished to integrate school guidance curriculum material into regular academic programming and therefore can and should be held accountable for their efforts.

Melding elements of school counseling into students' regular academic preparation seems like a daunting task. Does this mean that school counselors have to be experts in all academic disciplines? Certainly not! Rather, it means that school counselors should integrate elements of school counseling into academic disciplines with which they are comfortable. For example, professional school counselor preparation is at the master's degree level. That means that all professional school counselors have a baccalaureate degree in something, and their undergraduate major is likely related to something taught in the school in which they work. That's where a school counselor can begin. For example, a school counselor who had an undergraduate major in mathematics might work with math teachers in the school to develop lessons on how mathematics can be used to explain some aspects of human behavior (such as the probability of behavioral reactions to certain events). Similarly, a school counselor who had an undergraduate major in psychology can work with psychology or civics teachers to explain how principles of psychology actually become manifest in human behavior, or a school counselor who knows something about accounting can work with an economics teacher to help students learn about how fiscal matters, concerns, and resources impact family functioning. Instruction content must be appropriate to the levels of the students to whom it will be given; therefore, adapting important school counseling topics to regular school curriculum areas need not be complex.

Integrating school counseling topical material into regular classroom instruction may be challenging for school counselors, but it is relatively easy to be accountable for such activities. The accountability for such integration lies not in the academic outcomes of the activities but rather in the extent to which they are implemented in classrooms. That is, a school counselor is merely charged to integrate some of the school guidance curriculum into regular classroom activities. The school counselor is not responsible for ensuring that academic integration activities are successful in an educational sense or effective in regard to academic content learning or skill development; that is the responsibility of the respective teachers who present the lessons. Therefore, a school counselor's accountability is essentially a counting function; a school counselor can simply report how many of her or his suggested activities were integrated by teachers into their regular classroom instruction. Thus, the bottom line in regard to a school counselor's fulfillment of this professional responsibility is in the number of the integrations, not in the academic outcomes. Of course, the counts can be enhanced with additional information, such as the number of classroom periods during which the integrated topical material was presented and/or the number of students who received the lessons. However, the main point is that a school counselor should not fall into the trap of trying to be accountable for the effectiveness of the instruction. A school counselor need only be accountable for the extent of integration.

Effective collaboration requires a willingness to share credit, blame, rewards, and penalties.

—Stone & Dahir, 2006, p. 184

GROUP ACTIVITIES

In the *ASCA National Model* (ASCA, 2005), what are traditionally thought of as small-group counseling activities are not included in the school counseling curriculum subsection. Instead, the area is focused on other types of group activities. Presumably, most of a school counselor's functioning would be developmental and/or preventative in nature (because if they were remedial in nature, the activities would be best identified as counseling). Therefore, as is the case for large-group guidance activities, the primary purpose of such activities is likely to teach students about topical material (e.g., the characteristics of a person who is multiculturally sensitive) or to help students develop new skills (e.g., appropriate reactions to bullying behavior). It follows that many of the activities used to evaluate the effectiveness of large-group guidance activities, such as administering a test, having students respond to a simulation, just having students write about what knowledge or skills they learned in the group also are applicable in this context. The same assessment cautions also apply, such as the need to pay careful attention to whether the purpose of the group is to teach knowledge, skills, or both.

One type of group conducted by school counselors falls between remedial and developmental: groups conducted to increase students' academic motivation and performance. For example, Sears, Moore, and Young (2004) offered that

> a small group counseling plan shows school counselors how they can help students apply the self-regulatory cycle to five basic study skills: planning and using time more effectively, understanding and summarizing text material better, improving methods of note-taking, anticipating and preparing better for exams, and writing more effectively. (p. 781)

> These five essential academic skills can be taught successfully to elementary through high school students as long as the students understand they need to engage in task analysis before selecting the appropriate learning strategy or strategies and then self-monitor to determine the effectiveness of the chosen strategy, adapting whenever necessary. (p. 786)

Such group activities are in part remedial because they often address student behaviors that inhibited previous achievement of academic success and are in part developmental because they often present behaviors presumed to lead to better academic performance in school. However, the situation is complicated by the fact that motivation is an affective characteristic. Therefore, evaluation of the effectiveness of these types of groups is tricky, at best. Certainly, the degree of knowledge (e.g., more effective study habits) or skills (e.g., better test-taking behaviors) learned from the group can be assessed using some of the methods already presented. The real question is whether academic motivation actually has increased. Students' academic motivation is not changed easily or quickly. Therefore, in most cases, sufficient time must pass before the effectiveness of the group activities can be evaluated fairly and fully. Unfortunately, there is no good definition of "sufficient time" for this purpose. In any event, after an appropriate length of time, the effectiveness of the group can be evaluated best by examining whether each participant's academic behaviors (e.g., homework submission rate or classroom test scores) have improved. Simply put, change in academic motivation must be inferred from evident behavior change.

The thing I loved the most—and still love the most about teaching—is that you can connect with an individual or a group, and see that individual or group exceed their limits.

—Mike Krzyzewski

Sometimes, it is necessary to turn around students, for them to have increased academic motivation and hence do better in school. The euphemism "turn around" means that there has to be substantial *personal* change for the students, often in regard to self-concept, self-confidence, and self-perceived competence. For example, suppose you identify 12 students in your high school that are at risk for poor academic performance and/or dropping out of school. You know you need to do something extraordinary to turn around these students, so you look to additional resources in your area. Now suppose that you arrange to collaborate with a mental health counselor from a local mental health agency to provide a Ropes Course experience for the target students. A Ropes Course is an outdoor experience involving many challenging physical activities intended to help participants improve their conflict resolution, peer relationship, anger management, and problem-solving skills. If successful, such experiences also typically lead to enhanced perceptions of self among participants. You decide to monitor the students' absences from school and discipline referrals while in school over the 6-week Ropes Course, information that is readily available from school records. You also decide to monitor the students' weekly percentages of homework submitted, which involves getting data from the students' teachers and calculating the respective percentages. Of course, all of this is relatively easily accomplished through use of a spreadsheet program. A data form that you might use for this activity is shown in Figure 4.2. Note that you can examine both individual and group (aggregate) results from this activity. This format is basically a multiple-baseline-across-people, single-subject design (see Chapter 6), so graphs depicting individual and group results are easily constructed to show the results graphically.

Accountability for School Counseling - Curriculum Functions   129

Ropes Course Project

Student:	Referrals	Absences	Homework %	Referrals	Absences	Homework %	Referrals	Absences	Homework %	Referrals	Absences	Homework %	Referrals	Absences	Homework %	Referrals	Absences	Homework %
1	2	2	15	1	2	20	0	1	30	1	0	35	0	0	50	1	0	60
2	3	2	15	2	2	10	3	1	10	2	0	25	0	1	30	0	1	40
3	5	3	0	3	2	25	1	1	50	1	0	60	0	0	75	0	0	75
4	1	1	30	0	2	30	1	2	25	0	1	25	1	2	20	2	1	20
5	6	4	0	3	2	0	3	1	10	0	1	15	0	0	50	1	0	60
6	3	0	25	0	1	25	2	0	25	0	0	30	0	1	30	1	1	20
7	5	2	10	4	1	25	3	2	15	0	0	35	0	1	50	0	0	50
8	1	4	10	0	2	25	4	0	30	2	2	30	1	0	40	1	0	50
9	4	0	30	1	2	25	2	0	35	1	3	10	0	2	40	1	0	45
10	3	1	25	2	2	30	1	0	50	0	0	65	0	1	65	0	0	80
11	1	0	20	0	1	30	0	0	15	0	0	20	1	0	25	0	0	0
12	5	3	0	2	2	20	0	1	25	0	0	50	0	1	60	0	0	70

FIGURE 4.2. Data form for the Ropes Course Project.

Another type of accountability information that is commonly collected about small-group activities is student satisfaction with participation in the group. Data on student satisfaction with a group is relatively weak accountability information in that making students happy (i.e., pleased with the group experience) is not usually the primary purpose of the group activity. For most school counseling program stakeholders (e.g., teachers or administrators), student satisfaction with the group is at best tangential information. They think it's nice if the students enjoyed the group, but they are primarily interested in the extent to which the group achieved its purposes. However, there is one group of stakeholders for which information about group participation satisfaction is very important: students. That is, many students are hesitant to participate in school counselor group activities for a variety of reasons such as shyness, fear that they will have to disclose something they don't want to disclose, or fear of becoming embarrassed. Therefore, information about students' satisfaction with participation in group activities can be extremely valuable when it is disseminated to other students. Such information has good potential to increase other students' interest and willingness to participate in groups conducted by a school counselor.

Satisfaction with participation in a group experience is an attitude, and therefore is best assessed with some type of survey instrument. In general, attitude items should relate to the group process, not to potential outcomes. For example, an item such as "I learned new behaviors from participating in the group" is an outcome-oriented item. Such an item is not an attitude item because the appropriate responses to such an item are yes or no (i.e., either the respondent learned new behaviors in or from the group or did not); therefore, an attitude response scale is not appropriate for such an item. Following are some process-oriented items that could be used to assess participant satisfaction with a group activity:

> I felt comfortable talking in the group
>
> The other group members listened to what I had to say
>
> I was able to stay focused in the group
>
> I enjoyed the group activities
>
> The counselor made it easy to be in the group
>
> I liked listening to what my peers had to say

The counselor respected my feelings

Participating in the group was fun for me

The counselor made it safe to be in the group

Being in the group was a good way to spend my time

Each of these items could be followed by a Likert scale or a rating scale such as 1 = *not at all how I feel about the group* to 10 = *very much how I feel about the group*. Of course, all of these items are stated positively. In an actual satisfaction survey, it would be good to have some of the items stated negatively.

PARENT WORKSHOPS AND INSTRUCTION

A school counselor's work and interactions with parents or guardians are multifaceted and complex. The most common school counselor–parent or school counselor–guardian interactions are in the form of parent conferences. However, in this part of the *ASCA National Model* (ASCA, 2005), the focus is on more general interactions with parents and/or guardians (in particular, interactions both to solicit parents' perceptions of needs for the school counseling program and to inform them of the school counseling program activities). Here, too, there is little or no evidence of the extent to which school counselors engage in such public relations activities, even though they have long been recommended in the professional school counseling literature. Presumably, the admonishment is for school counselors to periodically conduct large-group meetings with parents/guardians of the children in their schools.

Conducting a large-audience meeting is one way to obtain input on parents' or guardians' perceptions of student needs to be addressed by the school counseling program. If such a method is used, the suggested needs should be recorded carefully and in detail; every effort should be made to understand and take note of each need exactly as it is presented. A school counselor's use of basic counseling skills, such as restating, clarifying, or summarizing parents' comments are particularly helpful in this regard. It is a good idea to have someone other than the meeting facilitator record the suggestions presented because the facilitator should maintain continuity of interaction with the audience. The needs identified should then be listed, perhaps in some order of priority as determined by the audience members. Being accountable for such an activity is relatively easy. At some point in the future, the school counseling program should be examined in regard to which and how many of the needs identified from the large-group meeting are being addressed specifically in the program. In other words, it should be possible to establish a one-to-one correspondence between each need identified and at least one specific school counseling program activity. If not, an identified need should be indicated as one that is not being addressed in the school counseling program. The accountability aspect of this is simply a reporting of the count of presented needs that are being addressed in the program. Of course, it is desirable to elaborate in any report the results on how each of the needs is being addressed; but again, that is a public relations function, not a method of accountability.

No matter how calmly you try to referee, parenting will eventually produce bizarre behavior, and I'm not talking about the kids. Their behavior is always normal.

—Bill Cosby

It should be noted that this is *not* a highly recommended way to determine parents' or guardians' perceptions of needs for the school counseling program, because the information generated is typically unwieldy and/or haphazardly obtained and presented. Better, more systematic, and more efficient methods of conducting needs assessments are presented in Chapter 8.

Informing parents/guardians of the components and activities of a school counseling program is a very good idea because it is a substantive and important public relations activity, and school counselors need as much good public relations as they can get. T. Davis (2005) wrote that

> when parents observe the school counselor being involved in the school process and actively engaged with students and faculty, they may better understand the counselor's effect on the academic program. Whether or not their children have indi-

> vidual or group exposure to school counseling services, this understanding goes a long way toward helping parents appreciate the benefits of having counselors in schools. (p. 198)

Theoretically, the recommended approach for this type of meeting is to present an overview of the various school counseling program elements, indicate how each is associated with a need that has been identified, and present any accountability evidence of the effectiveness of the respective activities. This recommended approach is theoretical to the extent that it necessitates that an effective needs assessment has been conducted and that accountability information is available, which is not often the case. Lacking either needs assessment or accountability evidence, the content of the presentation is simply an overview of the activities being conducted in the school counseling program.

Presenting the components of a school counseling program to parents or guardians is essentially a teaching activity in that information is conveyed with the intent that the recipients retain the information. As a teaching activity, the best way to determine if the audience members actually retained what was presented would be to give them a test. However, it would be tacky for a school counselor to quiz a group of parents or guardians. Fortunately, there is a better way. Theoretically, all of the components of a school counseling program potentially could be helpful to any student in the school (a point which should be made during the presentation). Therefore, parents or guardians attending the meeting can legitimately be asked which of the component activities of the school counseling might be of assistance to their child or children, either at the end of the meeting or as a follow-up activity. They could do this simply by checking off on a list those school counseling program elements they think might be helpful to their child or children. Hypothetically, all the parents/guardians who attended the meeting should check all elements of the program as potentially helpful to their child or children in the school. Of course they won't all check off every element on the list; however, the counts of the checks for each of the elements presented and listed (perhaps even presented as percentages of total respondents) gives information about how well they understood what was presented about each of the program components as well as the school counseling program as a whole. It's a subtle and indirect way of evaluating the presentation, but it's certainly better than giving the parents/guardians a test, and more importantly, better than not evaluating the activity.

Conclusion

Effective implementation of a comprehensive school counseling curriculum is a complex and often difficult task. Further, school counselors typically perceive widely varying degrees of perceived importance and usefulness for the various components of a comprehensive school counseling curriculum, which means that it is very hard to be motivated to implement some components. Nonetheless, implementation of the school counseling curriculum provides an important opportunity for professional interactions between school counselors and their colleagues in the schools. It is in effect a golden opportunity for school counselors to inform their colleagues about what school counseling is and how it relates to the other activities in schools. Given that potentiality, implementation of a comprehensive school counseling curriculum not only merits school counselors' attention, it is a source of accountability data that is likely to be received well by at least one important group of stakeholders.

For Thought and Deed

1. Use any of the popular Internet search engines to find information about teaching philosophies or orientations. Then write a brief (less than three page) description of your personal philosophy of teaching. Remember that any good philosophy of teaching statement takes into account the writer's beliefs about how people learn.

2. First, identify a topic of interest about which you would like to present as a large-group guidance unit to a group of students at a school level of your choosing. Then, identify and briefly explain some of the advantages and disadvantages of a school counselor and a teacher working together (i.e., collaborating) to develop and present a large-group guidance unit on that topic.

3. Create a 10-item survey that could be used to assess students' attitudes about participation in a large-group guidance activity.

4. Assume that, as a school counselor, you are going to lead a meeting of parents who have been invited to provide feedback on the school counseling program in your school. How would you introduce yourself to the audience, how would you explain the purpose of the meeting, and what ground rules for the meeting would you explain?

CHAPTER 5

ACCOUNTABILITY FOR SCHOOL COUNSELING INDIVIDUAL PLANNING FUNCTIONS

In earlier days of the school counseling profession, school counselors were commonly known as guidance counselors. Frank Parsons, considered the Father of Guidance is credited with having initiated use of the term (Beale, 2006). *Guidance counselor* was an appropriate title back then because people holding those positions did very little counseling, much less any developmental counseling. Instead, they spent almost all of their time trying to help students make appropriate academic and career (and occasionally personal) plans and decisions (i.e., they were busy giving advice as they tried to provide guidance). Obviously, the roles and work of the professional school counselor today have evolved significantly and substantially as the profession has developed. However, the need for and appropriateness of guidance activities remains. What may loosely be called "guidance" services are subsumed within the "Individual Student Planning" subsection of the *ASCA National Model* (ASCA, 2005):

> Individual student planning consists of school counselors co-ordinating ongoing systemic activities designed to help individual students establish personal goals and develop future plans.... Within this component, students evaluate their educational, occupational and personal goals. (p. 41)

Such individual planning services are delivered to students either individually or in small groups. In either case, however, the process typically involves use of both formal and informal student appraisal information in conjunction with school-counselor–provided advisement and/or counseling.

> *Identifying which students will benefit the most from individual counseling services can pose a tremendous challenge for professional school counselors.*
>
> —Newsom & Gladding, 2007, p. 170

INDIVIDUAL AND SMALL-GROUP APPRAISAL

The term *appraisal* is broad in scope and encompasses not only testing but also gathering input and feedback information from a variety of sources (Erford, 2007a; Whiston, 2005). Other-than-test (e.g., anecdotal or observed behavior) information about a student may come from teachers, parents, administrators, various school specialists (e.g., special education teachers or school psychologists), the student's peers, and, of course, the school counselor. While there is wide variation in the objectivity of these types of information, any of them is potentially significant and useful for a student. As a specialist in both testing and interpersonal communications, a school counselor should be able to help students understand the types and respective credibility of the information available to them and to help them make decisions and plans effectively, based on good information.

Students participate in many types of standardized testing in schools, and school counselors should be able to help them understand their test results. Most commonly, standardized test results are presented as normative data in which a student achieves a relative position within a norm group. In effect, a student is positioned within a presumably similar group of students. Therefore, a common goal of test result interpretation is to enable a student to understand her or his relative position and the implications thereof among a group of peers. Sometimes, students participate in criterion-referenced testing, in which a student's test results are indication of the number of competencies achieved from among those tested. The criterion-referenced test result interpretation goal is to enable a student to understand both how many and which specific competencies the student achieved.

The methods school counselors use to help students understand their standardized test results are many and varied (e.g., individual or group test interpretation sessions; use of charts, diagrams or other visual aids; use of written explanations for test interpretation), and may vary depending on the type of test. However, the basic accountability issue for school counselors is whether the students understand their respective test results after the test-result interpretation-assistance activities have been completed. In addition, it is desirable to know whether the students acted on the basis of the results received.

The simplest way to determine whether students really understand their test results is to use a brief, written questionnaire (akin to a semistructured interview or essay test procedure) to allow them to write what they think the test results mean for or about them. For example, you could give the students a written summary of their individual test results and then ask them to respond in writing to questions such as the following:

> For each of the areas on the test, how do your scores compare to those of other students like you?
>
> In which area did you receive the highest score?
>
> In which area did you receive the lowest score?
>
> Based on your scores, what kinds of things do you do best?
>
> Based on your scores, what kinds of things do you do less well?
>
> For each of the areas on the test, what does your score mean to you?
>
> What have you done as a result of your test scores?

For academic performance (e.g., achievement) tests, you might also ask students the following:

> Based on your test scores, in which academic subjects are you likely to do best?
>
> Based on your test scores, what are your best school skills?
>
> Based on your test scores, what would be some good courses for you to take?

For tests that measure characteristics of students, you might ask questions such as the following:

> What did you learn from your test scores about yourself as compared to other students like you?
>
> In which areas are you most like your peers?
>
> In which areas are you least like your peers?
>
> How do your test scores suggest how you behave?
>
> Which of your test scores would you like to change?
>
> What behaviors could you change to change your test scores?

You could score responses to questions such as these by assigning a category (e.g., as either "understands" or "does not understand" the test score), so that quantitative data can be gathered. Usually, it is best if someone other than you, the school counselor who provided the test-interpretation assistance activity, scores the responses, because it increases the credibility of the process. It also should be noted that this rather formal assessment of the effectiveness of a school counselor's test-interpretation assistance need not be conducted with all students to whom the assistance was provided. However, a sample of sufficient size should be used such that the results can be legitimately considered generalizable to all students who receive such assistance.

If students are able to understand fully and accurately the appraisal information made available to them, then they should be (a) able to establish goals and (b) aware of the decisions to be made and plans that have to be implemented to begin moving toward those goals. That is, they should be able to apply their understandings by turning them into behaviors. Statements of intention to behave in a particular way are certainly not a guarantee of behavior change, but they are a good beginning. Within the *ASCA National Model* (ASCA, 2005), goal setting and planning are addressed in regard to the educational, occupational, and personal realms of students' lives. Thus, these are the three realms of students' lives in which the appraisal information can be applied.

Papa requires that when one speaks with him one does not stop after telling only half the information.

—Anna Freud

As with facilitating of understanding test results, school counselors use a variety of methods to help students set goals, become aware of decisions that need to be made, and begin moving toward the goals. These methods include individual, small-group, and large-group interactions; use of media and/or technology; experiential activities (e.g., job shadowing); visitations (e.g., to colleges or businesses); mentoring activities; structured peer interactions, and many others. However, regardless of the methods used, the students are supposed to be able to set goals, identify important decisions that need to be made, and formulate initial plans to move toward their goals. Therein is the basis for school counselor accountability: Do the students actually set goals, identify decisions to be made, and begin planning?

Directly soliciting information from students by using a questionnaire is again the best way to obtain substantive accountability information. After you have conducted activities to help students set goals, you should query the students about whether they have done so. Questions should be specific to the realm of goal setting but parallel in format. For example, in regard to academic planning, you might have students who participated in a goal-setting activity provide written responses to questions such as the following:

> What is your final educational goal right now?
>
> What resources are available to you to help you achieve that goal?
>
> What decisions will have to be addressed for you to pursue this goal?
>
> Who can assist you to make those decisions?
>
> What course sequence will you take to achieve that goal?
>
> What is the very next step you will take to move toward that goal?

You might ask similar types of questions for the occupational/career and personal realms of students' lives.

Again, categories of responses should codify the students' responses. For example, for the first sample question, end-point educational goals might be categorized as high school graduation, community college or college/university graduation, or completion of a post–high school vocational training program. Here, too, it is probably best if a colleague scores the responses and a size sample sufficient to warrant generalization is used.

An alternative method for evaluating the effectiveness of activities intended to facilitate students' understanding of appraisal information or their goal setting and planning is to use an attitude survey. In general, attitude surveys are designed to assess students' attitudes about the effectiveness and usefulness of the activities in which they participated. The caution presented earlier applies here: Even though students may indicate that they understood and/or liked some activity doesn't necessarily mean that they behaved differently as a result of participation. Therefore, while attitudinal data may be good for fostering interest in the activities among other students, attitudinal data are not substantive accountability data for these types of activities.

INDIVIDUAL AND SMALL-GROUP ADVISEMENT

Providing advisement literally means giving advice. School counselors, like most adults, like giving advice; it engenders feelings of being helpful. However, giving advice to students isn't all that easy. For one thing, unsolicited advice is often ignored simply because it is unwanted; people have to be receptive to advice for it to achieve an effect. For another, even good advice will be rebuked if it isn't given at an appropriate time; sometimes people are ready to hear things and sometimes they are not. Thus, school counselors have been admonished to give students advice very sparingly and only with careful consideration of the timing for the advice giving (e.g., Myrick, 2002). Within the *ASCA National Model* (ASCA, 2005), the focus of "advisement" is on provision of various types of information to students in regard to their educational, personal, or occupational goal setting and planning. It is decidedly not on telling students how to behave. Thus, the purpose of advisement is to help students gain information from which to make decisions effectively and wisely, not to make decisions for the students.

Your modern teenager is not about to listen to advice from an old person, defined as a person who remembers when there was no Velcro.

—Dave Barry

School counselors use a variety of activities to provide information to students, including both direct and indirect methods. Direct methods typically include activities such as classroom guidance presentations and individual and small-group interactions. Indirect methods typically include activities such as maintaining and/or distributing print media (i.e., books, catalogs, pamphlets, flyers, or magazines), providing access to technological resources (i.e., Web sites or stand-alone informational software), posting written announcements for student viewing, sending written communications to parents, or maintaining a local school counseling Web site. However, regardless of the method used to disseminate information to students, the accountability questions include how the information was distributed, how much information was distributed, did the students who were supposed to receive the information actually receive it, did the students who received the information understand it, and did the students who received the information actually use any of it?

The amount of information that school counselors distribute to students, parents, administrators, and other stakeholders during an academic year is simply amazing. Equally amazing, however, is how most school counselors don't bother to be accountable for their work. At an absolute minimum, a school counselor should keep a running log (perhaps by placing a copy in a folder or box in the school counselor's office) of the informational materials distributed throughout a school year. Maintenance of the list should not be a major or complex activity; all that needs to be recorded is a very brief description of whatever was distributed, notation of how it was distributed, and notation of to whom it was distributed and when. Here, too, use of a spreadsheet software program makes this a simple record-keeping activity. Of course, the nature and amount of information from the log should be distributed as part of a school counselor's annual accountability activities report.

Everybody gets so much information all day long that they lose their common sense.

—Gertrude Stein

Determining whether students who were supposed to receive information actually received it is somewhat more difficult but certainly not impossible. For example, school counselors often distribute informational materials, particularly print media, to students in large groups. School counselors can simply keep track of how many informational materials were in fact given directly to students, perhaps on the master log of materials distributed. Similarly, if information is distributed through a Web site, the Web site should have a counter that records the number of hits during a given time period. Obviously, there is not a one-to-one correspondence between the number of hits and the number of people who actually visited the Web site, because some students may visit it more than once, and some people who visit it may not be among the intended recipients. Nonetheless, the count indicates the extent to which the Web site's information was accessed. It is not possible to determine how many students hear verbal announcements, however, it is possible to keep track of the number of announcements made as well as when they were made. Finally, school counselors give a lot of information through individual or small-group interactions. It is reasonable to assume that the people in those interactions receive the information; keeping track of what was disseminated and how many people received it through direct interactions is another way of generating accountability data.

It is indeed difficult to determine what proportion of students who received distributed information understood what was presented to them. However, querying a representative sample of students in writing or through the use of semistructured interviews can provide some information. In addition, there may be behavioral indicators of understanding. For example, if students are given information about how to do something, such as how to apply for college scholarships, keeping track of the number of students who acted correctly on the basis of the information (such as submitting an application for a college scholarship correctly and successfully) indicates the extent to which the information was understood.

Presumably, information is distributed in the context of advisement so that the students will act upon the information. Sometimes the students will use the information correctly, and sometimes they won't. However, the crux of the matter in regard to accountability lies in how many students were moved to do anything. Any noted behavioral indicators showing that some students attempted to do something as a result of having received the information is reasonable accountability data. However, richer and more credible accountability information relates to what students did and if what they did was appropriate to the information distributed. Although semi-structured interviews or written questioning would give such accountability information, that information would be a one-time snapshot of what the students did. For many types of information distributed, the expectation (and appropriate student response) is that the students will engage in a series of activities that are appropriate (i.e., they will initiate a process of action). A good way for you to obtain good accountability data for the activity processes in which students engage is to have a representative sample of students keep a journal of their respective activities. Of course, this would have to be done with students who were willing to share their journals after the activities (the requirements for which are presented in Chapter 9). The data derived from their journals could be interpreted in regard to what goals they set, what decisions they made, and what plans they made for future activities. If appropriately collected, summarized, and reported, such information would be particularly substantive and impressive accountability data for a school counselor's advisement activities.

For your information, I would like to ask a question.

—Samuel Goldwyn

CONCLUSION

Helping students find their own way in the world is a noble and important school counseling goal, one that requires school counselors to engage in a wide variety of activities. Many school counselor activities related to the goal fall into the realm of helping students with individual planning. The trick for counselors is to help students without just telling them what to do and also to be accountable for how they help students. Thus, being accountable for activities in regard to helping students with individual planning calls for school counselors to be creative in both what they do and how they are accountable for their actions.

For Thought and Deed

1. Use any of the popular Internet search engines to find ideas about how to help students perform better on tests (e.g., use "test preparation" as a keyword for a search). From you search, develop a list of stimulus behaviors in which students can engage to improve their performance on tests. Then, for each student stimulus behavior listed, develop a corresponding list of behaviors that would indicate that a student had actually engaged in each of the stimulus behaviors.

2. It is well known that any test score is not exact because of measurement error, which is frequently expressed as the standard error of measurement. Find any standardized achievement test suitable for use with students at a school level of your choosing, find the standard error of measurement for the test, and then write out how you would explain the standard error of measurement in regard to a particular student's score on the standardized test.

3. If a school counselor uses a semistructured interview as a means to determine whether students understood what was presented to them (such as test scores or informational materials), it was recommended that someone other than the school counselor compile the results of responses to the questions. Most likely, that someone else would be a teacher colleague of the school counselor. If a teacher colleague helps you, as a school counselor, it is advisable that you reciprocate by helping the teacher in some ways. What are some ways that you can reciprocate; that is, what are some professionally appropriate ways that you can help a teacher with her or his professional activities?

CHAPTER 6

ACCOUNTABILITY FOR SCHOOL COUNSELING - RESPONSIVE SERVICES

Professional school counselors are most recognized for what are identified in the *ASCA National Model* (ASCA, 2005) as "Responsive Services." These services include a school counselor's activities for consultation, individual and small-group counseling (sometimes referred to together as personal counseling), crisis counseling, referral, and peer facilitation. These services typically define school counselors to the largest groups of school counseling program stakeholders, such as teachers, parents/guardians, and students. Therefore, it is crucial that school counselors be particularly effective in their accountability for these services.

Many of the general accountability activities already presented are applicable to responsive services. For example, students can be surveyed toward the end of each school year to determine how many of them received services such as personal counseling, peer facilitation or mediation, or other activities that were part of the school counseling program. Similarly, keeping track of how many teachers and how many times teachers sought consultation from a school counselor is a good accountability activity. However, teachers also can be polled to determine how frequently they referred students for a school counselor's services and the number of times they sought consultation from a school counselor about students, which serves as a source of validation of the school counselor's data, thus strengthening it. These are examples of process data that demonstrate what services school counselors offer and how frequently people associated with the school use those services.

As a school counselor, you also can evaluate the effectiveness of your responsive services with rating scales, semistructured interviews, or other indicators of outcomes. For example, you can create a rating

145

scale to administer to students at the end of personal (either individual or small-group) counseling to measure students' degree of satisfaction with participation in those activities. Similarly, after consulting with teachers or parents/guardians, you can conduct brief, semistructured interviews to determine what the teachers or parents/guardians found most helpful and their degree of satisfaction with the activities. Further, you can observe and record students' behaviors that are presumed to have been affected by your interventions.

Even academic performance and school behavior records can be used, albeit cautiously and with proper consideration of the limits of inference, to evaluate responsive services. For example, the number of students sent to the office for fighting could be tallied before and after the implementation of a peer mediation program, or individual students' grades and attendance could be compared before and after they receive personal counseling. However, remember that although a school counselor's intent may be to demonstrate that her or his responsive services contributed to better academic performance, such data do not prove directly that those services alone caused the improvement. Some accountability activities that are specifically appropriate for use with responsive services activities are presented as follows.

CONSULTATION

The importance of the school counselor's role as a consultant has been widely acknowledged in the professional literature (e.g., Baker & Gerler, 2004; Cobia & Henderson, 2006; K. Davis, 2005; Gysbers & Henderson, 2006; Myrick, 2002), and a variety of consultation models suitable for use by school counselors have been identified (e.g., Brown, Pryzwanski, & Schulte, 1998; Kampwirth, 2006; Keys, Green, Lockhart, & Luongo, 2003). Consultation is an indirect service that involves a consultant working with a consultee for the benefit of a client (Kampwirth, 2006). The consultation process typically involves three individuals: the person providing the consultation, known as the consultant; the person receiving the consultation, known as the consultee; and the person receiving services from the consultee, known as the client. Thus, a school counselor, as a consultant, might collaborate with a teacher, as a consultee, to help her or him work more effectively with a student, as a client. Consultation is an indirect service because the consultant does not work directly with the client, the consultee does. In practice, school counselors operate both as consultants and consultees. That is, in addition to providing consultation services, they may seek consultation from another person (e.g., teacher, parent, school social worker, mental health counselor, or school psychologist) to help them with students they are advising or counseling. However, in such cases, they are providing direct services and should use appropriate methods to evaluate their effectiveness, as is suggested in the next section of this chapter. When teachers and parents/guardians seek consultation from a school counselor to help them work with their student or child, the school counselor is being asked to provide consultation services and therefore must evaluate the effectiveness of those services using methods appropriate for it.

The function of an expert is not to be more right than other people, but rather to be wrong for more sophisticated reasons.

—David Butler

Historically, school counselors often functioned, or were called upon to function, in the context of one of the expert models of consultation. In an expert model, the consultant literally is called upon to provide a solution to the client's problem. For example, in an expert model, a parent experiencing relationship difficulties with a child would ask the school counselor how to interact better with the child, the school counselor would tell the parent how to interact with the child, and then the parent would attempt to interact with the child as the school counselor recommended. But as Kampwirth (2006) noted,

> among human service personnel, particularly in the schools, there is general consensus that the expert model, defined as one in which a consultant, sometimes from outside the local school or district, unilaterally decides which interventions would be most appropriate for a teacher or parent to use, has limitations that make it less than ideal. (p. 16)

We think Kampwirth's comment is an understatement; the expert model of consultation is generally disdained in schools today. Alternatively, school counselor consultation today is generally conducted as an activity involving collaboration between the school counselor and the teacher, parent, or whomever as the consultee (Davis, 2005; Kampwirth, 2006; Keys et al., 2003). Kampwirth (2006) wrote that

> collaborative consultation is a process in which a trained, school-based consultant, working in an egalitarian relationship with a consultee, assists that person in her [his] efforts to make decisions and carry out plans that will be in the best interests of her [his] students. (p. 3)

In the collaborative model, a school counselor and the consultee work together with varying degrees of mutual responsibility and action. The benefits of collaborative consultation seem obvious, because as Kampwirth (2006) wrote, "In …schools…, people tend to be more likely to implement changes that they have been involved in discussing and creating" (p. 16).

Although school counselors sometimes initiate consultation activities with teachers or parents/guardians, school counselor consultation usually results from a request from a teacher or parent. The request for consultation is sometimes made directly and sometimes made casually and ranges from strong negative reactions to a student (e.g., "Help! That kid is driving me crazy!") to generalized feelings (e.g., "I wish I got along better with my class") to sincere and specific expressions of concern (e.g., "Something seems to be wrong with my student. Can you help me find out about that?"). Therefore, a first task for a school counselor is to determine if an actual request for consultation has been made. School counselors who provide unsolicited consultation will find themselves unpopular in a hurry, and certainly will not be appropriately accountable for providing unsolicited and unwanted advice.

Don't be troubled if the temptation to give advice is irresistible; the ability to ignore it is universal.

—Planned Security Magazine

The accountability focus for consultation activities should be on behavior change. A teacher, parent, or other stakeholder who seeks consultation from a school counselor is essentially asking for help on how to change a student's behaviors—even though it may be presented as "the student needs an attitude change!" Such requests are often clouded in elaborate description of a student's situation or behaviors and the requestor's frustration from the inability to deal with it effectively. However, at the heart of the request is a solicitation for assistance with how to act differently to change the student's behaviors. The teacher or parent wants to know how he or she can behave differently to make the situation better. In the context of the consultation activity, the teacher's or parent's discussion is usually filled with characterizations, emotions, and descriptions of the student's behaviors. However, eventually it all leads to "...and I don't know what to do" (i.e., how to behave). Certainly, a school counselor as a consultant should allow a consultee to express emotions about a difficulty. However, just as certainly, effective consultation moves beyond that to helping the consultee identify and, in some cases, actually practice new ways of behaving that have potential to resolve the difficulty. Therein is the key to accountability for the consultation. A school counselor has been an effective consultant if, and only if, the consultee engages in new behaviors.

School counselors' reputations rest heavily on their accountability in providing consultation. Unfortunately, they all too often fail this accountability test and instead fall into what Carlson and Dinkmeyer (2001) referred to as the useless triangle. The useless triangle is a situation in which the consultee (e.g., a teacher) complains about the student to the school counselor (as a consultant), but the consultee takes no responsibility for effecting change with the student. Instead, the consultee expects the school counselor to fix the student on the consultee's behalf. The unwary school counselor agrees and thus falls into the trap. This is a useless triangle because, in most cases, the problem behaviors are a result of the interaction between the student and consultee. Therefore, the student's behaviors can be changed most easily by the consultee changing the way she or he interacts with the student, not by the school counselor trying to change the student's behavior. Thus, when school counselors act as consultants with teachers or parents/guardians, they must focus their efforts on helping the teachers or parents/guardians change their own behaviors so that these changes will affect subsequent and associated changes in student's behaviors.

Although there are many methods school counselors can use to demonstrate their effectiveness in consultation, a primary one is the use of rating scales, sometimes as a reflection of perceptions and sometimes as a reflection of frequencies of specific student behaviors. Rating scales can be used quickly and easily to identify the extent of severity of the problem before and after consultation. For example, consider a mother who consults you because she is having trouble getting her 12-year-old daughter up in the morning in time to get ready for school and catch the school bus on time. Each morning the mother knocks on her daughter's door and yells at her, but many times the daughter manages to be late anyway, which results in the mother having to drive her to school, which in turn makes the mother late for work. The mother describes her daughter as irresponsible. Prior to formal initiation of the consultation process, you could ask the mother to rate how responsible her daughter is on a scale of 0 to 10, with 0 = *not at all responsible* and 10 = *fully responsible.* Consider that the mother gives her daughter an initial rating of 2. Alternatively, you could ask the mother to rate how frequently her daughter, on average, fails to get to school on time, such as 1 to 5 times per week.

Consultants are people who borrow your watch and tell you what time it is, and then walk off with the watch.

—Robert Townsend

During brief consultation, you learn what behaviors the mother has tried, what behaviors (if any) have worked, and what behaviors have been unsuccessful. You decide on a new strategy, involving the parenting approach called "logical consequences," in which the mother tells her daughter that the daughter is responsible for getting herself up and ready to go to school, and/or must suffer the consequences of not getting to school on time. However, the mother also tells her daughter that if she has to drive the daughter to school, she will charge her daughter taxi fare (i.e., money the daughter must provide from her own resources). During consultation, the mother rehearses with you how she will tell her daughter this plan and then agrees to try it for 1 week. After a week, you call the mother to see how it is working. The mother reports that she had to drive her daughter the first morning and therefore charged her taxi fare, but she hasn't had to drive her to school since. You ask her to again rate her daughter on responsibility. She now gives her daughter a 6. After another week, you repeat the evaluation procedure. The mother reports that the daughter is now showing much better responsibility in regard to getting ready for school and now rates her daughter an 8. Similarly, you might have had the mother rate how frequently, on average, the daughter has been late to school during the 2 weeks following the consultation activity.

Using a simple rating scale not only helps in the consultation process as the consultee sees improvement in the client but also provides accountability data. Of course, more complex rating scales can be used, depending on the goals of the consultation. For example, if multiple target behaviors are identified, then a rating scale could be developed with items corresponding to each of the behaviors. In addition, the consultee could be asked to provide ratings for each behavior on a different schedule, such as daily or weekly. However, regardless of the procedural plan, the data generated help both to provide consultation process assistance and to fulfill an accountability function.

As another example, suppose that you are an elementary school counselor and that a fourth-grade teacher comes to you, lamenting that things are not going well in the teacher's class. The teacher conveys that different students, at different times, cannot maintain focus during the various lessons and end up disrupting the class. The teacher wants your help to have the students in the class become more engaged in the learning process. In talking with the teacher, you find that what the teacher wants is for the students to ask more and better questions. You decide to use the Student Success Skills program (see www.studentsuccessskills.com) with the teacher and class to try to improve the level of students' engagement in the learning process. You decide that students will be more engaged in the class if they (a) ask more questions and (b) ask better questions (i.e., questions that include clarification or summarization of partially understood content, clarity of request, and appropriate presentation). The teacher's class in conducted daily from 8:00 a.m. until 10:00 a.m. You begin the process by observing the teacher's class for three different half-hour time periods on Monday, Wednesday, and Friday of the next week. During your observations, you record both the number of questions and the number of good questions the students ask. You then work with the teacher over the following weeks to present the Student Success Skills program for the students. After you have completed the program, you repeat your observation and recording activities. (Figure 6.1 shows how you could record your data.)

The Accountable School Counselor

STUDENT SUCCESS SKILLS PROJECT

Week Before	Total Number* of Questions Asked	Number of "Good" Questions Asked	Student Success Skills Activities	Total Number* of Questions Asked	Number of "Good" Questions Asked	Week After
Monday 8:30–9:00	3	2	XXXXXX	10	7	Monday 8:30–9:00
Wednesday 9:00–9:30	4	1	XXXXXX	8	5	Wednesday 9:00–9:30
Friday 9:30–10:00	3	1	XXXXXX	8	6	Friday 9:30–10:00
Totals	10	4	XXXXXX	26	18	XXXXXX

FIGURE 6.1. Data form for the Student Success Skills Project.

Single-subject designs are discussed at length in the next section, but it is noted here that they can be applied directly to consultation activities as well. Single-subject designs provide very strong evidence of effectiveness in consultation and therefore should be given very strong consideration by a school counselor who wants to evaluate her or his consultation effectiveness.

PERSONAL COUNSELING

Individual and small-group counseling are the services that most distinguish school counselors from other school and educational personnel. Unfortunately, they also are services that are often misunderstood and therefore cause school counselors credibility problems. Brown and Trusty (2005) wrote the following about individual counseling:

> The following are characteristics and qualities of sessions that would indicate that individual counseling is occurring:
>
> - There is a close psychological and emotional contact between the counselor and student.
> - The content of the session is confidential in nature.
> - A student's problem or concern is the major focus of the session.
> - The student's goal is behavior change, including coping and adapting by learning new skills.
>
> Of the qualities of individual counseling sessions, the one that bears most influence is the first, psychological and emotional contact. If close contact between the counselor and student exists, then counseling is necessarily occurring. (p. 288)

Goodnough and Lee (2004), referring to small-group counseling in schools, wrote that

> group counseling initiatives within a larger comprehensive school counseling program address developmental milestones, provide remediation, and promote a healthy climate within

the school. By developmental milestones we mean that professional school counselors can reasonably expect that most or all students would benefit from participating in groups designed to promote academic, career, or personal/social development.

Group counseling is remedial in nature when it addresses topics or issues that impair the learning and development of specific groups of students. Remedial groups help students develop coping skills to assist them in coming to terms with difficult personal and social issues.

Groups that address the culture and climate of the school...include issues related to diversity awareness, bias and prejudice reduction, conflict resolution, and respect of self and others. These groups may also address the cultural and institutional barriers to learning of certain groups of students (e.g., students of color, gay, lesbian, bisexual and transgendered youth; lower socioeconomic status students). (p. 174)

Thus, school counselors provide personal counseling to students for a wide variety of issues ranging from crisis to normal-development situations. The following strategies can be used to evaluate the effectiveness of individual and group counseling with students exhibiting any of a variety of concerns. We consider personal counseling to include individual or small-group counseling of 10 sessions or less, not including intake sessions, in which a school counselor decides whether to engage the student in counseling or to refer them to another professional. However, intake sessions also can be documented to yield accountability data, particularly in regard to the kinds of concerns presented to a school counselor.

Administrators, teachers, and other school personnel frequently lament that school counselors spend considerable time counseling students but that the students don't change. In effect, they are suggesting that school counselors have not demonstrated accountability for their personal counseling activities. This lack of understanding leads to stakeholders' misinterpretation of school counselors' activities, such as the incorrect conclusion that school counselors provide personal counseling to students when the students should be receiving therapy from more qualified professionals and that school counselors provide long-term personal counseling to a few students rather than short-term, very brief counseling to many students. Good accountability information would go a long way toward rectifying these commonly held misperceptions about what school counselors actually do in personal counseling with students.

I've experienced several different healing methodologies over the years—counseling, self-help seminars, and I've read a lot—but none of them will work unless you really want to heal.

—Lindsay Wagner

Unfortunately, sometimes school counselors agree to work with students whose problems are beyond the scope of their competence. For example, most school counselors are not trained or certified to treat eating disorders or well-established substance abuse problems, but they attempt to counsel students with such problems anyway. Good professional practice suggests that students with diagnosable problems (i.e., problems whose resolutions involve substantial personality change) should be referred to other professionals (e.g., a mental health counselor, counseling psychologist, clinical psychologist, or psychiatrist) with better training and/or more time available to help them. Accountable school counselors use short-term personal counseling only with students they are competent and qualified to counsel. Students with severe problems and/or who require long-term therapy should be referred to other mental health professionals. However, the referral source often wants a school counselor to provide supportive consultation, collaboration, or counseling. In such cases, both the consultation and counseling should be evaluated and reported for accountability purposes.

Some school counselors may provide long-term counseling to a few students on a weekly basis for a number of weeks, but most don't have the luxury to provide such interventions Kareck, 1998). Further, it is not recommended for most school counselors. For example, the *ASCA National Model* (ASCA, 2005) is clear in regard to long-term counseling when it states, "School counselors do not provide therapy" (p. 42). Therefore, a school counselor must ask the question, "If I agree to provide individual counseling to this student, will I likely be able to provide counseling a sufficient number of times to ensure satisfactory change in the time available or would the student be better served if I referred him or her to another professional?" The answer to that question determines the applicable type of accountability, either for the counseling or for the referral.

The good news is that many times school counselors are indeed effective in their individual and group counseling with students. The bad news is that they don't usually generate evidence of their effectiveness or share the results with stakeholders. One reason school counselors fail to generate effectiveness evidence for their personal counseling activities is fear and/or misunderstanding about confidentiality. Some school counselors fear that recording anything about their counseling activities risks violating confidentiality. Others fear that anything they write down or record might have to be surrendered to parents/guardians or lawyers if they are subpoenaed. It is true that school counselors can be called to testify in court and that their records can be subpoenaed by court order. However, this is an insufficient excuse to not keep records, including treatment plans and evaluative information. In fact, having written treatment plans and evaluations can be a viable defense *against* charges of malpractice (Remley & Herlihy, 2001).

The Family Educational Rights and Privacy Act of 1974 (FERPA), also known as the Buckley Amendment, guarantees parents/guardians or guardians of minors and students of majority age the right to view their child's educational records. Therefore, if counseling records (including accountability data) are kept in a student's school record (e.g., cumulative folder), they are part of the child's educational records. Counseling notes not kept in the school records and not seen by anyone but the school counselor are not regarded as educational records subject to parent or guardian review under FERPA (but the records could still be subpoenaed by court order). Therefore, documentation of counseling, including some types of accountability data, should be done in such a way that it will not libel or harm anyone if it becomes public (Remley & Herlihy, 2001).

If you choose to provide individual or group counseling to students, you should seek informed consent from both the student and the student's parents or guardians. However, some authorities suggest that it is probably not necessary to obtain parental consent just to provide personal counseling to students (Remley & Herlihy, 2001). Regardless of whether it is necessary for the provision of personal counseling activities, informed consent is necessary for gathering accountability information about the effectiveness of counseling activities (see Chapter 9).

Once engaged in counseling, the student and the school counselor should mutually agree upon a few primary counseling goals. As is true for consultation activities, broad goals should be converted into observable and measurable objectives. For example, you might work toward the following:

Goal—To improve the student's relationships with peers.

Objectives—In the next week:

1. The student will initiate conversations with at least two other students during lunch.
2. The student will participate in an after-school club.
3. The student will, with parent or guardian permission and supervision, invite another student to his or her house after school.

Counseling goals and objectives should be incorporated into a treatment plan, which also serves as the blueprint for the outcome evaluation of counseling. The treatment plan should include a brief description of the issue or concern that brought the student to counseling, the goals for counseling, the measurable objectives for counseling, and the counseling methods to be used. In a typical treatment plan, proposed activities are listed along with a column to indicate when these activities have been completed. (An example of a treatment plan is provided in Figure 6.2.)

The advantage of using a treatment plan is obvious: generating accountability data is built into it. To demonstrate accountability, a school counselor need only compile and report the number of objectives completed successfully. In Figure 6.2, this counting process is easy because the counseling objectives are specified as behaviors.

Being busy does not always mean real work. The object of all work is production or accomplishment and to either of these ends there must be forethought, system, planning, intelligence, and honest purpose, as well as perspiration. Seeming to do is not doing.

—Thomas A. Edison

Some of the accountability methods described for consultation also apply for personal counseling. For example, a semistructured interview could be used to gather more evidence of the effectiveness of

158　The Accountable School Counselor

COUNSELING TREATMENT PLAN

Student: _Sandra Argentia_ (grade _5_)　　　　　　　　Date: _9/25/08_

School Counselor: _Tracy Armstrong_

Counseling issue:

Teacher referred student to counseling for picking on others in classroom, fighting on playground, and for not having friends.

Counseling goals:

Decrease fighting and disruptive behavior, help him make friends, and improve his self-esteem.

Initial counseling objectives:

In the next two weeks, the student will be able to:

1. Identify his feelings and demonstrate how to express them appropriately.
2. List three things he can do instead of initiating fighting when he feels angry and wants to fight.
3. List three things he currently does that discourage friendships.
4. List three things he can do to encourage friendship.
5. List five personal abilities or characteristics of which he is proud.

Long-term counseling objectives:

In the next month, the student will:

1. Not be disciplined for fighting in school for at least one week.
2. Participate in at least one extra-curricular school activity.
3. Identify at least three students as his friends.

Counseling methods to be used:

Individual and small-group counseling, and parent and teacher consultation.

Proposed Actions:	Date Completed
Secure parental permission for counseling sessions.	9/26/08
Informed consent signed and returned.	9/27/08
Consulted supervisor about treatment plan	9/25/08
Individual counseling to establish trust and ascertain his strengths	9/27/08
Consult with teacher about classroom management	9/28/08
Consult with parent(s) about discipline style, opportunities for friends	9/31/08
Individual counseling to develop plan for making friends	10/01/08
Enroll in group counseling to learn new interpersonal skills	
Complete group counseling	
Terminate individual counseling	
Follow up with parent(s) and teacher	

FIGURE 6.2. Counseling treatment plan.

personal counseling. Students who received personal counseling could be asked to respond verbally or in writing to questions such as the following:

How have you changed as a result of our counseling sessions?

How has counseling helped you deal better with your problems?

How has the school counselor been most helpful to you?

What will you do to continue to deal better with your problems?

Similarly, parents/guardians and/or teachers could be interviewed to determine their perceptions of the impact of counseling on the student. For example, a teacher might be asked the following:

How has the student changed since counseling?

How is the student better prepared to work in your class as a result of counseling?

How is the student better adjusted personally and socially as a result of counseling?

And finally, parents/guardians could be asked,

How has your child changed since receiving counseling?

How does your child behave differently as a result of counseling?

How has your child's counseling benefited you?

Rating scales could also be devised and administered to students at the completion of counseling. Sample items for such a survey might include the following:

My counselor understands me and my problems.

SA   A   D   SD

My counselor does not really want to help me.

SA   A   D   SD

Counseling helped me understand myself better.

SA   A   D   SD

I feel better about myself because of counseling.

    SA   A   D   SD

I am not doing better in school because of counseling.

    SA   A   D   SD

I would recommend my counselor to my friends.

    SA   A   D   SD

Single-subject designs, also known as single-system or $N = 1$ designs, are a sophisticated and powerful way to demonstrate the effectiveness of counseling. Bloom, Fischer, and Orme (2003) wrote that

> the key distinguishing characteristic of single-system designs involves a planned comparison of a non-intervention (usually, a preintervention or baseline) period of observation with observations of the intervention period, or, in some cases, the postintervention period.
>
> *The underlying assumption is that if the intervention had not occurred, the pattern of events observed during the baseline likely would have continued to occur as before.* (p. 332) [emphasis added]

Bloom, et al., (2003) also commented that

> there are four main reasons for using single-system designs in every practice situation.
>
> First, these designs encourage practitioners to *assess* the case as objectively as possible, and to *monitor* these changes in the client targets and/or situation over time.
>
> The second purpose of single-system designs is to *evaluate* whether changes actually have occurred in targeted events.
>
> The third purpose of single-system designs builds on the second, but adds that the evaluation now concerns whether the practitioner's intervention could be *causally linked* to these observed changes.
>
> The fourth major purpose of single-system designs is to enable practitioners to *compare the effectiveness* of different interventions. (pp. 330-331)

In a single-subject design, instead of comparing measures of treatment and control group subjects, the intervention (treatment) single recipient serves as his or her own control (Fraenkel & Wallen, 2006; Ritchie, 1983). Briefly, the process begins with identification of a specific behavior (or sometimes behaviors) to be changed. Then, a baseline rate (i.e., frequency of occurrence) of the target behavior is established, either through observation or by another measurement technique. A treatment or intervention is then implemented. The target behavior is measured during the time of the intervention implementation to determine if the intervention affected the rate of the target behaviors (Kratochwill & Bergan, 1990). In addition, the target behavior is sometimes measured after the intervention has been concluded to determine whether the change has continued. A single-subject design is essentially a time-series design consisting of taking multiple measures of the target behavior at predetermined intervals before and during, and perhaps after, the intervention.

The first step in using a single-subject design is to operationally define the problem (i.e., to specify the specific target behaviors that are to be changed). Emphatically, the behaviors that are to be changed must be specified as actual behaviors, not generalized descriptions of behaviors. For example, "The student is disruptive in class" might be operationally defined as "The student gets out of seat during class without permission" or "The student interrupts other working students by poking and/or touching them." Similarly, "The student is not keeping up with the others" might be operationally defined as "The student does not hand in homework each day" or "The student does not complete weekly quizzes." Even broad psychological constructs can be operationally defined. For example, whereas the usual conceptual definition of a student's self-concept is the way the student views him or herself, an operational definition of a student's self-concept is the student's score on a standardized measure of self-concept.

[Single-subject designs] are most commonly used to study the changes in behavior an individual exhibits after exposure to an intervention or treatment of some sort.

—Fraenkel & Wallen, 2006, p. 306

Next, a baseline (i.e., pattern of relative frequency of occurrence) is established to show when and how often the target behavior occurs. For example, the disruptive student might get out of his or her seat as frequently as three times a day or as infrequently as three times a week, but either can be a legitimate baseline. You would record (likely from observation) instances of the target behavior over a period of time to establish the baseline. Alternatively, you might estimate the frequency of target behaviors in order to establish a baseline. The *best* procedure is to get an actual count baseline of the behaviors but allow that an estimate will suffice in some situations (Ritchie, 1983).

The next step is to establish a behavioral goal in regard to the target behaviors. Sometimes the goal is to reduce the frequency of a target behavior (e.g., decreasing the frequency of talking out of turn or touching other students inappropriately) and sometimes it is to increase the frequency of a target behavior (e.g., increasing the frequency of arriving to class on time or turning in homework as and when assigned). In any case, the behavioral goals must be *reasonable* and *observable* if the intervention is to have any chance of succeeding. For example, if a student leaves his or her seat inappropriately six times every class period, it is not advisable to establish a zero out-of-seat behavior goal for an initial intervention; reducing the out-of-seat behavior goal to no more than two times per period would be more appropriate and realistic. If the intervention is successful, then another goal can be established and the intervention repeated or intensified. Setting unrealistic or unobtainable goals sabotages the potential for success of the intervention and diminishes the potential for the school counselor to be accountable.

Deciding on an appropriate intervention is the next step. There are many possibilities (e.g., ignoring misbehavior, putting the student in time-out, applying principles of logical consequences) depending on the target behaviors and goals, but it is always important that a school counselor and/or whoever else is involved in providing the intervention be comfortable with it. For example, if a teacher is unwilling or unable to implement her or his part of the intervention, it surely will fail. In addition, whenever teachers and/or parents or guardians are involved in an intervention, success is more likely if they help develop the intervention.

After the intervention is completed, compare the two baselines to determine whether the intervention worked as intended. For example, if the goal was to reduce the frequency of a target behavior, there should be fewer occurrences of the target behavior during the intervention baseline data. Because the occurrence of each target behavior is tallied, it is easy to make the comparison. However, making a graph of the baseline data certainly gives visual enhancement to meanings and interpretations of the data. Typically, a graph with the target behavior frequency on the y-axis (vertical) and days on the x-axis (horizontal), with a daily (or other interval) data point (i.e., dot) representing the actual behavior frequency is prepared. An example of the A-B design is presented in Figure 6.3. For other good examples of how the data can be graphed as well as for more examples of application of single-subject designs, refer to Bloom et al. (2003) or Yarbrough and Thompson (2002).

Figure 6.3 illustrates an A-B design, in which the target behavior frequency during the baseline (i.e., "A") period is compared to the corresponding frequency during the treatment (i.e., "B") period. However, two variations of this single-subject design are more commonly used. One is the A-B-A design (i.e., baseline-treatment-baseline). For example, imagine that a student is habitually tardy to her classes. You observe that the student appears to be reluctant to interact with her peers be-

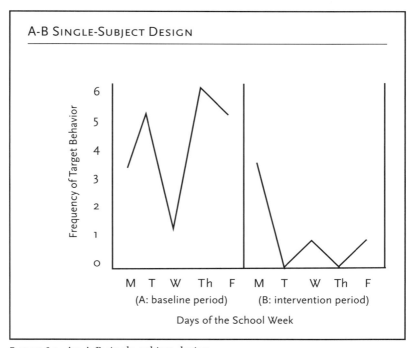

FIGURE 6.3. An A-B single-subject design.

tween class periods, and thus the student hangs back until the other students enter the class, thus making her tardy. You ask the student's teachers to keep track of how many times during the next 3 full weeks the student is late to her respective classes. The tardiness reports for the first week constitute the baseline condition measurements. Now suppose that during the second week you meet the student before or between classes, on a random basis, and encourage the student to get to class on time. You might even escort the student to her class, talking with her while you walk. This second week constitutes the treatment condition. During the third week, you stop meeting the student between classes. This third week is the second baseline condition. A graph of the results of this hypothetical scenario is presented in Figure 6.4.

The graph in Figure 6.4 shows that the results of this hypothetical situation contain both good news and bad news. The good news is that your treatment (i.e., encouraging the student to get to class on time) had the desired effect. The bad news is that the effect of your efforts diminished quickly when they were stopped (i.e., the student reverted to a relatively high rate of tardiness). Thus, this hypothetical scenario is a good example of a school counselor accountability activity and a bad

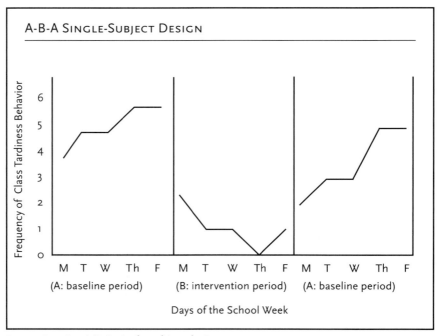

FIGURE 6.4. An A-B-A single-subject design.

example of school counselor practice (i.e., obviously, it is inappropriate and not feasible for a school counselor to meet with a particular student between classes on a long-term basis).

Let's revisit the same hypothetical scenario, but change the design and the treatment (intervention). Suppose the child's behavior is essentially the same (i.e., she is quite frequently tardy to her classes). However, in this example, you would have the teachers specifically record the frequency of the student's tardiness each day for 4 weeks. The first week would constitute the baseline condition. Now imagine a different intervention. Suppose you meet with each of the child's teachers and asks them to (a) stand at the student's classroom doorway before class and (b) intentionally and specifically say "hello" or otherwise greet positively the student as she approaches the classroom. In other words, the teachers would be asked to seek out, focus upon, and encourage the student to come into the class for a period of 1 week. This second week constitutes the first treatment (intervention) condition. For the third week, you ask the teachers to return to their normal between-class behaviors (i.e., to act as they typically did prior to the first intervention week). This third week constitutes the second baseline condition. Finally, you ask the teachers to engage in the same greeting behaviors during the fourth and subsequent weeks that they used during the second week. This plan is known as an A-B-A-B single-subject design. A graph of the results of this hypothetical scenario is presented in Figure 6.5.

The A-B-A-B single-subject design can dramatically demonstrate the effectiveness of the treatment if the frequency of the target behavior changes when the intervention is first introduced, reverts back to the baseline level when it is withdrawn, and then improves again when it is reintroduced. It also has the decided advantage of ending with the treatment still in effect. For example, in the hypothetical scenario, your intervention "leaves" the teacher's greeting the student before the respective classes. Obviously it is unlikely that the teachers will continue this special behavior for an extended period. However, if most or all teachers continue the greeting behavior for some time after the second baseline condition ends, it is likely that they will have changed the student's tardiness behaviors substantially (i.e., the student's get-to-class-on-time behaviors will generalize).

In addition to A-B, A-B-A, and A-B-A-B designs, school counselors can use multiple-baseline designs to document the effectiveness of counseling. For example, in a multiple-baseline-across-situations design variation, if a student exhibits the same target behavior (e.g., a

166　The Accountable School Counselor

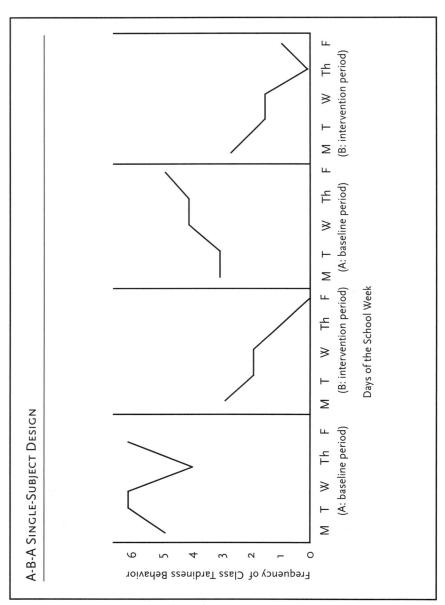

FIGURE 6.5. An A-B-A-B single-subject design.

disruptive behavior) in several classes, the school counselor could work with the teachers of those classes to operationally define the disruptive behavior and agree on implementing an intervention to reduce the number of disruptions. The same intervention and data-gathering techniques would be applied in each classroom. In brief, a multiple-baseline-across-situations design is used to investigate and change the *same target behavior* in different situations or contexts. Note that if a multiple-baseline-across-situations design is used, the results include a graph for each situation.

Another variation is to use a multiple-baseline-across-people design. This approach involves applying the *same intervention* to several students exhibiting the same target behavior in the same situation. For example, if several students are exhibiting the same disruptive behavior in a teacher's class, the counselor could help the teacher use an intervention that might stop each student's individual disruptive behavior. If a multiple-baseline-across-people design is used, a graph for each *person* is created to show the results. Note that the multiple-baseline-across-people design may be especially suitable to small-group counseling interventions if the group has relatively few students.

A third variation is to use a multiple-baseline-across-interventions design. In this approach, different interventions are focused upon the same target behavior sequentially (i.e., not at the same time), but different interventions are used to change the behavior. In each of these variations, the procedures are essentially the same in that appropriate prebaselines are established, interventions are conducted and baseline data are gathered during intervention, and appropriate postbaselines are established. If a multiple-baseline-across-interventions design is used, the results should be a graph for each *intervention*.

Because personal counseling is a unique but relatively visible school counseling program service, school counselors should take all the time necessary to evaluate it. No one else in a school is qualified to perform personal counseling services; therefore, it is hard for an administrator to dismiss a school counselor who can demonstrate accountability for personal counseling.

Crisis Counseling/Response

The *ASCA National Model* (ASCA, 2005) states that "crisis counseling provides prevention, intervention and follow-up ... to students and families facing emergency situations" (p. 43). It also casts a school counselor as a leader in developing crisis intervention plans for students in the school. By definition, crisis counseling cannot be scheduled, but plans can be made for the use of crisis counseling. When the need for crisis counseling or response arises, it takes priority over other activities.

Crisis situations usually involve a sudden, unplanned change in a student's life that affects his or her personal, social, and emotional well-being. Crises students might experience include injury or illness, physical abuse, loss of a friend or pet, pregnancy, or substance abuse reaction. Crisis also might involve change in student's family that impacts the student's functioning, such as parental announcement of a divorce, a death in the family, financial crises for the family, parental or sibling substance abuse, or domestic violence. In an effective summary, Cobia and Henderson (2003) described three categories of crises students may experience:

> Situational crises may be environmental catastrophes such as a tornado, fire, or other natural disaster; personal/physical, such as illness or accident resulting in disability; or interpersonal, such as family disruption through divorce or death. Transitional crises include such universal states as movement through developmental life phases or nonuniversal occurrences such as changes in social status....Cultural/social crises...are...those related to one's social or cultural milieu such as discrimination, and those resulting from a violation of social norms such as being the victim of abuse or some other type of crime. (pp. 127–128)

As a school counselor, you may be among the first to become aware of the crisis situation, and therefore must be prepared to take action. Sometimes all you can do is to comfort and support a student, which may involve only one or two short visits. In these cases, it is not necessary to develop a treatment plan. However, accountability is still appropriate, even though it might only involve recording the number of crisis counseling sessions and the types of issues encountered. School counselors needing more substantive evaluations of their crisis counseling can use semistructured interviews or even postcrisis rating scales. (Sometimes, a school counselor may be able to enroll a student in crisis in supportive group counseling, such as a grief group or group for children of divorce. Accountability methods discussed for personal counseling and groups also are suitable for these support groups.)

In many crisis situations, school counselors need to direct students and/or their family members to outside resources for more extensive help. Competent and professional school counselors have extensive referral resources readily available (e.g., mental health and health professionals, government agencies and organizations, community counseling agencies) to recommend to students and their families. Many school counselors keep a local database of referral resources that list pertinent information such as the address and phone number, kinds of issues treated, cost, and contact persons. School counselors should tally the number of referrals and reasons for referring students and/or families for treatment by other professionals. Other accountability procedures for referrals are discussed in the next section.

REFERRALS

Baker and Gerler (2004) captured the essence of why school counselors need to be good at making referrals when they wrote, "All professionals are limited in expertise and time" (p. 177). From essentially the same perspective, Studer (2005) wrote that

> it is not unusual for situations to arise that are beyond the knowledge and training level of the school counselor. In these situations, students are often better served through the expertise of other professionals either within the school setting or in the community. Counselors are expected to establish a network of outside experts for students who need help; and, if a referral is needed, three sources [to which a referral could be made] are recommended to be given to the student and/or parent. (p. 35)

Making a referral to a student is similar to consultation for a school counselor in that the school counselor, in a sense, gives responsibility for providing help to the student to another person (i.e., the professional receiving the referral). Thus, there are similarities between evaluating the effectiveness of consultation and referral activities. However, referral is decidedly different from consultation in that once the referral has been made, a school counselor rarely has input as to what the professional receiving the referral does with the student and/or family. This separation of the school counselor from the student creates a paradoxical situation for the school counselor in regard to being accountable for referral activities. This paradox makes generating evidence of referral effectiveness both simple and difficult.

The simple side of being accountable for referral-making activities is a record-keeping and counting function. That is, certainly a school counselor should keep a record of each student who is referred (although a specific name need not be recorded), the basis of the referral, (e.g., for psychotherapy or assistance with a medical condition), and the name of the professional to whom the referral was made. The accountability evidence for these activities is simply a compiled list of which types of students were referred for which reasons to which professionals during some given period of time.

The difficult side of being accountable for referral-making activities lies in the fact that school counselors are not only responsible for making referrals, they also are responsible for making *effective* referrals. That is, referrals that result in students getting the help they need, and thereby improving, from the professionals who receive the referrals. Simply put, a school counselor not only needs to make referrals, a school counselor needs to make *good* referrals.

School counselors refer students for a variety of reasons. Some of the most common reasons are similar across school levels, and some are unique to school level. For example, Ritchie and Partin (1994) surveyed school counselors in regard to the most common reasons underlying their referrals and found that elementary school counselors most often referred students for child abuse, family concerns, emotional concerns, and behavioral problems; middle school counselors most often referred students for family concerns, emotional concerns, child abuse, and behavioral problems; and high school counselors referred students most often for reasons including emotional concerns, alcohol and other substance abuse concerns, family concerns, and mental health concerns. Regardless of the reason for the referral, however, a school counselor should follow up on the referral. Follow-up contact (which is permitted within applicable ethical standards) allows the school counselor to determine whether the referred student actually received services from the professional to whom the student was referred. Obviously, if a student doesn't act upon the referral, it not a "good" referral, and in fact wasn't a referral at all. Therefore, through follow-up contacts, a school counselor should keep a record of how many students actually participated in the services intended from the referral. The number of students who participated in referral activities can be divided by the number of student referrals attempted to yield a completed referral percentage, which is one type of accountability evidence.

I'm not the smartest fellow in the world, but I can sure pick smart colleagues.

—Franklin D. Roosevelt

The most difficult part of being accountable for referrals is determining if students changed and improved as a result of being referred. Here, too, school counselors must be as specific as possible in describing the reasons for the referral, because those reasons become the basis for evaluating whether the student has changed. It is recommended that the reasons for the referral be stated behaviorally whenever possible.

Many of the evidence-gathering methods described previously can be used to obtain such data. For example, students and/or family members can be queried through a semistructured interview or a questionnaire *after* they have participated in the referral service to obtain information about the effectiveness of the service they received. Similarly, teachers, administrators, and/or parents or guardians can be queried about whether they are aware of changes in the student and/or the student's behaviors. Students also can be surveyed in regard to their attitudes about the referral activities and/or the referral process. However, again, asking about whether they liked what happened is considerably less credible than determining if changes actually occurred. In any case, the basic requirement is that school counselors should not only be accountable for making referrals but also for the effectiveness of the referrals they make.

Peer Mediation and Conflict Resolution

Sheperis, Weaver, and Sheperis (2004) wrote that

> peer mediation is a form of conflict resolution often used in school settings that involves use of a third-party, presumably an impartial person, to assist in resolving a dispute between two or more people.
>
> Peer mediation is a form of facilitated interpersonal communication that requires the application of problem-solving methods to achieve agreement between or among disputants. (p. 369)

Peer mediation has been promoted as a means to expand the services of school counselors by training students to help other students with their concerns (e.g., Myrick, 2002). Inevitable conflicts in increasingly diverse student bodies, growing tensions about how students should be educated and what they should be taught, and publicity over events such as extreme violence in schools have led educators to embrace a variety of conflict resolution programs. Originally called "peer facilitation" programs, early peer mediation models involved training students to become effective listeners and to facilitate and help other students resolve interpersonal and other issues (Myrick, 2002). Today, peer mediation programs are among the fastest growing conflict resolution programs in schools (Ripley, 2003; Sheperis et al., 2004). As a result, the models underlying them and the methods used in them are indeed diverse. Regardless of the model used, however, school counselors often are responsible for training peer mediators and for overseeing peer mediation programs in schools. Basically, peer mediators are students trained to help two or more other students who are experiencing a conflict achieve a mutually satisfactory resolution of their conflict. A peer mediator thus facilitates collaboration between the disputing parties to find a satisfactory resolution to their conflict.

Ripley (2003) noted that peer mediation and conflict resolution not only can diffuse immediate conflicts but also can increase achievement, invoke higher level reasoning, promote social development, improve problem-solving abilities, increase students' self-confidence, and strengthen interpersonal relationships among students. However, despite the growing interest in and promises of and for peer mediation, empirical evidence of its effectiveness is sketchy at best. Most of the support for peer mediation effectiveness in the professional literature is anecdotal and therefore highly subjective, generally unreliable, and often invalid. Further, the evaluation procedures that have been used to evaluate peer mediation effectiveness have been poorly construed and constructed and are not generalizable (Ripley, 2003). If schools are to continue to adopt peer mediation as a response to conflict among students, and if school counselors are to continue to lead in implementing such programs, they must be able to provide solid, empirical, and validly obtained evidence of the program's effectiveness. Fortunately, there are several ways to gather such evidence to determine the impact of peer mediation programs.

Conflicts can be conceptualized as either tractable or untractable (resolution resistant). Tractable conflicts are minor disputes in which a simple misunderstanding occurred. This type of conflict is usually solvable through mediation strategies.

—Ripley, 2003, p. 296

Evaluation of peer mediation effectiveness can occur during the training of peer mediators, during the implementation of a peer mediation program, and after the program has been implemented. Evaluation approaches include determining how well mediators learned mediation and conflict resolution skills, how satisfied students are after receiving mediation, how students who participate in mediation change their behavior, and how a peer mediation program affects the atmosphere and climate of a school.

If peer mediation is to work, peer mediators must have the skills to mediate disputes effectively. Therefore, assessing peer mediators' skills and attainment of abilities is one way to address a school counselor's accountability for peer mediation activities. Peer mediators often are selected for their potential to help their classmates cope with personal issues. Sometimes students are surveyed and asked to list the names of one or two students with whom they would feel comfortable sharing personal concerns. Sometimes teachers are asked to nominate students they feel would be good mediators. Regardless of the selection procedure, however, nominees should be interviewed by the school counselor or a panel including the school counselor who is going to lead the program, teachers, and students to determine their suitability for the role (Robinson, Morrow, Kigin, & Lindeman, 1991). Typically, those students selected are trained in effective listening and communication skills and problem-solving strategies. Therefore, students should be pretested before training to determine the level of their skills. After peer mediation training, they should be tested again to determine if (a) their listening effectiveness has improved and (b) if their listening skills are at a sufficient level to allow them to be successful mediators (Bell, Coleman, Anderson, Whelan, & Wilder, 2000). Note that both criteria should be fulfilled because some students may improve but still not have listening and/or mediation skills sufficient to warrant participation as a peer mediator.

Several means can be used to determine whether students have improved their listening, communication, and problem-solving abilities as a result of peer mediation training, and there are several instruments in the professional literature that have been used to evaluate such skills training (e.g., Myrick, 2002; Tindall & Gray, 1985), although some caution should be exercised in choosing among existing instruments, because some of them aren't strong psychometrically. There also are a number of counselor effectiveness scales in the professional literature, and some of them can be readily adapted for use in peer mediation training evaluation (e.g., *Counselor Rating Scale–Short Version or Counselor Effectiveness Scale*). Also, observation checklists can be used to rate peer mediators pre- and posttraining (e.g., Humphries, 1999). However, perhaps the best method is to use written simulations. Descriptions of both common and relatively rare student-to-student conflict scenarios can be developed, perhaps with local adaptation (e.g., in settings with which the students are likely to be familiar). You can ask the students being trained to select the most appropriate response from among a set of response choices or to develop their responses to the scenario without a prompt. In essence, you can use either a multiple-choice test or an essay test. The advantage of an essay test is that postevaluation discussions (during a feedback session) can be centered on how the students came to make the responses they did, how else they might have responded, and why some responses are effective and some are not.

You can also interview students and ask them standard questions about their role as a mediator. You can rate and compare their responses to the same questions after they have completed training. For example, you might ask the students to respond to the following situations:

> Jerry just learned that Andy asked Jerry's girlfriend to go to the dance with him and she agreed. Jerry is threatening to hurt

Andy physically if he takes her to the dance. How would you intervene?

Latisha claims that Marcia is saying bad things about her to Latisha's friends and that Marcia is ruining her reputation. She has vowed revenge on Marcia. How would you intervene?

The students' verbal responses to these scenarios could be rated on a scale in which 0 = *ineffective*, 1 = *somewhat effective*, 2 = *effective*, and 3 = *effective*. The ratings might be made only by you, the school counselor, or anonymously by some subset of the students being trained. Of course, such a rating scale also can be applied to evaluations of students' written responses for written simulations.

You can conduct a formative or ongoing evaluation of peer mediation by collecting process data. For example, each time a peer mediator is involved in a student-to-student conflict resolution activity, you should record the nature of the activity (without names of those in conflict), including the kind of dispute and the outcome of the mediation effort. You can collect then compile these data over an academic term or the entire school year. You can then present the results as evidence of the effectiveness of the program. In particular, a decrease in mediations may indicate that the program is teaching students to handle disputes on their own, which is one of the primary goals of peer mediation programs.

Another way to evaluate the effectiveness of peer mediation is to gather feedback from the students who use the peer mediator services. Their satisfaction with their mediation and with their peer mediator can be assessed through rating forms, checklists, written comments, or recorded oral comments (e.g., through a semistructured interview). These data also can be tallied to determine whether consumers of peer mediation are satisfied with the services they received. Further, opinions of school community members, including teachers, can be obtained through use of a survey to determine if they perceive positive results from a peer mediation program. Other forms of program evaluation, discussed in Chapter 8, also are applicable to evaluation of peer mediation programs.

According to the *ASCA National Model* (ASCA, 2005), "the techniques of peer mediation and conflict resolution are used to help students learn how to make changes in the way they get along with others" (pp. 42–43). Therefore, the most compelling evidence of effectiveness is measures of change in actual student behaviors. It is difficult to track the subsequent behaviors of individuals who have received peer mediation intervention, because peer mediation services are confidential. However, behavior patterns of a small number of students who have participated in peer mediation can be tracked to infer the effect of the peer mediation program. All schools keep records on discipline referrals, suspensions, and expulsions, including those student actions (such as fighting) that are presumably subject to reduction from a peer mediation program. Such data can be compared before and after the implementation of a peer mediation program, and/or periodically throughout it. Of course, a decrease in fighting may not be solely because of the peer mediation program activities. However, it can likely be inferred that the peer mediation program contributed to the decrease. In addition, improvements in school climate can be measured and at least in part attributed to a peer mediation program (Carruthers, Sweeney, Kmitta, & Harris, 1996). Other indicators that have been used to infer the effectiveness of peer mediation programs include changes in school attendance, school grades, and attitudes toward school (Tobias & Myrick, 1999). Finally, you can compare the frequencies of certain student behaviors and conditions (i.e., truancy, tardiness, and discipline referral rates) with another comparable school that does not have a peer mediation program (e.g., Barnett, Adler, Easton, & Howard, 2001).

CONCLUSION

Because the activities subsumed under the Responsive Services subsection of the *ASCA National Model* (ASCA, 2005) are commonly expected of school counselors, they force school counselors to be accountable for them. Stakeholders pay attention to a school counselor's responsive service activities, whether a school counselor wants them to or not! Therefore, it is important for a school counselor to develop and implement good, sound accountability activities for evaluation of these types of school counseling services. In some of the previous sections of this book, we have advocated that the results of a school counselor's accountability activities be used to promote the various aspects of the school counselor's functioning. Basically, that means that the school counselor can use the results of accountability activities to bring stakeholders' attention to what the school counselor is actually doing. Accountability for responsive services is at the other end of the spectrum; stakeholders will be looking carefully for evidence of a school counselor's effectiveness in providing these types of services.

For Thought and Deed

1. Although it is less popular today, some school counselors still find appropriate occasion to use the expert model of consultation. Assuming you will be called upon to provide consultation services to teachers, parents/guardians, or other school personnel, for which aspects of student development and/or behaviors would you legitimately be an "expert"?

2. One of the most common requests that teachers make to school counselors is for assistance with what they (overly simplistically) refer to as *disruptive students.* This catch-all term is one that frequently leads school counselors into the useless triangle trap, because a teacher has one set of behaviors in mind when she or he uses the term and the school counselor has another set of behaviors in mind when he or she works with the student. Engage several teachers in a conversation about what they consider to be disruptive classroom behaviors, and take note of the behaviors they relate. Be sure the focus of the conversations is on students' *behaviors*, not generalized comments about students' characteristics or attitudes.

3. Assume you have been asked by a school administrator to work with a child who is disrespectful to teachers. Describe a *single-subject A-B-A-B with multiple-baselines-across-situations design* that you could use to help the student and generate accountability data.

4. One of the typical outcomes of a peer mediation activity is a behavioral contract that is signed by the disputants at the conclusion of the activity, presumably because signing a contract is a strong indication of intent to behave in agreed upon ways. Create a hypothetical scenario that includes student disputants and a peer mediation activity intended to resolve the dispute, and then write a behavioral contract that could be used as the conclusion of the peer mediation process.

CHAPTER 7

Accountability for School Counseling - System Support Functions

Within the *ASCA National Model* (ASCA, 2005), "system support consists of management activities that establish, maintain, and enhance the total school counseling program" (p. 43). Thus, your various professional development, consultation and collaboration, and program management functions and activities are covered in this subsection. System support activities do not involve face-to-face work with students but nonetheless are appropriate and important parts of your work as a school counselor and your general professional functioning. Unfortunately, however, system support activities are among the least recognized activities in which you engage as a professional school counselor. Therefore, being accountable for these types of activities is particularly important for you so that various school counseling program stakeholders will understand the multifaceted nature of these work-related activities and realize that you engage in many of the same types of other-than-direct-service activities as do other education professionals.

Because there is some overlap of elements within the Responsive Services and System Support subsections (e.g., consultation and collaboration) in the *ACSA National Model*, only those topics not covered previously are addressed in this chapter.

Professional Development

In the Professional Development subsection of the *ASCA National Model*, you are charged to "update and share" your professional knowledge and skills with others (p. 43). The "update" part means that you

179

should regularly and systematically engage in activities that will enhance and improve your knowledge, skills, and overall functioning; that is, you should participate in what are commonly known as continuing education or professional development activities. Statements of advocacy for school counselors to engage in (postgraduation and/or postinitial certification) professional development abound within the school counseling literature, partly because professional development is covered in the ASCA National Standards (Campbell & Dahir, 1997) but more importantly because it is good sense for professionals to continue to improve themselves. You are of course advised to keep abreast of new information and skills that are necessary for continued effective functioning in your current school counseling situation. However, you also are advised to go beyond minimum professional development involvements, simply as a matter of professionalism. For example, Linde (2003) wrote that

> while [school] counselors must attend continuing education opportunities to renew national and/or state credentials, it is important to stay current with theories, trends, and information about clients and different populations. (p. 46)

Dollarhide (2003b) provided even more personalized instruction to school counselors:

> You will want to remain up to date with the professional literature from your professional associations. You must read new books that address the issues your students, families, and community are facing. Remain aware of new music, movies, TV shows, and images pervading our culture that send messages to students about how they should be—how they should act, feel, think, and look—and that send messages about how their families, schools, and community should be. You must commit yourself to lifelong learning. (p. 335)

Although professional development activities are advocated in the professional literature, there are few specific recommendations about the types of activities in which you as a school counselor should engage. For example, there is no specific encouragement anywhere in the *ASCA National Model* for school counselors like you to participate in your annual state school counselor association conferences or even in the annual ASCA national conference. Presumably, determining which professional development activities are pertinent and appropriate, when they are to be completed, and how you will participate is an individual decision. That being the case, concomitantly, you are free to choose any or all the professional development activities for which you will be accountable. Of course, our bias is that you should be accountable for all of them.

The most common type of professional development activity in which practicing school counselors engage is attending local, state, regional, or national conferences and meetings that focus on school counseling. School counselors who attend such conferences or meetings invariably learn new things and/or develop new skills by virtue of the sessions in which they participate. Further, assuming you attend such meetings, it is likely that you will use some or all of what was gained from participation in your day-to-day functioning as a school counselor. However, the important question is, how can you be accountable for your learning or skills development from such participation? The answer is to demonstrate that there is a change in how you do your daily work as a result of having the new knowledge or skills.

It is change, continuing change, inevitable change, that is the dominant factor in society today. No sensible decision can be made any longer without taking into account not only the world as it is, but the world as it will be.

—Isaac Asimov

You will have developed further professionally only if the knowledge and/or skills gained from engaging in a professional development activity somehow become manifest in your work as a school counselor. Therefore, your accountability task is to first identify and then to publicize how you are using what you learned, developed, or gained from participation. Perhaps the simplest way to be accountable is to disseminate the information (e.g., as an announcement) to various stakeholder groups. For example, you might distribute a school counseling program newsletter to various stakeholder groups on a regular basis (which is in and of itself a good means to be accountable and foster public relations). In addition, you should have a Web site for your school counseling program that can be used to disseminate your professional development information. Any communication about a professional development activity in which you engaged should include (a) the name of the events (and perhaps a little about others who attend such a meeting); (b) the general nature of the knowledge enhancement and/or skill development that resulted from your participation; and, most importantly, (c) how you are putting into practice your new knowledge and/or skills. In other words, you should convey how the knowledge or skills gained are being put to use to benefit students and/or others in the school. Of course, the distribution of this information also conveys the number of professional development activities in which you engaged during a given time.

One of the most common but least recognized ways you can engage in professional development is through reading, including reading professional information available on the Internet. Journals from professional associations, professional books and magazines, and Internet articles and resources are all valuable contributions to your professional knowledge and skills. In addition, continuing education activities on the Internet are increasingly becoming available and are a convenient way to enhance your professional knowledge and/or skills. Your professional readings should be disseminated for both public relations and accountability purposes. However, the most important information you can give is how you are doing things differently as a result of your professional reading. See Figure 7.1 for an example of opportunities for professional development.

Another pertinent activity for which accountability is needed and recommended is membership in professional organizations and associations for school counselors. We believe that holding membership in ASCA, your state school counselor association, ACA, and perhaps other professional organizations for school counselors is essential; such memberships are one of the hallmarks of a true professional. Ways to communicate such information, in an accountability context, include using letterhead stationery that includes your membership listings, posting your memberships information under personal/professional information on a Web site, and including your membership information as part of your e-mail signature information.

The same recommendations apply to the professional credentials you hold; information about your credentials should be evident to all. Many counseling professionals include acronyms after their names on professional written communications to indicate their credentials (e.g., LPC for licensed professional counselor, CSC for certified school counselor, or LSC for licensed school counselor). Achieving professional cre-

Accountability for School Counseling - System Support Functions

PROFESSIONAL DEVELOPMENT OPPORTUNITIES

During the next year you will have a variety of professional development opportunities available to you. It is unlikely that you will be able to participate in all of them, because of the costs and/or time requirements associated with them. However, it is important to consider all the opportunities and then to prioritize and select from among them those that will be of greatest benefit to you. For each of the categories following, list the professional development activity and the estimated costs (e.g., registration, travel, and accommodations expenses) associated with each activity.

Conferences, meetings, or training sessions:	Estimated Cost:	Priority:
National		
ASCA National Conference	1200.00	
Regional		
State		
State ASCA Conference	400.00	
Local		
Local area state ACA chapter meetings	0.00	
Distance (i.e., online or virtual) education activities		
Online home study CEU courses	0.00	
Professional resources:	Estimated Cost:	
Professional association memberships		
ACA	151.00	
ASCA	115.00	
State ASCA	45.00	
Books and other print media		
Professional reference books	250.00	
Professional journals and other subscriptions		
Software and other electronic resources		
Additional professional credentials		
NBCC certification fees	60.00	

FIGURE 7.1. Professional development opportunities.

dentials beyond the basic requirement for you to be a school counselor (i.e., state certification or licensure) is particularly notable for stakeholders. For example, by achieving recognition as a National Certified School Counselor (NCSC) from the National board of Certified Counselors (NBCC; see www.nbcc.org), you convey to stakeholders that you are well-qualified and recognized nationally for your professional competence. Similarly, are your graduate degree diploma and ASCA, state school counselor association (SCA), ACA, state counseling association (CA) membership and national certified counselor (NCC), NCSC, and state school counselor certificates in plain view in your office? They should be. Remember that disseminating your membership and credential information is not bragging. People are impressed by professional credentials. It is good professional practice for you to inform your various stakeholders of the nature and extent of your professional involvements.

PARTNERING AND TEAMING

Partnering and Teaming activities include your work with others in the community in ways that benefit the school counseling program and therefore, indirectly, students and/or other individuals associated with your school. Bryan and Holcomb-McCoy (2004), in addressing the most common example of partnering, wrote that

> school-family-community (SFC) partnerships are collaborative initiatives or relationships that actively involve school personnel, parents, families, and community members and organizations as equal and mutual partners in the planning, coordination, and implementing of programs and activities at home, at school, and in the community to help increase the academic, emotional, and social success of students. (p. 162)

Bryan and Holcomb-McCoy (2004, p. 162) also listed what they found to be the nine most common manifestations of SFC partnerships, including (a) mentoring programs, (b) parent centers, (c) family/community members as teachers' aides, (d) parent and community volunteer programs, (e) home visit programs, (f) parent education programs, (g) school–business partnerships, (h) parents and community members in site-based management, and (i) tutoring programs. Figure 7.2 shows

Accountability for School Counseling - System Support Functions   185

PARTNERS AND TEAMS

As a professional school counselor, you have or will have established relationships with other professionals and/or organizations (including agencies and businesses) in your community. List the primary professionals and/or organizations in your community with whom you partner or team. Then, rate their respective importance to you as a professional resource using a rating scale 1 = *relatively low importance* to 5 = *high importance*.

Professionals in the community with whom I currently have a working relationship:	Rating
Tom Kellerman (private practice)	4
Alexis Deloro (M.D.)	5
Sam Uldermis (County community resources dir.)	5
Mary Jane Onkosky (County commissioner)	5

Professionals in the community with whom I would like to have a working relationship:	Rating
Elayne Constanza (private practice	4
Jack Olingeria (private practice)	5
Theo Harrison (private practice – family)	4
Desmond Neubower (social worker)	5

Organizations in the community with which I currently have a working relationship:	Rating
Crisis Center	5
Teen Center	3
Alternative school (for at-risk youth)	4
Community legal services	3
Behavioral (mental) health services	4
Big Brothers/Big Sisters	4
County recreation department	4
Local council of churches	4

Organizations in the community with which I would like to have a working relationship:	Rating
Local area Kiwanis club	3
Local area Junior League	3

FIGURE 7.2. Rating partners and teams.

how you can document and rate the professionals and organizations with whom you partner.

The nature of your involvements in SFC programs, and other variations of partnering and/or teaming with community members and organizations, varies from having a minor and perfunctory role to being a highly active program participant, leader, and coordinator. Regardless, however, this is another set of activities for which it is relatively easy for you to demonstrate the *extent* of your participation, but also relatively difficult to demonstrate the *effectiveness* of your activities.

Partnering within the *ASCA National Model* (ASCA, 2005) specifically involves, "orienting staff, parents or guardians, business and industry, civic and social service organizations and community members in the comprehensive school counseling programs through such means as partnerships, newsletters, local media, and presentations" (p. 43). Essentially, these are public relations activities; therefore, accountability data such as the number of visitations or presentations made are easy enough to track and report. For example, frequently, it is possible to track the number of people who were involved in partnering activities, such as by recording the number of parents attending a meeting. Occasionally, it may even be possible that one of your activities leads directly to something obviously beneficial for the school counseling program, the school, and/or the students, such as a civic organization creating a scholarship for students in a school as a result of your work with that organization. Unfortunately, it is often difficult to determine the *direct* outcomes of your partnering activities (i.e., cause–effect relationships) because the results typically only become evident after a relatively long time, which means that other intervening factors may have caused the outcomes. You certainly should look for and seize any opportunity to show that your involvements in partnering activities have led directly to evident benefits for students or others in the school community. In addition, you should use whatever methods are available to generate evidence of accountability, including adapting methods used in your consultation or referral accountability activities to your partnering activities. However, do not spend excessive time trying to demonstrate your effectiveness for these types of activities. We are not suggesting that partnering is not important, but because of the complexities of demonstrating how you directly impacted the results of partnering activities, and the amount of time needed to do that, your time and energy may be better spent in other accountability activities.

Coming together is a beginning; keeping together is progress; working together is success.

—Henry Ford

"Community outreach" means that you serve as a liaison between your school counseling program (and perhaps the school in general) and various community agencies, employers, or other potential resources for the program (Taylor & Adelman, 2000). As with partnering, the primary accountability method for your activities as a liaison lie in keeping track of what was done, with whom, how frequently, and, perhaps, at what cost. But again, demonstrating your effectiveness for these types of activities beyond what is readily evident is not warranted.

The *ASCA National Model* (ASCA, 2005, p. 43) encourages school counselors to become involved in school and community advisory councils, committees, organizations, events, and the like. Basically, the idea is for you to show school counseling program support for other relevant activities by being involved in them. Again, being accountable for such activity can be relatively simple: keep track of the number of activities and the time spent participating in them, and because it is nearly impossible for you to generate evidence of *causal* effectiveness for these types of activities, your effort is better spent on other things.

In general, partnering and teaming are important school counselor activities, but it is difficult to generate causal and quantitative evidence of effectiveness. Typically, the best and most convenient accountability data are indicators of your time invested in participation. However, if you are called upon specifically to provide evidence of your effectiveness for these types of activities, consider using some of the other methods that have been suggested for gathering feedback from indirect service activities, such as written questions or semistructured interviews.

PROGRAM MANAGEMENT

The program management functions within the *ASCA National Model* (ASCA, 2005) encompass all the activities necessary to deliver the

188   The Accountable School Counselor

school counseling program and to keep it operating effectively and efficiently. As a school counselor, you perform various activities to make the school counseling program function, but the two areas in particular for which you should strive to be accountable are budget management and resource development.

BUDGET MANAGEMENT

To be effectively accountable for budget management, you first have to know the budget for your school counseling program. That may seem obvious, but most school counselors do not know the budgetary amounts specifically allocated to school counseling services. School budgets are anything but easy to understand. However, it is crucial that you know exactly how much money is allocated for school counseling services and how it is allocated at your school. It is common for some school funds to be allocated to guidance services in such a way that you will not have control over their use and expenditure. For example, the costs for state-mandated testing might be allocated to the guidance program, but because such testing is mandated, you do not have direct control over how those funds are spent. Similarly, funds for necessary record keeping (e.g., attendance, tardiness, truancy records) might be assigned to guidance services in the school budget, and you will not have control over those funds. The point is that you should have a thorough knowledge of the school counseling program budget so that you can be held accountable only for those portions of the budget over which you have control.

Most of what we call management consists of making it difficult for people to get their work done.

—Peter F. Drucker

Once you know how much money you have to operate your school counseling program, being accountable for how the money is spent amounts to applying some rather simple mathematics. For example, some of the money likely was spent for (physical) program resources, such as print media, tests, equipment, or software. What materials were obtained and at what cost for each? Other monies likely have been spent on program operations, such as positive behavior reinforcers (e.g., candy, stickers, or bulletin-board stars) for students who participated in behavior modification activities you conducted or associated with field trips or visitations you arranged or conducted. How much money was spent for each of these activities, and on what was it spent? There also might be human resource costs, such as those associated with bringing in speakers for classroom guidance activities. How much money was spent on human resources, and on whom was it spent? Finally, there may be office management costs for your school counseling program, such as for general office supplies, equipment maintenance, or long-distance telephone calls. How much was spent for each category of expenses? Figure 7.3 shows how you cankeep track of your program budget and of the monies that you do and do not control.

SCHOOL COUNSELING PROGRAM BUDGET

It is likely that you control the expenditure of some of the monies allocated to conduct your school counseling program, but it also is likely that monies are assigned to your school counseling program over which you have no control. Regardless of the degree of control, it is important to know the amount of the school counseling program budget, excluding salary allocations. Find out what your school counseling program budget actually is and then in the spaces below allocate the monies over the major categories.

School Counseling Program Budget Total:	$3,000.00
School counseling program monies I control	Amount
AV materials for students (e.g., films	$250.00
Computer supplies (e.g., software)	$150.00
Professional resources (e.g., books or kits)	$400.00
Assessment resources	$200.00
Total:	$1,000.00
School counseling program monies I do not control	Amount
Professional travel allowance	$250.00
Computer/Technical support	$500.00
Miscellaneous resources	$500.00
Total:	$1,250.00

FIGURE 7.3. School counseling program budget.

Stakeholders interested in school counselor budgetary accountability usually are primarily concerned with cost–benefit ratios. That is, they want to know the relationship between the number of students or others who benefited directly from each activity and the actual cost associated with each activity. For some of your activities, such as mass distribution of print media, it is relatively easy to determine the per-student expenditure (i.e., cost–benefit ratio); for most of your school counseling activities, however, determining cost–benefit ratios is difficult. Nonetheless, you should make every effort to provide those data whenever possible. For example, if computer technology (e.g., access to certain online resources or use of software) is made available through the school counseling office, keep computer-use logs to record of how many students used the services provided and how long they used them. Similarly, if costs were associated with a guest speaker's presentation, record the number of students who heard the speaker to determinate the of a cost–benefit ratio. You can similarly compute per-student costs for other for other school counseling program activities. Although it takes time, effort, and creativity for you to develop cost–benefit financial information, it is well worth it because stakeholders interested in financial matters want to know that they are getting as much bang for the buck as possible. What is perhaps more important, such information is essential when it is used as a basis for requesting additional funding for your school counseling program; that is, the best argument for additional funding is being able to demonstrate that current program funds are being used effectively, efficiently, and prudently.

RESOURCE DEVELOPMENT

Another way to demonstrate fiscal responsibility and accountability, is to secure external funding for some of the activities in your school counseling program. For example, some community businesses or agencies might provide funding for a specific activity, such as your peer mediation program, or financially sponsor speakers for your career education activities. And just as athletic departments and booster clubs solicit financial support from the community, school counselors can solicit funding for school counseling projects, as long as they are approved at the school system level. Further, your school counseling program advisory board might sponsor fundraising activities to support special projects such as the purchase of career education software. You might even obtain state or national grant monies for innovative and well-designed programmatic activities that have good potential for generalization to other schools or settings. Philanthropic organizations also are a possible source of external funding. Increasing numbers of school counselors are turning to grant writing as a means to help finance their school counseling programs; why not be among them? What better way to demonstrate the cost effectiveness of your program than to obtain external funding? If you are able to obtain additional funds, you can demonstrate an even higher level of cost effectiveness.

In-service Activities

The sharing part of the *ASCA National Model* (ASCA, 2005) relates to the recommendation that as a school counselor you should both attend local in-service training activities along with other school personnel *and* provide local in-service training for other school personnel. In regards to participation in local in-service activities, the accountability strategies for professional development activities apply here as well. That is, you should convey and explain to stakeholders how what you learned at the in-service training activity resulted in changing some of the ways you implement your school counseling program. The resultant change may be as mundane as dealing with student records in a new way or as complex as implementing new programmatic activities. However, no matter the significance of what was learned, the applications of the learning should be disseminated. (See Figure 7.4 for an example of identifying possible in-service activities.)

Most in-service activities provided by school counselors are information-giving sessions. The *stated* rationale for such activities is that teachers and other school personnel need to know the information so that they can do their jobs better and more efficiently (and therefore benefit students); the *unstated* rationale is that if teachers or others know the information, the school counselors' jobs will be easier. Regardless of rationale, information-giving in-service activities are not usually well received by school personnel. An alternative is to provide in-service training that helps teachers and others learn or develop new skills they can use in their respective work functions. The nature of skills training always involves more activity by the participants (i.e., they aren't just sitting there listening to someone trying to fill their

192 The Accountable School Counselor

IN-SERVICE ACTIVITIES

As a school counselor, there should be at least three in-service activities that you could lead and present for other professionals in your school. In the following spaces, list three in-service activities you could provide in your school with relatively little preparation, identify for whom the in-service would be provided, and indicate what resources would be needed to present the in-service activity.

Activity 1:	Basic responding skills for dealing with angry children	
	Target audience:	*Teachers in my school*
	Resources needed:	*None*
Activity 2:	Helping students explore the world of work by integrating activities into classes	
	Target audience:	*Teachers*
	Resources needed:	*Access to computers for participants*
Activity 3:	Explaining the ASCA National Model	
	Target audience:	*Local area school principals*
	Resources needed:	*Resources from ASCA, including several copies of the ASCA National Model and other information that can be distributed to attendees*

FIGURE 7.4. Three possible in-service activities.

brains with more stuff). Therefore, skills training is usually better received by participants.

Creative minds have always been known to survive any kind of bad training.

—Anna Freud

Being accountable for the provision of in-service training to other school personnel is more complex and primarily depends on follow-up activities after the in-service. Again, one type of in-service activity that school counselors frequently provide gives information about what is currently being done in the school counseling program. Such awareness-raising activities are difficult to evaluate directly. However, you can follow up with the participants through distribution of a questionnaire or even a personal interview to determine if any or how many of the participants are doing anything different (e.g., referring students to new school counseling program activities, referring students more frequently to current program activities, requesting specific types of assistance from the school counselor) as a result of the in-service training you provided.

Consider a more sophisticated example. Assume you have provided an in-service to train others in your school to do something different (e.g., to interact with students differently, to make referrals using a different process, or to integrate school counseling information and activities into regular classroom experiences). Such a training activity is much like a classroom guidance activity for students; that is, it is essentially a teaching activity. Therefore, your accountability would depend on how the participants put into practice that which you taught. Here, too, follow-up contact with the participants through a questionnaire, a behavior checklist, personal interviews, or even observation of participants' behaviors are good ways to determine if or how many of the participants are actually doing anything different as a result of the training that you provided.

Conclusion

The system-support functions and activities in which you engage are vital to the success of your school counseling program, but being accountable for them isn't very exciting. We suspect that the reason for this is because they seem to be distant from what school counselors prefer to do (i.e., to help kids directly). Everyone knows that these functions have to be fulfilled, but do stakeholders really care about them? We believe they do care about them, far more than you might imagine. A large portion of the stakeholders for your school counseling program know or care very much about the inner workings of a school counseling program. Put another way, they don't look at things the way you do; more likely, they view things from a consumer perspective. They want to know that what you do as a school counselor helps them achieve what they want to achieve, helps them do what they do better, and doesn't cost more than is absolutely necessary. These stakeholders are neither adversarial nor disparaging to your work or efforts. They simply have a different view of things and therefore have different sets of values and priorities. Therefore, it *is* important to demonstrate accountability for your system-support functions and activities, even though it may not be the most exciting thing you do.

FOR THOUGHT AND DEED

1. It is likely that in your graduate-level school counselor education curriculum there were courses you would have liked to take but were unable to take. Identify two courses that you would like to have taken during your program. Then, identify all the resources (e.g., academic programs, online offerings, professional workshops) that you could access to obtain preparation in those two educational areas.

2. Within the *ASCA National Model*, school, family, and community partnerships are viewed as resources to enhance students' academic, career, and personal/social developments. However, the one form of partnership cannot be equally effective for each of the three realms of student development; different combinations of partnerships would seem to be needed for each development realm. What are the relative emphases that should be given to school, family, and community resources in each of the three realms of student development?

3. What are the best possible sources from which you might obtain additional fiscal and/or physical resources for your school counseling program? What would you have to do to solicit these resources (i.e., to maximize your chances that these resources would be given to your school counseling program)? What would you have to give in return for those resources?

4. Identify two specific skills (i.e., behaviors) that you could teach to teachers and/or others in your school. Then, explain how you would teach each of these skills during two separate 1-hour in-service training sessions for teachers and/or others in your school.

CHAPTER 8

SCHOOL COUNSELING
PROGRAM EVALUATION

When most school counseling professionals hear the term *program evaluation*, they think of a process used to determine the effectiveness and/or outcomes of a whole school counseling program. That is an appropriate interpretation, but it is limited in scope. Program evaluation is actually a much broader concept and is more appropriately used to describe a wide variety of activities that yield important information about an entire school counseling program. The word *important* in this context means information that is useful for decision making about the program and/or the activities within it. For example, Fitzpatrick et al. (2004) defined *evaluation* as "the identification, clarification, and application of defensible criteria to determine an evaluation object's value (worth or merit) in relation to those criteria" (p. 5). In the present context, the evaluation object is your school counseling program. Note that this definition emphasizes application of "defensible criteria" as the basis of program evaluation. For your school counseling program, the defensible criteria against which your program should be evaluated are component elements of the *ASCA National Model* (ASCA, 2005) and of the ASCA *National Standards for School Counseling Programs* (Campbell & Dahir, 1997), and any local school or school-system standards or statements of expectation for your school counseling program.

Unrau et al. (2001, p. 67) cautioned that you should conduct an "evaluability assessment," which is defined as an assessment of a program's readiness to be evaluated, as part of a program evaluation process. In other words, your school counseling program has to be at a sufficient state of development so that it can be evaluated using accepted program evaluation techniques. More specifically, the mission statement, goals, objectives, elements, structure, schedule, resources, and primary activities for your school counseling program must be clearly

195

identified and in place before you conduct a program evaluation. In addition, restrictions and constraints that impact your program should be identified. In general, you can conduct effective program evaluation only when you have very good, thorough understanding of your school counseling program.

A considerable number of program evaluation methods and procedures have been presented in the professional literature. Fitzpatrick et al. (2004) provided a general summation of these methods:

> Evaluation uses inquiry and judgment methods, including: (1) determining **standards** for judging quality and deciding whether those standards should be relative or absolute, (2) collecting relevant information, and (3) applying the standards to determine value, quality, utility, effectiveness, or significance. It leads to recommendations intended to optimize the evaluation object in relation to its intended purpose(s) or to help stakeholders determine whether the evaluation object is worthy of adoption, continuation, or expansion. (p. 5)

One rather drastic possibility alluded to in this broad overview of program evaluation methods is that the evaluation process might lead to a recommendation that the program evaluated be discontinued. That's not likely to be the case for your program, because school counseling programs are likely here to stay. However, there is always the question of whether it will remain *your* school counseling program.

Popham (1993) provided summaries of various commonly used program evaluation models, including the following:

- **Goal Attainment Models** focused on the extent to which programs achieve the goals established for them. In Tyler's model, educational goals are specified as behavioral objectives, and the evaluation process involves determining the extent to which students achieved various behavioral objectives. Hammond's and Metfessel and Michaels' variations of Tyler's model incorporate refinements in the attribution of sources of influence in the degree of achievement of the behavioral objectives.

- **Judgmental Models Emphasizing Inputs** focused on external evaluators' conclusions and decisions about whether the allocation to and/or use of resources in a program is appropriate and/or successful for achieving of the program's goals.

- **Judgmental Models Emphasizing Outputs** focused on external evaluators' conclusions and decisions about whether current program operations, including resource allocation and use, are appropriate and/or successful in bringing about desired program outcomes. Scriven's Goal-Free Model seeks to determine all program outcomes, regardless of whether they relate to program goals. Stake's Countenance Model involves evaluations across three phases of program operation, including antecedents, transactions, and outcomes.

- **Naturalistic Models** focused on using information from program participants' personal perspectives. Stake's Responsive Evaluation model seeks to be particularly responsive to the needs of those for whom the evaluation is conducted (e.g., stakeholders). Eisner's Connoisseurship Model employs the assumption that human observation is the key data-gathering technique in a program evaluation process.

- **Decision Facilitation Models** focused on providing substantive information to stakeholders and other decision makers to be used to make significant decisions (e.g., termination) about the program. Provus' Discrepancy Model involves evaluating the discrepancies between what was proposed or intended and what actually happened in the program. Cronbach's model of educational evaluation emphasizes that the evaluator only provides information and that actual decisions should be made by stakeholders.

Each of these models for or general approaches to program evaluation can be used for evaluation of your school counseling program. And as with all evaluation processes, each has its advantages and limitations. In the main, however, these models are too complex to efficiently evaluate a school counseling program. Further, most of them are focused upon relatively specific aspects of a program, and, therefore, the methodologies associated with them also are relatively purpose-specific. VanZandt and Hayslip (2001) wrote that:

> [school counseling program] evaluation needs to be approached from two different perspectives: formative and summative. *Formative* evaluations provide information during the development and implementation phases of the program. Such information informs us about our needs and program highlights.

> *Summative* evaluations are more descriptive; they tell us what the program has accomplished and usually are aligned with program goals. (p. 140)

The CIPP model for program evaluation embraces VanZandt and Hayslips' recommendation and adds to it in important ways. Stufflebeam and associates' (1971) CIPP model is broad in scope and therefore provides a general framework for program evaluation instead of a specific set of procedures (Fitzpatrick et al., 2004; Gredler, 1996; Popham, 1997). CIPP is an acronym used to reflect four distinct types of evaluations within a general program evaluation model: Context, Input, Process, and Products evaluations. The four elements of the CIPP model are associated with four different types of decisions (Stufflebeam et al., 1971):

Context evaluation ------------ Planning decisions

Input evaluation ---------------- Structuring decisions

Process evaluation ------------- Implementing decisions

Product evaluation -------------- Recycling (continuation) decisions

The CIPP model seems to have found favor in much of the counseling profession, likely because it is readily adapted to a variety of school and other counseling programs. We also favor the CIPP model as a basis for school counseling program evaluation.

CONTEXT EVALUATIONS AND NEEDS ASSESSMENTS

In the CIPP model, context evaluation is essentially synonymous with needs assessment. Royse et al. (2006) wrote that

> needs assessments can provide valuable information for program planning, including what groups to target for services, the best ways to publicize or market services, estimates of the numbers of persons who could benefit from a specific program or service, information about the geographic distribution and

sociodemographic characteristics of potential clients, and barriers that may be encountered by clients. (p. 54)

Royse et al. (2006) also outlined the major steps in a needs-assessment process:

1. Development of understanding of the

    a. purpose of the needs assessment,
    b. geographic region (e.g., school, school system, community) for the needs assessment,
    c. stakeholders to be represented in the needs assessment,
    d. available resources for the needs assessment, and
    e. time available for the needs assessment.

2. Identification of the specific information sought.

3. Determination of whether the information sought exists or needs to be generated.

4. Determination of the methodology and/or development of the instrumentation.

5. Collection and analyses of the needs-assessment data.

6. Preparation of a needs-assessment report.

7. Preliminary dissemination of the needs-assessment report to stakeholders to obtain their feedback.

8. Final dissemination of the needs-assessment report.

In general, you can conduct a needs assessment from within two broad perspectives. One is to assess needs in regard to school counseling services that you are currently providing. The other is to assess needs in regard to school counseling services that you could provide if the need were evident or strong enough. Of course, a needs assessment also can identify school counseling services or activities that are being provided but for which a strong need is not evident.

Needs assessments are usually given to students because they are the primary recipients of school counseling services. However, needs assessments may also be used appropriately with other stakeholder groups such as parents, teachers and other school personnel, or persons in the local community. Needs assessments for students should be conducted on a regular basis (e.g., annually) because program-specific needs might change frequently. Needs-assessments for other stakeholder groups should be conducted periodically as needed and potentially helpful.

Needs assessments have been widely advocated and endorsed as good practice by ASCA and by numerous school counseling authorities. Unfortunately, however, there is scant evidence that school counselors typically engage in needs assessments for their school counseling programs. One unfortunate result is that there are few examples of needs assessment instruments in the school counseling professional literature. Perhaps one reason that needs assessments are not more common is that even the relative few that do exist do not have substantive psychometric quality (Thompson, Loesch, & Seraphine, 2003).

Development of a good needs assessment instrument does involve some focused work, but certainly it is not outside the realm of appropriate activity for a practicing school counselor, because the process itself is an accountability activity. For example, Thompson (2001) developed the Intermediate Elementary School Counseling Needs Survey (IESCNS) to assess the counseling needs of third-, fourth-, and fifth-grade elementary school students. The developmental process for the IESCNS is described in Thompson et al. (2003). In general, the items on the IESCNS were developed and clustered to represent the academic, career, and personal/social areas of student development as they are presented in the ASCA *National Standards for School Counseling Programs* (Campbell & Dahir, 1997). The IESCNS is presented in Figure 8.1.

In the IESCNS, the items are presented as student behaviors and/or self-perceptions, not as statements of explicit request for assistance with specific life conditions. The general levels of the various needs assessed for any particular student, or aggregate of students, must therefore be inferred from the results. This tactic was used because most elementary school-age students are not able to identify their needs very specifically and/or may not be willing to express them directly (Thompson, 2001). It is interesting to note that Thompson found that the three areas of needs which were to be assessed in the IESCNS were not easily differentiated, and she concluded that students who had high levels of counseling needs tended to have them in all three areas (Thompson, 2001).

Although there is no empirical support in the professional literature for this contention, we believe it likely that needs for students in middle or high schools, because of their developmental levels, can

INTERMEDIATE ELEMENTARY STUDENTS COUNSELING NEEDS SURVEY (IESCNS)

Instructions for Responding to Survey Items

Each of these statements expresses an idea that may or may not be true for you. To the right of each statement are four response choices:

SA = *strongly agree*
A = *agree*
D = *disagree*
SD = *strongly disagree*

Read each statement. **Circle** the response that describes your own feeling about the statement. You may choose not to respond to a question. Circle only one response for each item.

1.	I am smart.	SA	A	D	SD
2.	I like learning things at school.	SA	A	D	SD
3.	When I do well in school I feel proud.	SA	A	D	SD
4.	When I have good classroom behavior I learn more.	SA	A	D	SD
5.	I turn my school work in on time.	SA	A	D	SD
6.	I ask for help at school when I need it.	SA	A	D	SD
7.	I know my learning style.	SA	A	D	SD
8.	I choose to have good behavior at school.	SA	A	D	SD
9.	I learn from my mistakes.	SA	A	D	SD
10	I share what I have learned with other students.	SA	A	D	SD
11.	I study enough to earn good grades in school.	SA	A	D	SD
12.	I like to find out more about something interesting I learned in school, even if I do not need to.	SA	A	D	SD
13.	I decide what grades I want to earn at school and make a plan on how to earn those grades.	SA	A	D	SD
14.	After school, I finish my assignments and still have time to do other things I like to do.	SA	A	D	SD
15.	The things I learn at school will help me with the job I do when I grow up.	SA	A	D	SD
16.	I can find information about the jobs I might like to do when I grow up.	SA	A	D	SD
17.	I work well with other students in teams.	SA	A	D	SD
18.	I decide what I need to do and make a plan on how to do it.	SA	A	D	SD
19.	I know what I can do well.	SA	A	D	SD

continues

FIGURE 8.1 Intermediate Elementary Students Counseling Needs Survey (IESCNS).

202　The Accountable School Counselor

Intermediate Elementary Students Counseling Needs Survey (IESCNS) *(cont'd)*

20.	It is okay for others to act and think in a different way than I do.	SA	A	D	SD
21.	I understand that doing well in school will help me to do well in the job I do when I grow up.	SA	A	D	SD
22.	I like myself.	SA	A	D	SD
23.	I know how to set goals for myself.	SA	A	D	SD
24.	I like the way I look.	SA	A	D	SD
25.	I tell others how I feel.	SA	A	D	SD
26.	I act in appropriate ways, even when I get angry.	SA	A	D	SD
27.	I know the difference between good behavior and bad behavior.	SA	A	D	SD
28.	It is okay for others to have a different kind of family than I do.	SA	A	D	SD
29.	I communicate well with other students.	SA	A	D	SD
30.	I communicate well with my family.	SA	A	D	SD
31.	I know that communication involves talking, listening, and nonverbal behavior.	SA	A	D	SD
32.	I get along well with other family members.	SA	A	D	SD
33.	I can make and keep friends.	SA	A	D	SD
34.	I use a step-by-step way to solve problems.	SA	A	D	SD
35.	I think of a lot of ways to solve a problem before I choose the best solution.	SA	A	D	SD
36.	Before I solve a problem I think about what will happen.	SA	A	D	SD
37.	I can solve my problems in appropriate ways.	SA	A	D	SD
38.	I ask for help with my problems.	SA	A	D	SD
39.	I do what I think is right even if my friends say I should do something else.	SA	A	D	SD
40.	I know my telephone number and home address.	SA	A	D	SD
41.	I understand and follow the rules set by my school, my parents and the law.	SA	A	D	SD
42.	I tell others what I want and do not want.	SA	A	D	SD
43.	I know when to ask an adult for help.	SA	A	D	SD
44.	When bad things happen in my life, I know what to do to make them better.	SA	A	D	SD
45.	I know the difference between appropriate and inappropriate physical touching.	SA	A	D	SD
46.	I know the physical and emotional dangers of drug use.	SA	A	D	SD

Figure 8.1 *(continued)*.

Note. Copyright 2001 by Diane Wittmer Thompson. Reprinted with permission.

be assessed effectively through a more direct approach. That is, the items on a needs assessment for middle or high school students can be stated as behaviors or self-perceptions for which assistance is needed. For example, the basic Likert scale format (i.e., *Strongly Agree, Agree, Undecided, Disagree, Strongly Disagree*) can be used to indicate the need strength for specific areas of concern. Thus, a needs assessment for middle or high school students might start with statements such as the ones in Figure 8.2.

Johnson et al. (2006) made the important point that if you choose to develop a needs-assessment instrument for your school counseling program, remember that student needs are different from student wants. Student needs are aspects of students' functioning that can be, are being, and/or should be addressed in your school counseling program. Student wants are aspects of students' functioning with which they might like assistance but that are not appropriate for attention in your school counseling program. For example, it is appropriate for you

---

MIDDLE OR HIGH SCHOOL COUNSELING NEEDS ASSESSMENT

Please respond to each of the following items using a scale of SA = *strongly agree*, A = *agree*, U = *undecided*, D = *disagree*, SD = *strongly disagree*

I would like to have help to ...

develop better study skills	SA	A	U	D	SD
manage my time better	SA	A	U	D	SD
stay focused in a classroom	SA	A	U	D	SD
feel better about myself as a student	SA	A	U	D	SD
identify jobs that I might like	SA	A	U	D	SD
find out what I am good at	SA	A	U	D	SD
learn about different kinds of work	SA	A	U	D	SD
find a part-time job	SA	A	U	D	SD
get along better with my peers	SA	A	U	D	SD
feel better about myself	SA	A	U	D	SD
get along better with my parents	SA	A	U	D	SD
learn about students from other countries	SA	A	U	D	SD

FIGURE 8.2. Middle or high school counseling needs assessment.

to help students cope with their respective intrafamilial problems, but is not appropriate for you to try to resolve those intrafamilial problems for the students' families. Basically, the idea is to address only needs to which you can be responsive.

A wide variety of needs-assessment methods other than use of surveys or questionnaires are available to you. Some of the so-called impressionistic approaches (Royse et al., 2006) to data gathering in a program evaluation process are well-suited for needs assessment. In general, these approaches involve gathering information and/or data relevant to the program from people (including stakeholders) judged to be important sources of input for the program. Some of the impressionistic approaches also are well-suitable to program outcomes assessment (to be covered subsequently). A few of these methods are described in the following sections.

Focus Groups

A focus group is a small group of people presumed to be representative of a much larger group of people who are brought together specifically to provide their opinions about a topic. Popularized in the public media for their use in marketing research and public policy determination, focus groups also have a long history of use in educational program evaluation (Fitzpatrick et al., 2004; Gredler, 1996; Loesch, 2000). The focus-group approach to needs assessment can be an efficient, inexpensive, and (dare it be said?) sometimes even a fun way for you to collect evaluation information.

Parents, teachers, and students associated with your school are the stakeholder groups most commonly represented in focus-group activities for school counseling programs. However, it is sometimes appropriate to conduct focus groups with community members, agency representatives, or other stakeholder groups. Generally, focus group-members should be relatively unknown to one another, at least in regard to the particular topic to be discussed, so as to allow a broad representation of possible opinions. However, the persons who participate in a particular focus group should all be from the same school counseling program stakeholder group. That is, a focus group should not, for example, contain combinations of parents, teachers, or students. It also is important that the selection of the focus-group participants be unbiased. For example, it is not appropriate for you to select for a focus group only those students who have had active participation in your school counseling program activities, only parents who have had direct contact with you, or only teachers who have supported your school counseling program. To avoid biased selection, you would need to select participants through some form of randomized selection procedure, such as selecting every 40th name on a list of students in the school and then inviting either them or their parents to participate, or selecting every fifth name on a list of teachers in the school and then inviting them to participate until the group is of sufficient size.

A focus group consists of a relatively small number of homogeneous individuals who provide qualitative data during a moderated, interactive group interview.

—Popham, 1993, p. 195

An effective focus group contains between 6 and 12 participants (Fitzpatrick et al., 2004), and the typical time period for conducting a focus group is from 1 to no more than 3 hours. You should make participants aware of the time commitment when you invite them. Typically, you will initially invite participation by telephone. However, you should follow up your initial verbal invitation with a written and/or electronic invitation so that participants have a record of it.

Key informants are those persons who are informed... usually because they are involved with some sort of service with that population.

—Royse et al., 2006, p. 67

You should conduct the focus-group activity in a neutral environment that will allow participants to express their opinions honestly. For example, a focus group for teachers should not be conducted in your school's teachers' lounge, and a focus group for students should not be conducted in your office. The environment also should allow for a circular arrangement of seating, as opposed to the typical classroom configuration. You should schedule the meeting at a time convenient for the participants, most commonly right after regular school hours or in the evening. In general, you should make the meeting as convenient and as comfortable as possible for the participants.

In the context of needs assessment (or other type of evaluation) for your school counseling program, multiple focus groups should be used. That is, you should repeat the same focus-group activity with the same types of stakeholders on several occasions. A minimum of three such focus groups should be completed for your school counseling program, but more may be necessary if you are at a large school. The use of multiple groups helps increase and diversify the opinions provided. You should conduct the activities within a relatively short time frame, such as a 1- or 2-week period. A short time period is important so that all participants are responding to the same stimulus situation. Conducting focus groups with two or more different stakeholder groups, especially in a similar time frame, also is highly desirable. Comparing of the opinions from the respective stakeholder groups yields valuable information about the effectiveness of the school counseling program.

Selecting of a competent focus-group moderator or leader is crucial. The moderator must have good verbal communication and group facilitation skills, be a good listener, and be unbiased. In general, the moderator must be able to create a nonthreatening environment for the participants, facilitate the group's achievement of the purposes of the activity, and not influence the information derived from it. One effective way for you to implement a focus-group approach is to collaborate with another school counselor; a school counselor from another school can conduct focus groups at your school, and you can conduct focus groups at the other school counselor's school. If this tactic is used, it is best if you and the other school counselor work at the same school level (e.g., elementary, middle, or secondary) so that, as moderators, you both are likely to understand the activities about which opinions are being sought and the nature of the comments rendered.

An alternative might be for you to use school counseling interns from a local area counselor education program (if available). This approach has several advantages, including that the school counseling interns likely are unbiased in the situation, possibly can conduct the activities in a very short time frame, and certainly would gain a valuable professional experience by their participation.

> *The role of the leader is facilitate discussion by posing initial and periodic questions, moderating the responses of more vocal members, and encouraging responses of quieter members.*
>
> —Fitzpatrick et al., 2004, p. 352

It should go without saying that you should *not* be the moderator for focus groups for your school counseling program. The credibility of the results of using focus groups to evaluate a school counseling program is contingent upon two factors: unbiased selection of diverse but representative persons from a stakeholder group and unbiased conduct of the data-gathering procedure. If you conduct focus groups for your school counseling program, bias (or at least allegations of it) cannot possibly be avoided. In addition, it is highly unlikely that the participants in a focus group will provide open and honest opinions if they know that they are evaluating the work of the moderator.

An example of how you or a colleague might introduce a needs-assessment focus-group activity to participants is presented in Figure 8.3.

NOMINAL GROUP TECHNIQUE

An alternative needs-assessment (and other program evaluation) method for your school counseling program is the nominal group technique (NGT). The term *nominal* is in the title because the participants are a group in name only; the members of the group do not interact in the ways that are typical of small-group interaction (e.g., as they might in a focus group). In fact, in this day and age of electronic communications, the members of a nominal group may never meet face to face. The purpose of using the NGT is to provide equal opportunity for members of the group to generate ideas about a stimulus topic. It can be thought of as a structured brainstorming technique.

There are usually between 6 and 12 NGT participants for each instance of implementation of the procedure. The group participants are selected so as to be representative of a larger group. For example, three students from each of four grades in a high school might be selected to represent students in the school. The participants are told at the beginning that they are free to offer whatever ideas come to them and that

208 The Accountable School Counselor

INTRODUCTION TO A NEEDS-ASSESSMENT FOCUS GROUP

[Turn on audiotape recorder.]

Hello and Welcome! The gift of your time to help us is greatly appreciated.

My name is _____ and I am a school counselor at _____ school. I am collaborating with _____, who is the school counselor at this school, to collect input and feedback on the school counseling programs at our respective schools. I am facilitating several meetings like this at this school and s/he is facilitating several meetings like this at the school at which I work.

The purpose of this meeting is to obtain your opinions about some services that could be provided through the school counseling program at this school. It is important to understand that the school counseling program at this school is designed to provide services to *all* children in the school, not just those who may have some type of special situation. You were not selected because of anything your child has done or because of any characteristic of your child. Rather, you were invited to participate in this meeting simply because you have a child who attends this school.

In a minute or so I will be asking for your opinions about some specific activities and services that could be a part of the school counseling program at this school. However, before starting that activity, I would like to explain about the audiotape recording. I would like to make an audiotape of this meeting so that I can develop an accurate record of your comments. Please allow me to explain how I will do that. After the meeting, I will listen to the audiotape and then write down your responses to the various questions I will ask. I will do this alone; no one else will listen to the tape. I will write only your responses and I specifically will *not* write down names of those who comment. It is your opinions that are important to us, not who offered them. The various opinions presented will then be put into a summary report that will be shared with the school administration. Names of the participants at these meetings will *not* be included in the report. The audiotape will be destroyed after the report has been compiled. We hope this approach will allow you to offer honest opinions while allowing us to get helpful information in a way that it can be used best.

If anyone objects to making an audiotape of this meeting, I will turn off the tape recorder and attempt to take notes on your comments. If you do not object to making an audiotape of this meeting, please sign and date the form I will now give to each of you. Are there any questions about the audiotape recording process or how the audiotape will be used? [*Informed consent is covered in greater detail in Chapter 9.*]

continues

FIGURE 8.3. Introduction to a needs-assessment focus group.

School Counseling Program Evaluation 209

> Thank you for your cooperation. Now I will ask for your opinions about some specific activities and services that could be provided as part of the school counseling program at this school. After that, I will ask for your opinions about the school counseling program here in general, what it should do to help students and also how it can be improved to better help children.
>
> Let's start with things related to students' academic or classroom work. What kinds of services or help would you like the school counselor to provide for students in regard to their academic performance? What are your priorities among them?
>
> [*Continue discussing various school counseling program activities and services that could be provided.*]

FIGURE 8.3. (*continued*).

they are not to criticize or comment negatively about the ideas offered by others. The topical stimulus is usually presented as a question. For example, the NGT facilitator (not you!) might pose the question: What can the school counselor(s) in this school do to be helpful to the students in this school? The question is usually given to the participants in writing so that they can maintain focus on the topical stimulus. If a face-to-face meeting is conducted, a U-shaped seating arrangement is best, and you should give participants index cards or small pieces of paper to write on. A flipchart or projected computer screen should be at the end of the room to allow the participants to view the generated ideas.

The NGT proceeds through several stages. In the first stage, the participants record (in writing or electronically) as many responses as possible to the stimulus question. This is a silent activity, and no discussion or electronic communication among members is permitted; communication is limited to the NGT facilitator. In the second stage, each participant presents his or her ideas to all other participants. Duplicate items are then eliminated, and the remaining items are numbered (but not in any priority). Next, each item is explained further (verbally or electronically) by the item contributor. Discussion of the ideas presented is not permitted during this item-explanation stage. In the fourth stage, the items are open to discussion (or electronic communication), but not to debate. That is, participants may comment on the items presented and share their opinions, but they are not allowed to argue about whether the item should be on the list. In the fifth stage, each participant selects and then prioritizes from the list her or his top five items, with 1 being the highest priority. The next step is for the votes (i.e., prioritization numbers) to be recorded by the respective items on the list. Next, the sum of the votes for each item on the list is computed. At this point, (verbal or electronic) discussion, but again not debate, of the items and their respective vote totals is permitted. In the seventh and final stage of the NGT, each participant again independently identifies his or her top five items from the list, assigns a rank order to each of them, and assigns a relative importance rating (1 = *low importance* to 10 = *high importance*) for each of her or his items. The data from the NCT activity are aggregated (i.e., combined and averaged for the respective items), and the result is a prioritized and evaluated list of the programmatic needs of the participants.

Criticism may not be agreeable, but it is necessary. It fulfils the same function as pain in the human body. It calls attention to an unhealthy state of things.

—Winston Churchill

To gain a fully comprehensive perspective on the programmatic needs for a school counseling program, you should use the NGT with several different groups of stakeholders. For example, you can conduct the NGT with additional groups of students, students having particular characteristics, parents, and teachers and other school personnel. The combined result of using the NGT across stakeholder groups is a well-documented list of the programmatic needs to which the school counseling program should be responsive.

Remember that, regardless of the type of needs assessment you conduct, it may not be possible for your school counseling program and/or you to be responsive to all the needs identified. Needs assessments are invaluable in determining what *should* be done in or by a school counseling program; however, what you *should* do may not always align with what you *can* do. Therefore, if or when it becomes necessary to establish priorities among identified needs, you may find it helpful to use the NGT or another technique (such as the Delphi technique, to be discussed subsequently) to determine which identified needs will actually become programmatic goals.

After an appropriate, ordered list of needs has been developed, it is time to move on to the next phase of the CIPP process. That is, it is

School Counseling Program Evaluation   211

time to determine what you will need to address the identified needs effectively and successfully.

INPUT EVALUATIONS

In simple terms, input evaluation is a process used to determine what resources are available to do whatever is needed or desired. Here, it involves the examination of available resources for your school counseling program. Resources that are typically examined include human, environmental, and fiscal resources. Unfortunately, input evaluations are uncommon in the school counseling profession, but as an accountable school counselor, you should conduct input evaluations periodically to demonstrate that your program is being conducted effectively within the limits of the resources available and/or to identify additional needed resources. Of course, conducting an input evaluation activity is in and of itself an accountability activity.

I was provided with additional input that was radically different from the truth. I assisted in furthering that version.

—Oliver North

Most school counselors are quick to lament that they do not have sufficient resources to accomplish what they want to accomplish in their respective school counseling programs. But can that condition be demonstrated through evidence?

Any input evaluation procedure you use should focus on the identified needs for your school counseling program. The needs–resources linkage is part of what makes the CIPP model integrated, as opposed to a series of separate steps. It is inappropriate for you to evaluate available resources, simply in regard to what you (or others) think you would like to be doing; input evaluation should focus on programmatic needs that are to be fulfilled. For example, your needs assessment may show that there is need for individual or small-group counseling, large-group guidance, and/or peer facilitation or mediation program activities for students in a school. Obviously, somebody has to be able to provide those services effectively, but not all school counselors are good at everything. Therefore, assessment of your competencies, and perhaps assessment of the competence of the school counselors with whom you work, is needed to determine the relationship between the needs and the competencies of the human resources that are available. The inability of the available school counselors or you to perform all the needed services effectively might demonstrate a need for more or different human resources with different competencies.

Are school counselor-to-student ratios too large? Maybe. The professional school counseling literature certainly suggests that the average ratio is too large, with the computed ratio being the numbers of school counselors divided by the total numbers of students across schools in the United States. However, evidence is needed to back up that contention. For example, not all students in a school routinely receive school counseling services and/or participate in school counseling program activities. Therefore, the number of different students who actually receive substantive school counseling services (as opposed to causal interactions) within a particular time period (e.g., an academic year) can be determined by careful record-keeping of which students are involved in which activities. The *ASCA National Model* recommends that you maintain a school counseling calendar as a means of documenting your school counseling activities, which a good resource upon which to record the numbers of students you interact with each day. Then, if you know the number of different students for whom you provided professional services during an academic year, you know your school counselor-to-student ratio (i.e., one-to-number of different students). Such information may be helpful in supporting the need for additional human resources. However, be careful in how you use a calculated student-to-school counselor ratio. For one thing, your work with teachers, parents, community members, or others are not reflected in that ratio. In addition, that ratio does not reflect how much time you spend with each student. Thus, that ratio is *not* a very accurate indicator of what you actually do.

As the number of students who receive relatively substantive school counseling services is determined, so can the information be related to environmental and fiscal data. For example, the square footage of your office and other space over which you have direct control can be readily computed. Dividing that square footage by the number of students who are served gives a ratio that can be compared to other ratios, such as the average ratio of teacher-to-classroom square footage. Those data *might* be evidential support for the need for more or different space for your school counseling program. Similarly, you could compute your school counseling department's per-student budget expenditure. Dividing your total school counseling program monetary allocation by the number of students who are served will give you a per-student expenditure figure. That per-student expenditure figure can be compared to the average per-student allocation for classrooms instruction and might serve as the basis for a requested increase in your school counseling program budget. However, be careful about both the numbers you generate and how you use them. You may find that your resources are much better than you think, and subject to reduction.

Restoring responsibility and accountability is essential to the economic and fiscal health of our nation.

—U.S. Senator Carl Levin

Evaluation of resources is important because the limitations of available resources in effect establish the boundaries for your school counseling program. Basically, you can only do as much as your resources will allow. However, even if your resources are minimal, it is crucial to determine if you are using those resources as effectively as possible. And, in particular, it is important to determine if you are using resources effectively while they are being expended. In other words, you want to be able to alter how you are using your resources while you are implementing your school counseling program if you find that you are not using your resources as effectively and efficiently as possible. The idea of reviewing what you're doing while you're doing it leads directly in to the next component of the CIPP model.

PROCESS EVALUATION

The term *process evaluation*, commonly known as "formative evaluation," involves evaluating a program as it is occurring (Stufflebeam et al., 1971). The goal of process evaluation is to determine if a program process that is currently being conducted should continue as it is being conducted or be changed (presumably for the better). Process evaluations also are conducted relatively infrequently in school counseling programs. We wonder why? Perhaps because many school counselors misinterpret the focus of process evaluation. That is, many school counselors believe that their various school counseling program activities are of such short duration that it is not feasible to collect information and also modify their activities as they are doing them. But individual activities are not the focus of process evaluation; it is a *program* evaluation process. Therefore, although process evaluation can be applied to the relatively few specific school counseling activities that last a relatively long time, more appropriately it should be applied to broad-scale cluster activities within the school counseling program. For example, at a minimum, you should conduct process evaluations of your collective academic, career, and personal/social development activities for students. In addition, process evaluation is appropriate for other large-scale, continuing activities in your school counseling program, such as a peer facilitation or mediation program or a teacher-as-advisor (TAP) program. The obvious implication is that process evaluations are most appropriate for relatively long-term (e.g., semester or academic year), ongoing school counseling programmatic activities.

There are no evaluation procedures specific to process evaluation. Royse et al. (2006) wrote that

> formative evaluation does not rely on a specific methodology or set of procedures. Instead, its focus is on acquiring information that would be useful for program improvement—whatever that would be. This information may come from interviewing staff or clients, reviewing records and progress notes, or participant observation. One could expect formative evaluators to look for glitches, breakdowns, lengthy delays, and departures from program design. They may find such problems as communication difficulties among staff, communication difficulties between administration and staff, poor client participation in a program, or a need for additional inservice training to standardize what is provided as intervention.
>
> There is no single recipe for formative evaluation. (p. 117)

Basically, the idea underlying formative evaluation is to find out what is working and/or what is not working as your school counseling program activities are being implemented. One implication in process evaluation is that you must gather data and make decisions relatively quickly. Therefore, process evaluation procedures should be developed before you begin the program activity so that they are ready to be used when appropriate. In addition, although process evaluation activities usually are conducted according to a preplanned schedule, they are sometimes developed as the need for them becomes evident. However, the use of process evaluations on a scheduled basis is recommended and is by far the most common approach.

Many of the data-gathering methods already presented can be used for process evaluation purposes. For example, stakeholders can be queried through the use of surveys or questionnaires. However, more commonly, process evaluation methods are more personalized, and include methods such as semistructured interviews, focus groups, or large-group discussion forums. You likely will find the latter particularly suitable for obtaining process evaluation information quickly and efficiently. However, you should be careful not to allow a few outspoken individuals to dominate the feedback given.

Objectivity (or lack of it) is a major consideration in process evaluation as it is in any other evaluation activity. However, because you are likely the person who is implementing the school counseling program activities that are being subjected to process evaluation, it is not a good idea for you also to be the person doing process evaluations. Process evaluation has much greater credibility if someone other than the process implementer conducts the evaluation. We advise you to have a colleague conduct any process evaluation for your activities; however, this does not mean that you should be entirely separated from the process. For example, certainly you should provide the process evaluator with information about the goals and objectives you are trying to accomplish and about the resources available to accomplish those goals and objectives (again, note the integration of components of the CIPP model). In addition, you should provide input to the evaluator about which aspects of the process you want evaluated as well as encourage the evaluator to take note of influencing factors that you may not have identified.

Process evaluation procedures can be extremely helpful to improve both the effectiveness and efficiency of your activities, and therefore we encourage you to conduct process evaluations for your school counseling program. We caution that you should have an objective viewpoint when you receive the results of process evaluations, however, because you might not like the results! But that's not really the point, is it? Whether you like the results is irrelevant. What matters is that you use the results to improve what goes on in your school counseling program.

> *The fact that a study examines program outcomes, or effects, however, tells us nothing about whether the study serves formative or summative purposes. The formative and summative distinction comes first, then, to help focus our attention on the judgment to be made or the action to be taken.*
>
> —Fitzpatrick et al., 2004, p. 22

After you have determined what you are trying to do (needs assessment), what resources you have to do it (input evaluation), and whether what you are doing is working (process evaluation), all that remains is to determine what actually happened as result. Specifically, you need to know the overall major outcomes of your school counseling activities.

PRODUCT EVALUATION

In the CIPP model, *product* is used as a synonym for *outcomes*. In general, this means an evaluation of the extent to which all the major program emphases within your school counseling program are fulfilling the needs (as related to goals) the program was intended to address. However, good outcome evaluation gives more complete information than just the extent to which programmatic goals were met. As Gredler (1996) wrote, "The [product] evaluation should document both intended and unintended effects and negative as well as positive outcomes" (p. 48). Thus, good outcome measurement yields data on what worked as well as what didn't work.

In product evaluation procedures, as in process evaluation procedures, it is important to have a clear understanding of what is being evaluated, which should lead to a clear understanding of the appropriate types of outcome data. For example, Unrau et al. (2001) wrote that

> outcomes are sometimes confused with outputs. Outputs are completed products or amounts of work done resulting from internal program activities. For example, number of clients served, the total hours of counseling services provided, and the number of crisis calls received. The pressure to collect program

School Counseling Program Evaluation   217

> outputs typically comes from program funders. While *outputs* focus on the results of program operations, *outcomes* focus on the results of client change.
>
> The distinction between outputs and outcomes is important to understand because high outputs are not always associated with positive outcomes, and *vice versa*. (p. 75)

In this context, we believe that, historically, school counselors have focused far too much on outputs in their program evaluation activities. For example, the school counseling literature emphasizes that a school counselor should have a good calendar. The *ASCA National Model* includes that "school counselors develop and publish a master calendar of school counseling events to ensure students, parents or guardians, teachers and administrators know what and when school counseling activities are scheduled and when and where activities will be held" (ASCA, 2005, p. 57). Assuming that all the events on your school counseling program calendar are conducted as scheduled, counts of the various activities conducted are simply outputs data, because they do not represent the impacts (i.e., outcome data or behavioral results) of those events. Similarly, Standard 7, "School Counselor Performance Standards," of the *ASCA National Model* requires the following:

> The professional school counselor is responsible for establishing and convening an advisory council for the school counseling program.
>
> 7.1   The professional school counselor meets with the advisory council.
>
> 7.2   The professional school counselor reviews the school counseling program audit with the council.
>
> 7.3   The professional school counselor records meeting information. (p. 64)

Presumably, if you meet with your advisory council one time, share with them any program information or data you have, and take any kind of notes on the session, you have fulfilled this performance standard. Further, you can count the meeting as a type of outputs accountability data. But wouldn't it be better (and far more impressive) to be able to describe what school counseling program changes resulted from the meeting? Figure 8.4 is presented to help you identify the outputs

STAKEHOLDERS, OUTPUTS, AND OUTCOMES

For each of the major stakeholder groups listed in the left-hand column, identify two types of outputs data and two types of outcomes data that you think would be of particular interest to the respective stakeholder groups.

Stakeholder Group	Outputs Data	Outcomes Data
Parents & Families	Reports of time spent counseling students	Number of students whose grades improved
	Number of students who completed college applications	Number of students accepted at colleges
School Administrators	Calendar of activities	Number of children whose grades improved
	Number of teacher consultations	Number of teachers who behave differently
Teachers	Calendar of activities	Identified students less disruptive in class
	Number of students counseled	Number of students with increased attendance
School Board Members	Calendar of activities	Number of students awarded scholarships
	Number of programmatic activities	Number of students in service learning activities
Other School Personnel	Number of consultations	Changes in students' test scores
	Number of students counseled	Decreases in discipline referrals
Students	Number of programmatic activities	Numbers of students involved in prog. activities
	List of career guidance materials available	Number of students getting part-time jobs
Community Members	Number of programmatic activities	Changes in students' test scores
	Calendar of activities	Number of students in service learning activities
School Counseling Professionals	Calendar of activities	Journal article
	Number of conferences attended	New counseling program offerings
Self	Calendar of activities	List of accomplishments with students
	Number of conferences attended	List of new knowledge and skills

FIGURE 8.4. Stakeholders, outputs, and outcomes.

and outcomes you think would be important to your various stakeholder groups.

Please do not misinterpret our message. We *do* believe that program outputs should be determined and presented as part of a product evaluation procedure for your school counseling program, and we encourage you to gather such data. However, we also believe that outputs data are a weak type of data for your accountability purposes. In our opinion, what matters most is what happened (i.e., how did people behave differently) as a result of your school counseling activities; that is, the outcomes of your activities are most important.

It is worth noting that good outcome evaluation is a relatively objective process in that it is focused on program results. Further, the results of good outcome evaluation procedures can become suspect when too much subjectivity is allowed to enter into the process. Outcome evaluation data reflect what happened, not why the results were the way they were. Conjectures about why certain results were found are highly subjective and are not intended to be a part of good outcome evaluation.

There are two possible outcomes: if the result confirms the hypothesis, then you've made a measurement. If the result is contrary to the hypothesis, then you've made a discovery.

—Enrico Fermi

A wide variety of data-gathering techniques can be used for (product) outcomes evaluation procedures, including most of the ones already presented in this book. Remember, however, that product evaluation is a part of program evaluation, and therefore is focused upon the broad, large-scale clusters of your school counseling activities. In general, there are two ways to generate product evaluation data. One is to go after it directly. For example, you could use the NGT to get information about the results of your individual or small-group counseling activities, or you could survey teachers about the general outcomes of your teacher consultation activities. Another way is to compile results from your individual activities. For example, if you used a single-subject data gathering procedure to change the same behavior for different students on different occasions, you could combine the results into a composite presentation. Similarly, you could combine the results of all your teacher consultation activities into a composite report. Most likely, you will use both generalized and compiled methods to generate an effective product evaluation report.

Helpful information about school counseling program evaluation is available from so-called traditional sources, such as books and professional journals, and nontraditional sources, such as the Internet. For example, the National Center for School Counseling Outcome Research (http://www.umass.edu/schoolcounseling/) has a free Listserv that you can and should join. This center provides summary reports, resources (e.g., the School Counselor Activity Rating Scale), and training opportunities. Other Internet sources provide guidelines for programmatic evaluation. Take advantage of these resources and be on the lookout for others as they become available.

CONCLUSION

Hopefully, it is obvious that there are many, many different ways to generate program evaluation data and information and that the methods presented throughout this book can be applied successfully in many different contexts. Indeed, the methods of generating accountability data are limited only by your imagination and creativity in applying them. With practice, your expertise in generating program evaluation data will develop rapidly. Being accountable becomes easier as it becomes a part of your normal functioning.

FOR THOUGHT AND DEED

1. Draw a schematic (i.e., picture with dimensions and objects) of what would be your perfect school counseling program work area in your school. What would be the major physical space areas (e.g., as office, small-group counseling, resource areas) in your program area and how much space would be allocated to each major area? What would be the essential equipment and other physical resources you would have in this school counseling area?

2. An easy way to conduct a needs assessment is to develop a checklist of matters or concerns for which you might be of assistance, and then have group respondents check off those concerns for which they would like as-

sistance. For example, to conduct a needs assessment of the teachers in your school, you might start with the instruction to "Put a check mark next to each item on the list that we might work together on to attempt to resolve the situation." The items on the list would be concerns, issues, problems, or difficulties faced by teachers (e.g., items such as "a student who is habitually late to class" or "a parent who does not respond to my phone calls"). Create a list of items that might be on this checklist (i.e., develop a teachers' needs assessment checklist). Remember that the more specific and behavioral the items, the easier it will be to provide assistance.

3. Assume you want to use focus groups to obtain evaluative information about your school counseling activities related to fostering students' career development. Further assume that you want to have three groups each for students, parents, and community members. Describe how you would go about selecting the participants for each of these stakeholder groups. What would be the discussion-starting question you would ask of the groups?

4. The *ASCA National Model* booklet contains a "Program Audit Form" (ASCA, 2005, pp. 131–141) for investigation of the extent to which a school counseling program reflects the components and elements of the *ASCA National Model*. Complete that form as the items apply to your school counseling program. What are the major strengths of your school counseling program? What areas of your school counseling program need more attention?

CHAPTER 9

Implementing an
Accountability Plan

Before we can discuss what is involved in starting and then conduct-ing your accountability activities, there is one topic that needs atten-tion: informed consent. We know that informed consent is a topic and set of procedures that most school counselors would like to avoid, and whether you as a school counselor use informed consent procedures depends on your particular situation. We can't make the decision for you, but we would be remiss in our professionalism if we did not offer some comments and guidance.

About Informed Consent

The requirements for informed consent participation in a research ac-tivity trace to The National Research Act of 1974 and the Family Edu-cational Rights and Privacy Act of 1974 (also known as the Buckley Amendment). These federal legislative acts reflect four primary human rights principles, including that individuals participating in a research project must be (a) made fully aware (i.e., have understanding) of the nature of the activities in which they are being asked to participate, (b) made fully aware of how the information obtained from or about them will be used, (c) guaranteed that participation is completely voluntary and that cessation of participation will not have negative consequences, and (d) given written explanation of the nature of the participation re-quested and their legal rights in regard to participation. There, general requirements are delineated as a set of specific elements that must be included in any informed consent form. Note that in the case of minors (i.e., generally, students under the age of 18), the authority to allow par-ticipation falls to their parents or legal guardians.

223

Since 1974, additional federal legislation (e.g., the Hatch and Grassley Amendments) and numerous judicial decisions have clarified the requirements for informed consent. However, even today there remain many misunderstandings about what is and is not required for informed consent participation. Our best advice to you is to consult with an appropriate school-district-level professional who can inform you about informed consent procedures in general, policies specific to your school district, and resources for understanding informed consent procedures.

At issue is whether your accountability activities constitute research as interpreted within the context of the Federal guidelines for informed consent. In general, if you are conducting your accountability activities as part of your normal and regular contractual responsibilities, it is not likely that you will need to use formal informed consent procedures. However, if you are conducting an accountability activity for a purpose that is not part of your normal and regular contractual responsibilities (e.g., if you are doing the activity to generate data for a journal article you plan to publish), then you will need to use formal informed consent procedures. Again, *we urge you to consult with an appropriate school-district-level professional who can inform you about informed consent procedures in general, policies specific to your school district, and resources for understanding informed consent procedures before you begin an accountability activity.*

Note that there is not a standard informed consent form; there is no government office that distributes it, no library in which the document can be found, and no Web site from which it can be downloaded. Informed consent forms are created for each specific activity for which participation is desired, *and they must be activity specific.* You cannot legally or ethically create a general or blanket informed consent form to be used for all of your accountability activities. In the majority of cases, the informed consent form is presented in the form of a letter. However, any form of written communication that contains the essential information is permitted.

Organizational, agency, or institutional review boards or committees that are responsible for implementing informed consent procedures frequently recommend, and in some cases require, using assent forms for activities involving students of secondary school age (i.e., teenagers in general; Jacob & Hartshorne, 2006). An assent form is essentially an informed consent form given directly to the participant. Use of an assent form is based on the idea that, while only parents or legal guardians have the legal right to determine whether their child participates in an accountability activity, secondary school–age children are often mature enough to have a say about whether they participate. Thus, use of an assent form allows students to decline to participate, even though their parents may have given permission for them to participate. The idea is that no one should coerce a student into participating in an activity because the student's parents or guardians have given permission. In most cases, an assent form is the same as the corresponding informed consent form, except that it is addressed to the student instead of to the student's parents or guardians. Examples of informed consent forms are provided in Figures 9.1 and 9.2. Note that in these examples, italics have been used to indicate where a choice of word (such as a male or female pronoun) is necessary.

ADOPT A POSITIVE SELF-PERCEPTION ABOUT BEING ACCOUNTABLE

Being accountable for your professional activities isn't easy for any school counselor, but it is easier for some than for others. What's the difference between those for whom being accountable is relatively easy and those for whom it is not? Are those school counselors who find it relatively easy to be accountable more intelligent, better skilled, better educated, or more dedicated? Do they have more supportive administrators, brighter students, more resources, better facilities, or more professional ambition? Probably not. More likely, the answer lies in the differences in their perspectives about themselves and their work. If indeed perception is reality, then having an appropriate perspective is essential to being accountable. But how can school counselors achieve an appropriate and functionally effective perspective on being accountable? Of course, there is no simple way to recommend how to achieve the right perspective, no magic pills or bullets. However, there are things that school counselors can do to improve their perspective. First among these is to adopt a positive perspective!

Character consists of what you do on the third and fourth tries.

—James A. Michner

226   The Accountable School Counselor

INFORMED CONSENT FORM FOR AN INDIVIDUAL COUNSELING RESEARCH ACTIVITY

Date

[school name]

[school mailing address]

Dear Parent or Guardian,

I talk and work with children individually as a part of the school counseling and guidance services I routinely provide in our school. It is helpful to gather information that allows me to evaluate the effectiveness of my activities and to share the results of the evaluation with others. Therefore, I am writing to request your permission to gather information from your child.

I plan to talk with your child for approximately one-half hour per week for each of the next 6 weeks. The purpose of our talks will be to help your child understand *his/ her* feelings, with the intention that such understanding will eventually help *him/her* improve *his/her* academic performance in our school. Your child may experience some very mild discomfort in talking about some things, but your child will not be pressured in any way to disclose anything that *he/she* does not want to disclose. I will arrange to hold the meetings at times that will not interfere with your child's academic work. I will ask your child to complete a questionnaire that questions how *he/she* feels about *him/herself* before I first talk with your child and again after I have completed talking with *him/her*. After we have finished our talks, I also will ask your child to respond to seven questions that will allow your child to indicate whether *he/she* found it helpful to talk with me. Your child does not have to respond to any question that *he/she* does not want to answer. I would be happy to provide a copy of these questionnaires for your review if you would like to see them.

I plan to work with and gather information from at least nine other students in our school in the same way. When I obtain information from a minimum of 10 students, I will develop a manuscript I plan to submit to a journal for professional school counselors. Your child will be kept anonymous in this manuscript, and your child's identity will be kept confidential to the extent provided by law. Your child's information will be identified by a code number, and only I will know the code number assigned to your child.

You and your child have the right to withdraw consent for your child's participation at any time without consequence. There are no known risks or immediate benefits for participation. No compensation is offered for participation. Group results of this activity should be available in *[month/year]* upon request. If you have any questions about this activity, please contact me at *[address and telephone number(s)]*. Questions or concerns about your child's rights in regard to participation in this activity may be directed to *[name, address, and telephone number(s) of the school-system person responsible for informed consent procedures]*.

continues

FIGURE 9.1. Informed consent form for an individual counseling research activity.

> Please sign and return this copy of this letter in the enclosed envelope. A second copy is provided for your records.
>
> Thank you for your assistance.
>
> Sincerely,
>
>
> *Ima Kounzlar*
>
>
> I have read the procedure described above. I voluntarily give my consent for my child, [_____*child's name*_____], to participate in *Ima Kounzlar's* study of the effectiveness of individual counseling to help children understand their feelings about themselves. I have received a copy of this description.
>
>
> _____   _____
>
> Parent/guardian   Date
>
>
> _____   _____
>
> 2nd parent/guardian or witness   Date

FIGURE 9.1. (*continued*).

Some school counselors commonly use many different excuses to avoid accountability activities, such as "I have too many other things to do," "Nobody cares about the results anyway," "There's no way they can fire me," and the ever popular, "Children are more important than data." But often these excuses are merely behavioral manifestations of more complex underlying dynamics centered on self-perception. That is, many school counselors simply feel incompetent about their ability to be accountable. They "never understood statistics," "don't remember all that testing stuff," and "had a bad professor for their research course." The conditions reflected in comments such as these all may be true; however, they are indicators of condition, not of competence. Figure 9.3 allows you to identify how you might have changed as a professional since becoming a school counselor.

You have probably noticed that we have neither discussed nor recommended the use of particular research designs or statistical analyses. That was not an oversight or omission on our part. Rather, we did not include those topics because research and evaluation are not the

228　The Accountable School Counselor

Informed Consent Form for a General Research Activity

Date

[school name]

[school mailing address]

Dear Parent or Guardian,

I sometimes conduct professional research studies in conjunction with the counseling and guidance services I routinely provide to children in our school. It is helpful to me to gather information from students in our school for these research activities. Therefore, I am requesting your permission to gather information from and about your child.

During this academic semester, I will be conducting a series of activities intended to help children perform better on standardized tests. The activities planned include large- and small-group interactions, classroom presentations and discussions, test preparation homework exercises, and the distribution of a handbook containing suggestions and ideas for how to take tests effectively. To show whether the activities were effective and successful, it is necessary for me compare each student's scores (i.e., percentile rankings) for all sections of the statewide comprehensive assessment test from last year with those achieved this year. In addition, I wish to examine whether the activities generalize to positively impact performance on regular class room work. This will involve comparing each student's grade point average from the preceding 9-week grading period with that achieved for the next 9-week grading period. I plan to gather these types of data from as many of the students in your child's grade level as possible. Therefore, my specific request is for permission to use your child's statewide test percentile rankings from last year and this year and your child's grade-point-average data from the previous and next 9-week grading period for my research.

When I obtain sufficient information, I will develop a manuscript to be submitted to a professional journal for publication. Your child will be kept anonymous in this manuscript, and your child's identity will be kept confidential to the extent provided by law. Your child's information will be identified by a code number to match former and current test and academic performance data, and only I will know the code number assigned to your child. Only group data will be included in the developed manuscript.

You and your child have the right to withdraw consent for your child's participation at any time without consequence. There are no known risks or immediate benefits for participation. No compensation is offered for participation. Group results of this activity should be available in [month/year] upon request. If you have any questions about this activity, please contact me at [address and telephone number(s)]. Questions or concerns about your child's rights in regard to participation in this activity may be directed to [name, address, and telephone number(s) of the school-system person responsible for informed consent procedures].

continues

FIGURE 9.2. Informed consent form for a general research activity.

> Please sign and return this copy of this letter in the enclosed envelope. A second copy is provided for your records.
> Thank you for your assistance.
>
> Sincerely,
>
> *Ima Kounzlar*
>
> I have read the procedure described above. I voluntarily give my consent for my child, [_____*child's name*_____], to participate in *Ima Kounzlar's* study of the effectiveness of a set of activities intended to help children improve their scores on standardized tests and in the classroom. I have received a copy of this description.
>
> | | |
> |---|---|
> | _____ | _____ |
> | Parent/guardian | Date |
> | _____ | _____ |
> | 2nd parent/guardian or witness | Date |

FIGURE 9.2. *(continued)*.

same thing and are not interchangeable processes. The difference between them is in regard to purpose. McGannon et al. (2005) made the difference clear when they wrote that

> the primary purpose of research is to add knowledge to a field and to contribute to the growth of theory. The primary purpose of evaluation is to help stakeholders make judgments or decisions. Research is intended for knowledge and evaluation is intended for use. (p. 6)

It is fine, and indeed admirable, for a school counselor to do research. However, our interest here is in promoting evaluation, for specific school counseling program activities or for the entire program. Therefore, don't think that you have to do a research study to be accountable or to evaluate your school counseling program. Rather, think that all you have to do is an evaluation project to generate evidence of what happens as a result of your activities. That type of project should seem easier to undertake—because it is.

230 The Accountable School Counselor

THE NEW ME?

Take some time to think about who and what you were professionally before you became a school counselor. What did you know the most about, what did you do best, and what did you want to achieve professionally? Now think about who and what you are as professional right now. How have you changed? List three things that are different for and/or about you since you became a school counselor.

1. Better relationship and interpersonal skills _____

2. Greater confidence in my ability to help others effectively _____

3. Significantly more knowledge of things that actually are helpful students _____

FIGURE 9.3. "The New Me?"

To be an appropriately credentialed school counseling practitioner, you must have successfully completed a graduate-level master's-degree academic program. Did you know that by virtue of having a master's degree you are in at least the upper 8% of the educational attainment hierarchy in the United States? (For current, interesting, information on the proportions of persons achieving various academic degree levels in the United States, search by "educational attainment" or "Digest of Education Statistics" at www.nces.ed.gov). Most school counselor preparation programs now require a minimum of 48 semester, program-relevant credit hours to receive a master's degree in school counseling. Therefore, one result of your level of educational preparation as a school counselor is that you are among the most educated people in school systems. People who achieve a master's degree in school counseling are neither stupid nor incompetent; those degrees are hard to come by. Achievement of a master's degree is indication of you having demonstrated acquisition of a wide variety of important and useful cognitive, academic, behavioral, professional, and even interpersonal and social skills. Most importantly, by virtue of being a school counselor, you have demonstrated the ability to learn and to change your own behavior in needed ways. Thus, any school counselor is competent to be effective in accountability activities, and that includes you! You may have to learn or relearn a few things and/or change a few behaviors to be successful in accountability activities, but competence is not an issue. You might have to sharpen some skills a bit, but you do have, like any school counselor has, the competence to be accountable.

RESIST BEING RESISTANT TO BEING ACCOUNTABLE

Changing, such as becoming accountable to your stakeholders, is not always easy. Sometimes, change is scary because it means venturing into the unknown. By definition, the unknown may be positive or negative, and so there is risk involved. Thus, many people, including many school counselors, resist change because it is simply easier, and likely safer, to keep doing what has been done in the past. But if you seek the easy path through life, you have chosen the wrong vocation—school counseling is hard work! The professional life of a school counselor is fraught with changes, some of which are foreseen and many of which are not. And as for safety, the long-term repercussions of staying immersed in a comfort zone for the present are almost always negative. Therefore, as Isaacs (2003) wrote, "It is worth reminding school counselors that they need to recognize and challenge their own resistance to change in preparing to engage in more accountable practices" (p. 291). Isn't it ironic that you as a school counselor spend much of your professional time and effort trying to get others (e.g., students, teachers, administrators, parents) to change, but how much time do you spend working on your own change? It is now time to take charge of your professional life and to direct and conduct your life so that the changes are positive.

EMBRACE CHANGE

Obviously, change can be for better or worse. However, in the majority of cases, positive change results from intentional action. That is, while people are sometimes just plain lucky, more often good things happen to people because they do things to make things happen in ways that will be beneficial to them. Therefore, the way to make an accountability activity a positive experience is to decide that it is going to be positive and behave in ways that will make it positive. After all, even if the results of an accountability activity aren't quite as positive as had been hoped, there is still both professional and personal benefit, merely from having carried out the activity!

Fear is your greatest obstacle—so question your fear. If it does not serve your greatest life then do not make it your master.

—Joy Page

While adopting a positive (can-do) attitude is the first and most important step toward being accountable, there are many other steps that facilitate achievement of success in the activity. However, before some of those steps are discussed, there is another important topic that needs attention.

DEVELOP AN ACTION PLAN

Assuming you choose to be accountable for your professional school counseling activities, the first question you must confront is, for which of your professional activities or functions do you want to be accountable? Most school counselors do several things very well, but none do everything well. However, it is impossible and unrealistic for you to be accountable for your many professional functions simultaneously. Indeed, such behavior likely would diminish the effectiveness of all of your professional activities. Therefore, the best results are achieved when the focus of the accountability activities remains clear and unencumbered. This means that you should engage in various accountability procedures sequentially, not simultaneously. But the question remains, where to begin?

To maximize the likelihood of success for the accountability activity, you should begin by conducting an accountability activity related to whichever professional function you perform best. Start from a position of strength. Obviously, determining which professional function you perform best requires some self-evaluation. Therefore, we created a school counselor self-evaluation form to facilitate this process (see Figure 9.4). It was created to reflect 15 professional functions in which school counselors commonly engage. In completing the form,

SCHOOL COUNSELOR SELF-EVALUATION FORM

Use a scale of 1 = *low* to 10 = *high* to rate your current level of functioning for each of the following school counselor roles and functions. Then provide a brief description of the evidence to support your self-rating.

Self-Ratings:		Evidence:
9	Classroom guidance	*Teachers frequently invite me to do classroom guidance in their classes*
8	Small-group counseling	*Teachers report change in students who participated in the groups I conducted*
8	Appraisal/testing	*Principal requested my service as coordinator of the state testing program in our school*
7	Advisement	*Student registration for classes was conducted in a shorter time*
9	Consultation with teachers	*Several teachers recommended to other teachers that they talk with me*
10	Consultation with parents	*Fifty-percent increase in parents wanting to meet and/or talk with me*
8	Individual counseling	*Academic performance of the students with whom I met increased for 80% of them*
9	Crisis counseling	*Students reported that I was helpful during their time of need for emotional help*
9	Referrals	*Students whose families were assisted are doing better academically*
10	Peer-facilitation activities	*Students are running the peer mediation program almost by themselves*
5	Professional development	*I only attended one conference this year*
8	Staff relations	*My guidance secretary completed a county-wide in-service on working in a school counseling program*
5	Community relations	*Spoke at meetings of several community groups and received positive feedback*
	Program management	
	Conducting in-service	

FIGURE 9.4. School counselor self-evaluation form.

respond within the context of a recent time period, such as the last 6 months or the preceding school year. Establishing a time frame context for the self-ratings helps you to keep your current activities in proper perspective.

To complete the form, first provide the numeric ratings on the left column of the page. Try to be as realistic as possible in the self-ratings. After the numeric self-ratings, complete the entries for the "Evidence" column on the right side of the page. Here, too, try to be as realistic as possible. Unless an accountability activity for one or more of the functions listed has been completed, it is likely that the evidence listed at this point will be relatively subjective. For example, evidence such as "student W *seemed* happier after individual counseling," "the class *applauded* after the classroom guidance unit," "teacher M voiced appreciation for my work with student K," "student H *appeared* to get along better with other students after small-group counseling," or "teacher P *appreciated* the advice about how to work with student G's parents" might be provided. The purpose of providing the evidence is to get a sense of support for the self-ratings given for each of the functions. That is, like most school counselors, you know intuitively what you do well and what you don't do so well; you feel when you have been successful in an activity and when you have not. Writing those feelings brings the evidence into consciousness, which should facilitate making reasonably accurate self-ratings.

After you have completed your self-ratings in Figure 9.4, use Figure 9.5 to rank order the various functions from the one you do best to the one you do least well. Assign a rank of 1 to the school counseling function you do best and a rank of 15 to the one that you do least well. During your first attempt at making these rankings, you will likely find ties (i.e., the same self-ratings) for some of the functions because, again, you do several things very well. However, for this purpose, differentiation should be forced; each function should have a separate ranking from 1 to 15.

Next, identify and think about the activity with the highest ranking (i.e., the activity with your rank of 1). This is the type of activity that you should select for your first accountability project. Your accountability activity is most likely to be successful if it is focused on an activity that you believe you do well. Your subsequent accountability activities should follow in the rank order developed (at least until the rank order changes) to increase the likelihood of success and feelings of competence in your various accountability activities.

BEST-TO-LEAST-BEST SCHOOL COUNSELING ACTIVITIES

Assign a rank of 1 to the school counseling activity you do best, a rank of 2 to the school counseling you do next best, and so forth for all the activities listed following. No ties allowed!

_____ Classroom guidance
_____ Small-Group counseling
_____ Appraisal/testing
_____ Advisement
_____ Consultation with teachers
_____ Consultation with parents
_____ Individual counseling
_____ Crisis counseling
_____ Referrals
_____ Peer-facilitation activities
_____ Professional development
_____ Staff relations
_____ Community relations
_____ Program management
_____ Conducting in-service

FIGURE 9.5. Best-to-least-best school counseling activities.

FOCUS ON A SPECIFIC PURPOSE

Having identified a type of activity that is likely to yield positive and meaningful results, the next step is to determine a specific activity to be conducted and evaluated. Completing the following sentence (as a purpose statement) may be helpful:

The purpose of this activity is to determine the effectiveness of

_____ (*specify a particular activity*) by

_____ (*specify a particular method of assessment*).

A time frame also should be included in the purpose statement. For example, if you evaluate a classroom guidance unit to help children learn effective ways to cope with bullying behavior, the purpose statement might be written as follows:

> The purpose of the this activity is to determine the effectiveness of *a classroom guidance unit on responding to bullying behaviors* [specific activity] *by having each student in the class list three behaviors* [specific method of assessment], *at the end of the unit* [time frame] *that can be used to respond to bullying behaviors.*

Similarly, if the purpose of an activity you use is to help a parent spend more time helping his or her child with homework, the purpose statement might be written as follows:

> The purpose of this activity is to determine the effectiveness of *individual parent consultation to increase a parent's time spent helping a child with homework* [specific activity] *by having the child report the average daily amount of time the parent spends helping with homework during 1 week before and the 6th week after the parent consultation* [time frame and specific method of assessment].

And as a final example, if the purpose of an activity is to relate a professional development activity to your school counseling practice, the purpose statement might be written as follows:

> The purpose of this activity is to determine the effectiveness of *test performance enhancement activities for teachers learned at a professional conference and presented to teachers at the last school in-service workshop* [specific activity] *by asking teachers to self-report how many of the activities they have used in the 6 weeks following the inservice workshop* [time frame and specific method of assessment].

Notice that in each case, the purpose statement indicates the specific activity to be evaluated, the nature of the data that will be obtained, and a time frame. Thus, writing a purpose statement is a good way to capture the essence of what will be done and to clarify what will be involved.

DETERMINE NEEDED RESOURCES

Almost all accountability activities require human, physical, and material resources. For example, if a classroom guidance unit is to be implemented, both a cooperative teacher and a classroom are necessary. Similarly, if a test, survey, or questionnaire is to be administered, they have to be obtained or created. Therefore, after you have determined the nature of the activity to be evaluated and written the purpose statement, the helpful next step is to specify the resources available or needed. Figure 9.6 should help you in this regard.

ACCOUNTABILITY PROJECT NEEDED RESOURCES

Think about an accountability project you would like to conduct. What will you need to complete the project successfully? What is the availability of the resources you will need? Complete the following for the human, physical, and material resources you will need to be successful in your project.

	Available	Needed	If needed, how and when obtained?
Human resources:			
Cooperative teachers	✓		
Statistics consultant	✓		
Research consultation		✓	*Contact former research methods professor by e-mail next week*
Material resources:			
Student surveys		✓	*Copy from accountability book CD; duplicate at school on Wednesday*
DVD of movie Hoot	✓		
DVD player		✓	*Make arrangements with school's A/V coordinator*
Physical resources:			
Classrooms	✓		

FIGURE 9.6. Needed resources for an accountability project.

238   The Accountable School Counselor

It is important to list each and all needed resources, even if they are readily available, to avoid unnecessary disruption to the accountability activity. For example, it is likely that you would use your office for individual counseling which, presumably, is readily available. However, is the office used for any other purposes? Are there times when it may not be available for individual counseling? If so, you should identify an alternative location to be used, if necessary. Similarly, it is always inappropriate to assume that a teacher, who has been receptive to school counseling activities, will be cooperative for a particular accountability activity. Therefore, you should contact the teacher to solicit his or her agreement to schedule the conduct of a classroom guidance unit, allow students to be out of his or her class, behave in a particular way as an intervention, provide particular types of student information, or cooperate in whatever way is needed. Of course, there also are always cost considerations for material resources, and availability of materials should be investigated carefully before it is assumed that they can be readily obtained. In sum, the availability of necessary human, material, or physical resources should be determined fully before they are characterized as available.

Determine the Measurements

Obtaining good data (remembering that data can be numbers or words) is at the heart of an effective accountability activity. Therefore, careful thought and specific attention must be given to how the data will be obtained. In general, data are obtained either directly, through self-report of the participants (e.g., by students completing a test, survey or questionnaire) or indirectly, through data provided by people other than the participants (e.g., observational or opinion data from teachers, parents, or other school personnel). In either situation, it is important that the data-gathering procedure be defensible as accurate (i.e., valid), consistent (i.e., reliable), and appropriate. For standardized tests and measures, support for these characteristics usually is found in the professional literature. For observational techniques (e.g., counting specific behaviors within a specific time period), it may be necessary to establish the needed measurement attributes through pilot tests or preparatory training activities. For the development of situation-specific tests, surveys, or questionnaires, it may be necessary to field test the instruments and/or seek consultation from persons known to have expertise in instrument development.

ESTABLISH A TIME SCHEDULE

As a school counselor, you are very busy and have many responsibilities that might take priority over your accountability activity. Therefore, it is important to establish a reasonable and somewhat flexible schedule for your accountability project because of the many factors that might disrupt your schedule.

In general, the time needed for an accountability activity can be divided into three phases: planning, implementation, and completion. The planning phase is the time needed to get ready for the activity. It includes activities such as obtaining resources, determining when the accountability activities can be conducted, giving attention to possible interruptions in the schedule, and determining who will participate in the activities and when they will be available to participate. Your planning phase also might include activities such as professional reading or consultation with other professionals. The implementation phase includes conducting the accountability activity and data gathering. The completion phase includes activities such as analyzing data, writing a report of the accountability activities, and preparing for dissemination of the results. The completion phase also might include working with consultants (e.g., statistical or writing consultants) or peers to clarify what was found and to determine how best to present the information effectively to various stakeholder audiences.

It is impossible to overemphasize the importance of having a good time schedule. Time management is a problem for all school counselors, not because they don't have good time-management skills, but rather because their work is always subject to unforeseen interruptions. Therefore, it is crucial that the schedule be sufficiently extensive and flexible to allow for possible interruptions.

It also is extremely important that the time for your accountability activity be dedicated time, which means that it should be a priority among your activities. For example, if 2 hours per week for 10 consecutive weeks are scheduled for your accountability activity, then every possible effort should be made to ensure that the time allocated is not usurped by other activities. One way to help ensure that the time for your accountability activity is dedicated is to negotiate the time priority with your administrator (i.e., your boss, who for most school counselors is their school's principal). In other words, you should reach agreement with your administrator that the time can and will be allocated specifically and exclusively for your accountability activity, except in the case of dire emergency. Such an agreement is not always achieved easily; however, as competent professionals, most administrators will be able to see the value and importance of accountability activities, and will reach agreement on their priority.

I am definitely going to take a course on time management... just as soon as I can work it into my schedule.

—Louis E. Boone

MONITOR PLAN IMPLEMENTATION PROGRESS

As some poets and song writers, and more than a few school counselors, have noticed, time seems to slip away quickly. Probably the most common reason school counselors give for not being accountable is that they don't have time. Time is precious and must be guarded carefully and fiercely. Nowhere is the need for such protection of time more evident for you than in the conduct of your accountability activity. Therefore, it is crucial to monitor the implementation of an accountability activity as it is progressing.

Self-monitoring is helpful but rarely fully effective. It is simply too easy to rationalize all the reasons why a schedule has or can change. Therefore, a good way to monitor progress on an accountability activity is to have a friend or colleague do the monitoring. This can be accomplished most effectively by giving the person a checklist of what was to have been done by corresponding particular dates (and of course, generation of this checklist also helps with planning in the first place). Ask the person who has the checklist to make periodic inquiries about the progress of the activity. If for some reason there is a delay in the progress, make a new schedule and give it to the person. Most people, school counselors included, don't like to apologize for delays, and so this is a good way for you to stay on task.

Another tactic that may be helpful is to build in rewards for achieving various progress-achievement points in the schedule. For example, treating yourself to lunch or dinner at a favorite restaurant or allowing time for a favored leisure activity can serve as incentives to progress efficiently through the accountability activity components. Similarly, checking off activity components as completed will be a rewarding and satisfying feeling for you and will serve to maintain your motivation and focus in the process. Although effective completion is the ultimate goal of an accountability activity, efficiency and steady progress also are important considerations.

Try Parallelism

People working toward the same or closely-related goals often find comfort in knowing that others share the vision and/or are sharing the same experiences, even though they are not working together directly. This idea can be called "parallelism," and it is different from collaboration. In collaborative activities, two or more school counselors might work together to either accomplish the same task or accomplish tasks that are integrally related. For example, you might collaborate with a colleague at your school to provide various school counseling services to students who have poor attendance records. Each of you would provide some of the services, and at the end you would pool your data to see if the school counselors improved the students' attendance records. Parallelism is a bit different. The "parallel" is that two school counselors are doing essentially the same thing but are not actually working together. For example, colleague school counselors at other schools might also be providing specific school counseling services to help students have better attendance records. You could even use the same accountability activities and procedures. In this case, you wouldn't be working with those colleagues, but all of you would be on the same path to the same goal.

The ACA has recently begun a Practice Research Network (PRN, Bradley, Sexton, & Smith, 2005) that exemplifies this type of parallelism. In the ACA-PRN, (primarily mental health) counselors from across the United States are collecting data and doing research on their professional counseling practices with clients who present with essentially the same problem. This is a powerful approach to counselor accountability for several reasons. First, it is work with clients who have actually sought counseling, as opposed to samples of convenience (e.g., university students) that are usually common to such research. Second, the PRN participants are sharing the vision in that they are all working toward the same goal. Third, the composite results of their efforts are likely to be substantive. And finally, each PRN participant can take comfort in knowing that others are doing and experiencing the same things.

So, one thing you can do to make your school counseling accountability activities a little easier is to find out what your colleague school counselors (wherever they may be) are doing for accountability activities. Another is that you can make your colleagues aware of your activities. In this age of electronic communications, it shouldn't be too difficult to find out or get the word out. And when you do learn of what others are doing, take comfort in knowing that other school counseling professionals share your vision.

Reap the Benefits of Being Accountable

We started this book with the idea that being accountable means being able to provide substantive evidence that your school counseling activities bring about desirable change in one or more students. And again, substantive evidence in this context means information that is more than mere verbalized opinion that something good happened. An effective accountability activity generates *evidence*. However, the benefits of an accountability activity are realized only when the results are communicated and disseminated effectively. Therefore, the first step in achieving some of the primary benefits of your accountability project is to create a written report of the activity. It is perhaps tempting to skip writing a report and just to tell people about the activity. However, just telling people limits the distribution of the results, minimizes the perception of all the work involved and of its importance, and, most importantly, increases the likelihood that what was done and found will be misinterpreted. Alternatively, an effectively written report increases the likelihood that what was done and found will be considered important, minimizes the possibility that the information conveyed will be misinterpreted, and facilitates development and implementation of all other means through which the information can and/or will be disseminated. It also enables you to bring the whole activity into coherent perspective and to gain understanding of the significance of the endeavor.

If you believe in yourself and have dedication and pride—and never quit, you'll be a winner. The price of victory is high but so are the rewards.

—Paul "Bear" Bryant

The written report of an accountability activity need not be a complicated document, but it does need to be complete and informative. It should communicate what was done; provide the schedule for what was done; describe who was involved (generally, excluding names of participants); include a fairly complete description of the activity that was evaluated, the results, and the major implications of the results. Inclusion of diagrams, charts, tables or other graphics always is desirable because it helps to clarify and enhance what is being communicated. Anecdotal (i.e., personal opinion or observation) information may be included but should be kept to a minimum because it detracts from the credibility of the results. A well-written report communicates the facts and is not a forum for expression of personal opinions or feelings. Your written report should be distributed to all persons who are likely to have interest in it; that is, the appropriate stakeholder groups for your school counseling program. Most likely, this group will include your school administrators and teachers but also might extend to school board members, parents, or others who have an interest in the effectiveness of school activities.

The written report also serves as the basis for other types of communication about the accountability activity. For example, if a public presentation is to be made to a school board meeting or to teachers at a school meeting, some elements of the written report might serve as the major elements of a PowerPoint presentation. The written report also might serve as the document from which an abbreviated summary is developed, such as one that might be distributed to parents or legal guardians at a PTA or similar meeting. If a speech is to be given about the activity, it can be developed most effectively by reference to the most important points in the written report.

Importantly, the written report should serve as the basis for communication of the results in broader professional contexts. For example, the written report might be developed further to be submitted as a manuscript for consideration for publication in a professional journal. Similarly, the written report might be used as the basis for an application to present a program on the accountability activity at a professional conference or convention. The written report might even be extended into an application for external funding (i.e., a grant) for similar activities. And finally, the written report might serve as an application for a professional recognition, such as those awarded by local, state, or national professional school counseling organizations. An outline to help you develop an effective written report is presented in Figure 9.7.

Go to the Top of the RAMP

We strongly believe that the primary benefit you will achieve as an accountable school counselor is freedom in and control over your professional school counseling activities. By providing evidence that your school counseling activities make positive differences in students' lives, your efforts and work will be recognized by your stakeholders as contributing substantively to the educational mission of your school. This increased positive recognition will in turn encourage and challenge you to be an even better school counselor. Good school counselors and their school counseling programs ought to be recognized, even beyond local stakeholders. A national recognition that you and your school counseling program can achieve that is entirely in concert with being accountable is for your program to be designated as a Recognized ASCA Model Program, identified by ASCA (2005) as a RAMP.

The application and criteria for your school counseling program to be recognized as a RAMP are available from the ASCA Web site (www.schoolcounselor.org). Some of the requisite application materials include descriptions of your program and its major components, activities, and operating policies. However, the most significant information required is a description of how your school counseling program addresses the various ASCA National Standards for Students (Competencies and Indicators; ANSSCI), as presented in an appendix of the *ASCA National Model*. The ANSSCI represent behavioral manifestations of

Implementing an Accountability Plan   245

ACCOUNTABILITY REPORT

A. Stakeholders to receive report

    a. _____

    b. _____

    c._____

B. Activity title _____

    1. Location for activities: _____

    2. Preparation time: _____ hours

    3. Direct-contact-with-students time: _____ hours

    4. Data collection and analysis time: _____ hours

    5. Activity schedule: _____

C. People involved

    1. Teachers: _____

    2. Administrators: _____

    3. Other school personnel: _____

    4. People from community: _____

D. Resources used

    1. Money: _____ dollars

    2. Physical materials: _____

    3. Human resources: _____

    4. Other resources: _____

E. Outputs and outcomes

    1. Outputs data obtained:

        a. _____

        b. _____

        c. _____

    2. Outcomes obtained:

        a. _____

        b. _____

        c. _____

F. Significance/importance of results

    1. To students: _____

    2. To Stakeholders: _____

FIGURE 9.7. Outline for an accountability report.

the principles inherent in the *ASCA National Model.* The ANSSCI are subdivided into the academic, career, and personal/social realms of student development. Within each of these three areas are primary standards (e.g., "Standard A: Students will acquire the attitudes, knowledge and skills that contribute to effective learning in school and across the lifespan"). The primary standards are in turn subdivided into second-level standards (e.g., "A:A1 Improve Academic Self-concept"). Finally, the second-level standards are further subdivided into specific component standards, usually behavioral (e.g., "A:A1.1 Articulate feelings of competence and confidence as learners"). Achievement of RAMP status does not require that all of the ANSSCI specific component standards be addressed in the school counseling program. However, clearly the intent is that most of them be addressed in a RAMP. An important component of the required RAMP application information is provision of evidence of the effectiveness of various programmatic activities intended to address various ANSSCI specific component standards. It is not sufficient in a RAMP application to merely inform what is being done to address various ANSSCI specific component standards; evidence of the outcomes of the activities must be provided. That is accountability, exactly as we have been presenting it in this book.

Examples of how information might be provided for two of the ANSSCI specific component standards are presented in Figures 9.8 and 9.9. Each of these examples contains the same elements: (a) identification of targeted students, (b) description of the school counseling service/activity provided, (c) identification of who provided the service/activity, and (d) description of outcome(s) measurement process and results. It should be evident that this type of information can be gathered easily in the context of your accountability activities and collected over time to be included in your RAMP application.

Achievement of RAMP designation for your school counseling program would be laudable and would put you at the forefront of the school counseling profession. However, it is a goal that can be achieved only after you have become an accountable school counselor. Thus, as we have emphasized throughout this book, being accountable should be the foundation for your activities and for achievement of your professional goals, whatever they may be.

Implementing an Accountability Plan   247

RESPONSE FOR AN ANSSCI SPECIFIC COMPONENT STANDARD—1

Personal/Social: A2: 8—Learn how to make and keep friends

Students in Grades 3–5

Service:

As near as possible to the beginning of each school year, teachers and the school counselor conduct peer introduction and ice-breaker activities for students in the third-, fourth-, and fifth-grade classrooms. These large-group guidance activities are focused on teaching students how to introduce themselves to other students, meeting and greeting other students, and basic interpersonal communication skills. Students work in groups and dyads to practice meeting and interacting with other students, especially students they have not known previously. The activities also include having students discuss what makes a good friend and what does not make a good friend. The students are informed that they should contact the school counselor if they are having difficulty making friends or are having difficulties in their relationships with their current friends. The students also are encouraged to participate in school-related extracurricular activities as a way to increase their numbers of friends.

Who:

The large-group guidance activities currently are colead by the school counselor and the classroom teacher. The plan is to (eventually) have the classroom teacher lead the activity with the school counselor serving only as a consultant for the activity.

Outcome(s) Measurement:

Prior to the initiation of the large-group guidance activities, the school counselor asks each student to list as many as three students with whom she or he would like to spend time outside of school. The responses are then structured as a sociogram. Six weeks after each large-group guidance activity is conducted, the school counselor again asks the students in the class the same question. These results also are structured as a sociogram.

Both sociograms for each classroom are examined by the school counselor and respective classroom teacher to identify social isolates. Students thus identified are contacted individually and seen by the school counselor. The two sociograms also are examined by the school counselor to determine if there are changes in the students' respective choices. The numbers of new choices are counted for each classroom as indication of the formation of new friendships among the students.

FIGURE 9.8. A response for an ANSSCI specific component standard.

248   The Accountable School Counselor

RESPONSE FOR AN ANSSCI SPECIFIC COMPONENT STANDARD—2

Personal/Social: A2.4—Recognize, Accept, and Appreciate Ethnic and Cultural Differences

Students in Grade 9

Service:

The school counselor collaborates with the ninth-grade Language Arts (e.g., English) teachers to promote multicultural appreciation and sensitivity among students in the respective classes. The school counselor presents two large-group guidance activities (one class period each) on understanding and appreciating people from differing cultures. During the first activity, a PowerPoint presentation that shows people from and in different cultural backgrounds is used as a prelude to large-group discussion of the different circumstances in which people of the world live. Students are encouraged to share their opinions about people of different cultural backgrounds. During the second activity, a PowerPoint presentation that shows examples of stereotyping, segregation, and/or bigotry (e.g., "colored only" water fountain signs) is presented as a prelude to large-group discussion of discrimination practices, how they arise, and their effects.

The classroom teachers support these large-group guidance activities by incorporating coverage of discrimination and its ramifications into their regular curricular activities. For example, some teachers require readings (e.g., *I Know Why the Caged Bird Sings*) into their class assignments. Similarly, some teachers incorporate quiz or test essay questions based on the school counselor's large-group guidance activity into their course assessments.

Outcomes Measurement:

Prior to the first school counselor activity, the school counselor presents to students five broad cultural identifiers (Asian, African American, European, Hispanic, and Middle Eastern) and asks the students to list up to 10 words that come to mind when they hear or see those identifiers. The same task is presented to the students by the school counselor 2 weeks after the classroom teachers have completed their respective coverage of discrimination in their classes.

The school counselor and the respective teachers work together to classify the words listed by the students. Each word is designated as "negative" (i.e., having a derogatory connotation), "positive" (i.e., having a flattering connotation), or "neutral" (i.e., having neither a negative nor positive connotation). The numbers of words in the respective designations are counted for each classroom for both the before and after assessments. Shifts in the numbers in the respective designations in each classroom are determined by subtracting the before numbers from the after numbers.

FIGURE 9.9. ANOTHER RESPONSE FOR AN ANSSCI SPECIFIC COMPONENT STANDARD.

Conclusion

If you as a school counselor are accountable for your professional activities, you are not necessarily the best school counselor around. However, all the best school counselors are accountable, and any school counselor who is accountable is, at the very least, a better school counselor. The various stakeholder groups to and for which you should be accountable are increasing their expectations and demands for accountability, and it is wise for you to be aware of and responsive to this trend.

You and other school counselors can learn relatively quickly both how to conduct accountability activities effectively and efficiently and how to integrate such activities into your normal functioning. Although initial efforts to be accountable may seem burdensome, you will learn rapidly how to overcome initial fears, trepidations, and difficulties. As a truly effective school counselor, you will soon find that being accountable is second nature, and you will view being accountable as an integral part of the successful delivery of your school counseling services and program.

The benefits you, other school counselors, and the school counseling profession stand to gain from being accountable are immense, as are the dire consequences of not being accountable. Each and every school counselor who views him- or herself as a professional school counselor should contribute to the overall effort and share in the rewards for being accountable. When you have taken the time and effort to complete that first, little, and simple accountability activity, you will have taken a major step in the right direction. The time to begin is now!

If I were required to guess off-hand, and without collusion with higher minds, what is the bottom cause of amazing material and intellectual advancement..., I should guess that it was the modern-born and previously non-existent disposition on the part of men to believe that a new idea can have value.

—Mark Twain

FOR THOUGHT AND DEED

1. Identify two school counselors who have generated some type of accountability evidence for one or more of their respective professional activities. Make appointments to talk with each of these school counselors. Ask them about their experiences in being accountable. What were the activities like for them? How did they feel about the activities when they started and when they finished them? What were the biggest obstacles in their activities? Who and/or what was helpful to them? Compare and contrast their respective responses to questions such as these.

2. List some rewards that you could give yourself for engaging in and completing an accountability project. Now, list them in order of priority. Think about how nice it would be to use them as incentives to complete an accountability project. So what is stopping you from conducting the activity?

3. Back in the 1960s, artist Andy Warhol said, "In the future everyone will be world-famous for 15 minutes." If you had your 15 minutes to be famous as a school counselor, which of your professional accomplishments would you acknowledge and highlight, and why? Would one of them be that you knew, and could prove from an accountability study, that you were good at some school counseling activity? So what is stopping you from conducting the activity?

4. Now that we have covered all these different ideas about being an accountable school counselor, it's time to daydream a bit. Briefly describe an accountability activity that you think would be fun to conduct. So what is stopping you from conducting the activity?

REFERENCES

American Counseling Association. (2005). *What is a school counselor: A resource guide for parents and students.* Alexandria, VA: Author.

American School Counselor Association. (2004). *Ethical standards for school counselors.* Alexandria, VA: Author.

American School Counselor Association. (2005). *ASCA national model: A framework for school counseling programs* (2nd ed.). Alexandria, VA: Author.

American School Counselor Association. (2006). *The role of the professional school counselor.* Retrieved May 12, 2006, from www.school-counseling.org

Asimov, I. (2006). *Brainyquote.* Retreived August 21, 2006, from www.brainyquote.com/quotes/quotes/i/isaacasimo124394.html

Astramovich, R. L., Coker, A. K., & Hoskins, W. J. (2005). Training school counselors in program evaluation. *Professional School Counseling, 9*(1), 49–54.

Aubrey, R. F. (1977). Historical development of guidance and counseling and implications for the future. *Personnel and Guidance Journal, 55*(6), 288–295.

Baker, S. B., & Gerler, E. R., Jr. (2004). *School counseling for the twenty-first century* (4th ed.). Upper Saddle River, NJ: Merrill/Prentice Hall.

Barnes, P. E., Friehe, M. J., & Radd, T. R. (2003). Collaboration between speech–language pathologists and school counselors. *Communication Disorders Quarterly, 24*(3), 137–142.

Barnett, R. V., Adler, A., Easton, J., & Howard, K. (2001). An evaluation of Peace Education Foundation's conflict resolution and peer mediation program. *School Business Affairs, 67*(7), 29–39.

Barry, D. (2006). *Brainyquote.* Retrieved September 12, 2006, from www.brainyquote.com/quotes/quotes/d/davebarry102386.html

Bauman, S. (2006). Using comparison groups in school counseling research: A primer. *Professional School Counseling, 9,* 357–366.

Beale, A.V. (2006). The roots of the profession. *ASCA School Counselor, 43*(6), 72–74, 76, 78, 80, 82, 84, 86–87.

Bell, S. K., Coleman, J. K., Anderson, A., Whelan, J. P., & Wilder, C. (2000). The effectiveness of peer mediation in a low-SES rural elementary school. *Psychology in the Schools, 37*(6), 505–516.

Berra, Y. (2006). *Brainyquotes.* Retrieved July 14, 2006, from www.brainyquote.com/quotes/quotes/y/yogiberra132510.html

Bloom, M., Fischer, J., & Orme, J. G. (2003). *Evaluating practice guidelines for the accountable professional* (3rd ed.). Boston: Allyn & Bacon.

Boone, L. E. (2006). *Brainyquote.* Retrieved August 9, 2006, from www
.brainyquote.com/quotes/quotes/l/louiseboo177150.html

Bradley, L. J., Sexton, T. L., & Smith, H. B. (2005). The American Counseling
Association Practice Research Network (ACA-PRN): A new research
tool. *Journal of Counseling and Development, 83*(4), 488–491.

Brown, D., Pryzwansky, W., & Schulte, A. (1998). *Psychological consultation: Introduction to theory and practice* (4th ed.). Boston: Allyn &
Bacon.

Brown, D., & Trusty, J. (2005). *Designing and leading comprehensive school
counseling programs.* Belmont, CA: Brooks/Cole.

Bryan, J., & Holcomb-McCoy, C. (2004). School counselors' perceptions of
their involvement in school-family-community partnerships. *Professional School Counseling, 7*(3), 162–171.

Bryant, P. (2006). *Thinkexist.* Retrieved June 29, 2006, from http://
en.thinkexist.com/quotation/if-you-believe-in-yourself-and-have-
dedication/347124.html

Burnham, J. J., & Jackson, C. M. (2000). School counselor roles: Discrepancies between actual practice and existing models. *Professional School
Counseling, 4*(1), 41–49.

Butler, D. (1997). *Reader's digest quotable quotes* (p. 130). Pleasantville,
NY: Reader's Digest.

Campbell, C. A., & Dahir, C. A. (1997). *The national standards for school
counseling programs.* Alexandria, VA: American School Counselor
Association.

Carlson, L. A., & Yohon, T. I. (2004). Professional school counseling advocacy: Marketing and beyond. In B. T. Erford (Ed.), *Professional
school counseling: A handbook of theories, programs, & practices*
(pp. 79–88). Austin, TX: PRO-ED.

Carruthers, W. L., Sweeney, B., Kmitta, D., & Harris, G. (1996). Conflict
resolution: An examination of the research literature and a model for
program evaluation. *The School Counselor, 44*, 5–18.

Chata, C. C., & Loesch, L. C. (2007). Future school principals' views of the
roles of professional school counselors. *Professional School Counseling, 11*(1), 35–41.

Churchill, W. (2006). *Brainyquote.* Retrieved May 25, 2006, from http://
www.brainyquote.com/quotes/quotes/w/winstonchu103863.html

Clark, F. A. (1997). *Reader's digest quotable quotes* (p. 60). Pleasantville,
NY: Reader's Digest.

Cobia, D. C., & Henderson, D. A. (2003). *Handbook of school counseling.*
Upper Saddle River, NJ: Merrill/Prentice Hall.

Cobia, D. C., & Henderson, D. A. (2006). *Developing an effective and accountable school counseling program.* Columbus, OH: Merrill/Pren-
tice Hall.

Cosby, B. (2006). *Brainyquote.* Retrieved September 1, 2006, from www
.brainyquote.com/quotes/quotes/b/billcosby156772.html

Curcio, C. C., Mathai, C., & Roberts, J. (2003). Evaluation of a school district's secondary counseling program. *Professional School Counseling, 6*(4), 296–303.

Dahir, C. A., Sheldon, C. B., & Valiga, M. J. (1998). *Vision into action: Implementing the national standards for school counseling programs.* Alexandria, VA: American School Counselor Association.

Davis, K. (2005). School-based consultation. In C. Sink (Ed.), *Contemporary school counseling: Theory, research, and practice* (pp. 297–326). Boston: Houghton Mifflin.

Davis, T. (2005). *Exploring school counseling: Professional practices and perspectives.* Boston: Houghton Mifflin.

DeVoss, J. A., & Andrews, M. F. (2006). *School counselors as educational leaders.* Boston: Houghton Mifflin.

Dinkmeyer, D., Jr., & Carlson, J. (2001). *Consultation: Creating school-based interventions* (2nd ed.). Philadelphia: Brunner-Routledge.

Dollarhide, C. T. (2003a). Educating and advocating with parents, colleagues in the schools, and colleagues in the community (Blocks 8, 9, 10 of the DAP model). In C. T. Dollarhide & K. A. Saginak (Eds.), *School counseling in the secondary school* (pp. 241–256). Boston: Allyn & Bacon.

Dollarhide, C. T. (2003b). Professional issues. In C. T. Dollarhide & K. A. Saginak (Eds.), *School counseling in the secondary school* (pp. 323–342). Boston: Allyn & Bacon.

Dollarhide, C. T., & Lemberger, M. E. (2006). "No child left behind": Implications for school counselors. *Professional School Counseling, 9*(4), 295–304.

Dollarhide, C. T., & Saginak, K. A. (2003). *School counseling in the secondary school.* Boston: Allyn & Bacon.

Drucker, P. F. (2006). (1977). *Peter's quotations: Ideas for our times* (p. 104). New York: Bantam Books.

Edison, T. A. (2006). *Brainyquote.* Retrieved September 30, 2006, from www.brainyquote.com/quotes/quotes/t/thomasaed131294.html

Ekstrom, R. B., Elmore, P. B., Schafer, W. D., Trotter, T. V., & Webster, B. (2004). A survey of assessment and evaluation activities of school counselors. *Professional School Counseling, 8*(1), 24–30.

Elmore, P. B., & Ekstrom, P. B. (2004). What assessment competencies are needed by school counselors? In B. T. Erford (Ed.), *Professional school counseling: A handbook of theories, programs, & practices* (pp. 399–406). Austin, TX: PRO-ED.

Erford, B.T. (2007a). *Assessment for counselors.* Boston: Lashka Press.

Erford, B. T. (2007b). *Transforming the school counseling profession* (2nd ed.). Columbus, OH: Merrill/Prentice Hall.

Espey, W. R. (1997). *Reader's digest quotable quotes* (p. 158). Pleasantville, NY: Reader's Digest.

Estonian Proverb. *Reader's digest quotable quotes* (p. 109). Pleasantville, NY: Reader's Digest.

Fairchild, T. N. (1993). Accountability practices of school counselors: 1990 national survey. *The School Counselor, 40,* 363–374.

Fairchild, T. N., & Seeley, T. J. (1995). Accountability strategies for school counselors: A baker's dozen. *The School Counselor, 42,* 377–392.

Family Educational Rights and Privacy Act of 1974, 20 U.S.C.A. § 1232g, 34 C.F.R. Part 99.3 Fed. Reg. 56 § 117.28012.

Fermi, E. (2006). *Brainyquote.* Retrieved October 9, 2006, from www .brainyquote.com/quotes/quotes/e/enricoferm125836.html

Fitch, T., Newby, E., Ballestero, V., & Marshall, J. L. (2001). Future school administrators' perceptions of the school counselor's role. *Counselor Education and Supervision, 41,* 88–99.

Fitzpatrick, J. L., Sanders, J. R., & Worthen, B. R. (2004). *Program evaluation: Alternative approaches and practical guidelines* (3rd ed.). Boston: Pearson Education.

Ford, H. (2006). *Brainyquote.* Retrieved September 9, 2006, from www .brainyquote.com/quotes/quotes/h/henryford121997.html

Fraenkel, J. R., & Wallen, N. E. (2006). *How to design and evaluate research in education* (6th ed.). Boston: McGraw-Hill.

Freud, A. (1977). *Peter's quotations: Ideas for our times* (p. 124). New York: Bantam Books.

Freud, A. (2006). *Brainyquote.* Retrieved May 15, 2006, from www .brainyquote.com

Frith, G. H., & Clark, R. (1982). Evaluating elementary counseling programs: 10 common myths of practitioners. *Elementary School Guidance and Counseling, 17,* 49–51.

Gates, B. (2006). *Brainyquotes.* Retrieved June 14, 2006, from www .brainyquote.com/quotes/quotes/b/billgates104353.html

Goldwyn, S., (2006). *Brainyquote.* Retrieved August 20, 2006, from www .brainyquote.com/quotes/quotes/s/samuelgold100166.html

Goodnough, G. E., & Lee, V. V. (2004). Group counseling in schools. In B. T. Erford (Ed.), *Professional school counseling: A handbook of theories, programs and practices* (pp. 173–182). Austin, TX: PRO-ED.

Goodnough, G., Pérusse, R., & Erford, B. T. (2003). Developmental classroom guidance. In B. T. Erford (Ed.), *Transforming the school counseling profession* (pp. 121–151). Upper Saddle River, NJ: Merrill/Prentice Hall.

Gredler, M. E. (1996). *Program evaluation.* Englewood Cliffs, NJ: Merrill/ Prentice Hall.

Guindon, M. H. (2003). Assessment. In B. T. Erford (Ed.), *Transforming the school counseling profession* (pp. 331–335). Upper Saddle River, NJ: Merrill/Prentice Hall.

Gysbers, N. C. (2004). Comprehensive guidance and counseling programs: The evolution of accountability. *Professional School Counseling, 8*(1), 1–14.

Gysbers, N. C. (2005). Closing the implementation gap. *ASCA School Counselor, 43*(2), 37–41.

Gysbers, N. C., & Henderson, P. (2006). *Developing and managing your school guidance program* (4th ed.). Alexandria, VA: American Counseling Association.

Gysbers, N. C., Lapan, R. T., & Jones, B. A. (2000). School board policies for guidance and counseling: A call to action. *Professional School Counseling, 3*(5), 349–355.

Gysbers, N. C., Lapan, R. T., & Stanley, B. (2006). No fear results evaluation. *ASCA School Counselor, 43*, 34–37.

Hadley, R. G., & Mitchell, L. K. (1995). *Counseling research and program evaluation.* Pacific Grove, CE: Brooks/Cole.

Hagborg, W. J. (1992). A counseling report card: A study of parental satisfaction. *The School Counselor, 40*, 131–135.

Hanson, W. E., & Claiborn, C. C. (2006). Effects of test interpretation style and favorability in the counseling process. *Journal of Counseling & Development, 84*(3), 349–357.

Hatch, T., & Bowers, J. (2002). The block to build on. *ASCA School Counselor, 39*(5), 12–17.

Havens, J. (2003) Student Web pages—A performance assessment activity they'll love! *Phi Delta Kappan, 84*(9), 710–711.

Herr, E. L. (2003). Historical roots and future issues. In B. T. Erford (Ed.), *Transforming the school counseling profession* (pp. 21–38). Upper Saddle River, NJ: Pearson Education.

Hoffer, E. (1998). *Simpson's contemporary quotations* (p. 118). Boston: Houghton Mifflin.

Houser, R. (1998). *Counseling and educational research: Evaluation and application.* Thousand Oaks, CA: Sage.

Hughes, D., & James, S. (2001). Using accountability data to protect a school counseling program: One counselor's experience. *Professional School Counseling, 4*, 306–309.

Humphries, T. L. (1999). Improving peer mediation programs: Student experiences and suggestions. *Professional School Counseling, 3*, 13–20.

Hughey, K. F., Gysbers, N. C., & Starr, M. (1993). Evaluating comprehensive school guidance programs: Assessing the perceptions of students, parents, and teachers. *The School Counselor, 41*, 31–35.

Inman, R. (1997). *Reader's digest quotable quotes* (p. 135). Pleasantville, NY: Reader's Digest.

Isaacs, M. L. (2003). Data-driven decision-making. *Professional School Counselor, 6*, 288–295.

Jacob, S., & Hartshorne, T. S. (2006). *Ethics and law for school psychologists*. Hoboken, NJ: Wiley.

James, W. (1977). *Peter's quotations: Ideas for our times* (p. 340). New York: Bantam Books.

Johnson, L. S. (2000). Promoting professional identity in an era of educational reform. *Professional School Counseling, 4*(1), 31–40.

Johnson, S., Johnson, C., & Downs, L. (2006). *Building a results-based student support program*. Boston: Lahaska Press.

Kampwirth, T. J. (2006). *Collaborative consultation in the schools: Effective practices for students with learning and behavior problems* (3rd ed.). Upper Saddle River, NJ: Pearson.

Kareck, T. J. (1998). Making the time to counsel students. *Professional School Counseling, 1*, 56–57.

Keller, H. (1997). *Reader's digest quotable quotes* (p. 25). Pleasantville, NY: Reader's Digest.

Keys, S. G., Green, A., Lockhart, E., & Luongo, P. F. (2003). Consultation and collaboration. In B. T. Erford (Ed.), *Transforming the school counseling profession* (pp. 171–190). Upper Saddle River, NJ: Merrill/Prentice Hall.

King, M. L., Jr. (2006). *Brainyquotes*. Retrieved September 8, 2006, from www.brainyquote.com/quotes/quotes/m/martinluth106169.html

Kleppner, O. (1977). *Peter's quotations: Ideas for our times* (p. 100). New York: Bantam Books.

Kratochwill, T. R., & Bergan, J. R. (1990). *Behavioral consultation in applied settings*. New York: Plenum Press.

Krzyzewski, M. (2006). *Brainyquote*. Retrieved August 4, 2006, from www.brainyquote.com/quotes/quotes/m/mikekrzyze295882.html

Lapan, R. T. (2001). Results-based comprehensive guidance and counseling programs: A framework for planning and evaluation. *Professional School Counseling, 4*(4), 289–299.

Lapan, R. T. (2005). Evaluating school counseling programs. In C. Sink (Ed.), *Contemporary school counseling* (pp. 257–294). Boston: Houghton Mifflin.

Lapan, R. T. (2006). Moving forward. *Professional School Counselor, 9*, ii–iii.

Larson, D. (2006). *Brainyquote*. Retrieved May 22, 2006, from www.brainyquote.com/quotes/quotes/d/douglarson104630.html

Levin, C. (2006). *Brainyquote*. Retrieved July 22, 2006, from www.brainyquote.com/quotes/quotes/c/carllevin167850.html

Lewis, A. C. (2003). New hope for educational research? *Phi Delta Kappan, 84*(3), 339–340.

Lincoln, A. (1997). *Reader's digest quotable quotes* (p. 102). Pleasantville, NY: Reader's Digest.

Linde, L. (2003). Ethical, legal, and professional issues in school counseling. In B. T. Erford (Ed.), *Transforming the school counseling profession* (pp. 39–62). Upper Saddle River, NJ: Pearson.

Linn, R. L., & Miller, M. D. (2005). *Measurement and assessment in teaching* (9th ed.). Upper Saddle River, NJ: Pearson.

Loesch, L. C. (2000). Counseling program evaluation: Inside and outside of the box. In D. C. Locke, J. E. Myers, & E. L. Herr (Eds.), *Handbook of counseling* (pp. 513–525). Thousand Oaks, CA: Sage.

Marx, G. (1977). *Peter's quotations: Ideas for our times* (p. 330). New York: Bantam Books.

McCall, W. A., (1992). *How to measure in education.* New York: Macmillan.

McCully, C., & Miller, L. (1969). *Challenge for change in counselor education.* Minneapolis, MN: Burgess.

McGannon, W., Carey, J., & Dimmitt, C. (2005). *The current status of school counseling outcome research* [Research Monograph]. Amherst: University of Massachusetts, Center for School Counseling Outcome Research.

Melton, B. (2003). Critical collaboration = Strong programs. *ASCA School Counselor, 40*(3), 4.

Michener, J. A. (1997). *Reader's digest quotable quotes* (p. 64). Pleasantville, NY: Reader's Digest.

Moore, J. L., III (2005). A call for greater collaboration between the counseling psychology and school counseling professions. *Journal of Counseling & Development, 83,* 504–508.

Morrow, E. R. (1977). *Peter's quotations: Ideas for our times* (p. 328). New York: Bantam Books.

Myrick, R. D. (2002). *Developmental guidance and counseling: A practical approach* (4th ed.). Minneapolis, MN: Educational Media.

Myrick, R. D. (2003). Accountability: Counselors count. *Professional School Counseling, 6,* 174–179.

Newsome, D. W., & Gladding, S. T. (2007). Counseling individuals and groups in school. In B. T. Erford (Ed.), *Transforming the school counseling profession* (2nd ed.). Upper Saddle River, NJ: Pearson.

No Child Left Behind Act of 2001, 20 U.S.C. 70 § 6301 *et seq.* (2002)

North. O. (2006). *Brainyquote.* Retrieved October 21, 2006, from www .brainyquote.com/quotes/quotes/o/olivernort161416.html

Nugent, W. R., Sieppert, J. D., & Hudson, W. W. (2001). *Practice evaluation for the 21st century.* Belmont, CA: Thompson Brooks/Cole.

Page, J. (2006). *Brainyquote.* Retrieved August 30, 2006, from www .brainyquote.com/quotes/quotes/j/joypage205620.html

Paisley, P. O., & Hubbard, G. T. (1994). *Developmental school counseling programs: From theory to practice.* Alexandria, VA: American Counseling Association.

Parsad, B., Alexander, D., Farris, E., & Hudson, L. (2006). High school guidance counseling. *Education Statistics Quarterly, 5*(3), 1–6. Retrieved May 14, 2006, from http://nces.ed.gov/programs/quarterly/vol_5/5_3/3_4.asp

Partin, R. L. (1993). School counselor's time: Where does it go? *The School Counselor, 40,* 274–281.

Partin, R. L., Huss, S. N., & Ritchie, M. H. (2003). *An update on school counselor's time.* Unpublished manuscript, University of Toledo, Toledo, OH.

Peter, L. J. (1997). *Peter's quotations: Ideas for our times* (p. 105). New York: Bantam Books.

Planned security magazine. (1997). *Reader's digest quotable quotes* (p. 130). Pleasantville, NY: Reader's Digest.

Popham, W. J. (1993). *Educational evaluation* (3rd ed.). Boston: Allyn & Bacon.

Popham, W. J. (2001). New assessment methods for school counselors. In G. R. Walz & J. C. Bleuer (Eds.), *Assessment issues and challenges for the millennium* (pp. 277–280). Greensboro, NC: CAPS Press.

Remley, T. P., Jr., & Herlihy, B. (2001). *Ethical, legal, and professional issues in counseling.* Upper Saddle River, NJ: Prentice Hall.

Ripley, V. V. (2003). Conflict resolution and peer mediation in schools. In B. T. Erford (Ed.), *Transforming the school counseling profession* (pp. 297–315). Upper Saddle River, NJ: Merrill/Prentice Hall.

Ritchie, M. H. (1983). Brief behavioural consultation. *School Psychology International, 4,* 237–244.

Ritchie, M. H. (1990). Counseling is not a profession—Yet. *Counselor Education and Supervision, 29,* 220–227.

Ritchie, M. H. (1997). Writing for publication in the helping professions. In L. Loesch & N. Vacc (Eds.), *Research in counseling & therapy.* Greensboro, NC: ERIC/CASS.

Ritchie, M. H., & Partin, R. L. (1994). Referral practices of school counselors. *The School Counselor, 41*(4), 263–272.

Robinson, S. E., Morrow, S., Kigin, T., & Lindeman, M. (1991). Peer counselors in a high school setting: Evaluation of training and impact on students. *The School Counselor, 39,* 35–40.

Roosevelt, F. D. (2006). *Brainyquote.* Retrieved June 3, 2006, from www.brainyquote.com/quotes/quotes/f/franklind135682.html

Roosevelt, T. (1977). *Peter's quotations: Ideas for our times* (p. 415). New York: Bantam Books.

Rowan, C. T. (2006). *Brainyquotes.* Retrieved July 12, 2006, from www.brainyquote.com/quotes/quotes/c/carltrowa131291.html

Royse, D., Thyer, B. A., Padgett, D. K., & Logan, T. K. (2006). *Program evaluation: An Introduction* (4th ed.). Belmont, CA: Thompson Brooks/Cole.

Sandburg, C. (1977). *Words about words.* Retrieved August 20, 2006, from www.wordspy.com/waw/20000131081504.asp

Schmidt, J. J. (2002). *Counseling in schools: Essential services and comprehensive programs* (4th ed.). Boston: Allyn & Bacon.

Sciarra, D. T. (2004). *School counseling: Foundations and contemporary issues.* Belmont, CA: Thompson Brooks/Cole.

Sears, S. J. (2005). Large-group guidance: Curriculum development and instruction. In C. Sink (Ed.), *Contemporary school counseling: Theory, research, and practice* (pp. 189–213). Boston: Houghton Mifflin.

Sears, S. J., Moore, J., III, & Young, A. (2004). Helping students improve their learning and study skills. In B. T. Erford (Ed.), *Professional school counseling: A handbook of theories, programs, & practices* (pp. 781–789). Austin, TX: PRO-ED.

Shaw, M. C. (1973). *School guidance systems: Objectives, functions, evaluation, and change.* Boston: Houghton Mifflin.

Sheperis, S., Weaver, A., & Sheperis, C. (2004). The evolution and application of peer mediation in schools. In B. T. Erford (Ed.), *Professional school counseling: A handbook of theories, programs, & practices* (pp. 369–377). Austin, TX: PRO-ED.

Simcox, A. G., Nuijens, K. L., & Lee, C. C. (2006). School counselors and school psychologists: Collaborative partners in promoting culturally competent schools. *Professional School Counseling, 9*(4), 272–277.

Sink, C. (2005). Comprehensive school counseling programs and academic achievement—A rejoinder to Brown and Trusty. *Professional School Counseling, 9*(1), 9–12.

Smith, J. M. (2004). Adolescent male views on the use of mental health counseling activities. *Adolescence, 39*(153), 77–83.

Stein, G. (2006). *Brainyquote.* Retrieved May 19, 2006, from www.brainyquote.com/quotes/quotes/g/gertrudest107878.html

Stone, C. B., & Dahir, C. A. (2006). *The transformed school counselor.* Boston: Houghton Mifflin.

Stone, C. B., & Dahir, C. A. (2007). *School counselor accountability: A MEASURE of student success* (2nd ed.). Upper Saddle River, NJ: Pearson.

Studer, J. R. (2005). *The professional school counselor: An advocate for students.* Belmont, CA: Thompson.

Studer, J. R., Oberman, A. H., & Womack, R. H. (2006). Producing evidence to show counseling effectiveness in the schools. *Professional School Counseling, 9*(5), 385–391.

Stufflebeam, D. L., Foley, W. J., Gephart, W. J., Guba, E. G., Hammond, R. L., Marriman, H. O., et al. (1971). *Educational evaluation and decision-making in education.* Itasca, IL: Peacock.

Taft, R. A., Mrs. (1977). *Peter's quotations: Ideas for our times* (p. 478). New York: Bantam Books.

Taylor, L., & Adelman, H. S. (2000). Connecting schools, families, and communities. *Professional School Counseling, 3*(5), 298–307.

Thompson, D. W. (2001). The development of a survey instrument to assess the counseling needs of intermediate elementary school students (Doctoral dissertation, University of Florida, 2001). *Dissertation Abstracts International, 62*(10), 3305.

Thompson, D. W., Loesch, L. C., & Seraphine, A. E. (2003). Development of an instrument to assess the counseling needs of elementary school students. *Professional School Counseling, 6*(1), 35–39.

Tindall, J. A., & Gray, H. D. (1985). *Peer power: Becoming an effective peer helper: Book 1. Introductory program.* Muncie, IN: Accelerated Development.

Tobias, A. K., & Myrick, R. D. (1999). A peer facilitator-led intervention with middle school problem-behavior students. *Professional School Counseling, 3,* 27–33.

Townsend, R. (2006). *Brainyquote.* Retrieved July 31, 2006, from www.brainyquote.com/quotes/quotes/r/roberttown165640.html

Trevisan, M. S., & Hubert, M. (2001). Implementing comprehensive guidance program evaluation support: Lessons learned. *Professional School Counseling, 4,* 225–228.

Twain, M. (2006). *Thinkexist.* Retrieved June 28, 2006, from www.thinkexist.com

Unrau, Y. A., Gabor, P. A., & Grinnell, R.M., Jr. (2001). *Evaluation in human services.* Belmont, CA: Thompson Brooks/Cole.

U.S. Department of Education National Commission on Excellence in Education. (1983). *A nation at risk.* Washington, DC: U.S. Government Printing Office.

U. S. Department of Education. (2006). *No child left behind: Expanding the promise: Guide to President Bush's FY 2006 education agenda* Washington, DC: Author. (ERIC Document Reproduction Service No. ED484218)

Vacc, N. A., & Loesch, L. C. (2000). *Professional orientation to counseling* (3rd ed.). Philadelphia: Brunner-Routledge.

VanZandt, Z., & Hayslip, J. B. (2001). *Developing your school counseling program: A handbook for systemic planning.* Belmont, CA: Wadsworth.

Wagner, L. (2006). *Brainyquote.* Retrieved August 30, 2006, from www.brainyquote.com/quotes/quotes/l/lindsaywag222124.html

Wall, J. E. (2004). Students, technology, and testing: Why counselors must care. In B. T. Erford (Ed.), *Professional school counseling: A handbook of theories, programs & practices* (pp. 475–481). Austin, TX: PRO-ED.

Ware, W. B., & Galassi, J. P. (2006). Using correlational and prediction data to enhance student achievement in K-12 schools: A practical application for school counselors. *Professional School Counseling, 9*(5), 344–356.

Whiston, S. C (2003). Outcomes research on school counseling services. In B. T. Erford (Ed.), *Transforming the school counseling profession* (pp. 435–447). Upper Saddle River, NJ: Merrill/Prentice Hall.

Whiston, S. C. (2005). *Principles and applications of assessment in counseling* (2nd ed.). Belmont, CA: Thompson Brooks/Cole.

Whiston, S. C., & Sexton, T. L. (1998). A review of school counseling outcome research: Implications for practice. *Journal of Counseling and Development, 76,* 412–426.

White, E. B. (1977). *Peter's quotations: Ideas for our times* (p. 455). New York: Bantam Books.

Winfrey, O. (2006). *Brainyquote.* Retrieved August 12, 2006, from www .brainyquote.com/quotes/quotes/o/oprahwinfr143005.html

Wittmer, J., Thompson, D. W., & Loesch, L. C. (1997). *Classroom guidance activities: A sourcebook for elementary school counselors.* Minneapolis, MN: Educational Media.

Wrenn, C. G. (1962). *The counselor in a changing world.* Washington, DC: American Personnel and Guidance Association.

Yarbrough, J. L., & Thompson, C. L. (2002). Using single-participant research to assess counseling approaches on children's off-task behavior. *Professional School Counseling, 5*(5), 308–314.

ABOUT THE AUTHORS

Larry C. Loesch, PhD, NCC, is a professor in the Department of Counselor Education at the University of Florida. Dr. Loesch has published over 100 professional journal articles, 11 book chapters, and 7 books, and has made over 85 professional program presentations. He served as editor of *Measurement and Evaluation in Guidance* and on the editorial board of *Counselor Education and Supervision*. Dr. Loesch has served as the president of the Florida and national Associations for Measurement and Evaluation in Guidance, Florida Counseling Association, Chi Sigma Iota, and Southern Association for Counselor Education and Supervision. He was a board member for the Council for the Accreditation of Counseling and Related Educational Programs and has been an evaluation consultant for the National Board for Certified Counselors since 1980. He was a corecipient of the American Counseling Association's 1983 Research Award and its 1992 Arthur A. Hitchcock Distinguished Professional Service Award. He is a charter member of Chi Sigma Iota's Academy of Leaders and received the 1998 Chi Sigma Iota Sweeney Professional Leadership Award. In 2001, Dr. Loesch served as a Fulbright Scholar in Bratislava, Slovakia. Dr. Loesch was selected to be a Fellow of the American Counseling Association in 2004.

Martin H. Ritchie, EdD, LPC, is professor and coordinator of school counseling in the Department of Counselor Education and School Psychology at The University of Toledo. After working as a school counselor in Virginia, he moved to Australia, where he trained school counselors and helped develop one of the country's first elementary school counselor training programs. He has written and presented on school counseling issues on the state, national, and international levels and has over 50 refereed publications. He served as editor of *Counselor Education and Supervision* and on the editorial board of *The Professional School Counselor*. He is cofounder and past president of the International Association for Marriage and Family Counselors and is a recipient of their Professional Development Award. He has served as president of the Ohio Counseling Association and the Ohio Association for Counselor Education and Supervision. He has received the Ohio Counseling Association's Research and Writing Award, the Charles Weaver Award for long and distinguished service, and the Herman J. Peters Award for exemplary leadership to the counseling profession.